REA FR OF ACPL

8-19-63

THINE FOREVER

Daily Devotions
Following
Luther's Small Catechism

Collated and Edited by
August G. Suechting

✠

Augsburg Publishing House
Minneapolis 15, Minnesota

1962 Printing

Copyright, 1950
The Wartburg Press
Assigned to Augsburg Publishing House, 1961

Made in the United States of America

1232021

To
THE CONFIRMED YOUTH
OF AMERICA

FOREWORD

For some time the collator of this devotional book has looked in vain for a suitable gift to the newly confirmed, a book that would keep alive the teachings received during instruction, a book written for them expressly that would stimulate loyalty to the church and their Lord.

The aim of THINE FOREVER is just that. Its meditations are based on Dr. Martin Luther's Small Catechism, supplemented by a number of kindred subjects related to the Christian life.

The collator wishes to express his deep gratitude to all who have cooperated so willingly to make this book possible, both as contributors of devotions and planners of special sections. Many pastors and synodical officials have participated in this intersynodical undertaking. This has been a much greater task than was anticipated; several years have been invested in its completion, and the reader will note that a number of contributors have been called to their eternal rest prior to publication.

Many hours and much careful thought were devoted by Prof. T. S. Liefeld to editing, reviewing, and coordinating the entire manuscript for its final form. His interest and able counsel are gratefully acknowledged. A special word of appreciation is due Pastor E. C. Dolbeer, who has prepared all the devotions not otherwise credited at the end of the book. Thanks should also be expressed to Dr. R. Neumann for his editorial help and to my daughter Esther for her typographical assistance.

THE EDITOR.

PREFACE

To write a preface to a book of devotions is no easy task, especially when it bears so multicolored a presentation as this collation by the Rev. Mr. Suechting. Here, however, we introduce a unique product intended for the confirmed youth of the Lutheran Church. This fact makes the publication one of highest value, for what greater pursuit can we follow than to gain and retain our young people for the Church of Jesus Christ! These brief devotions by a variety of Lutheran clerical contributors lean on the classic of the Lutheran Church, Dr. Martin Luther's Small Catechism. They appeal to the best in the youth of the church. If followed in practice day by day and line upon line these testimonies to the faith in Christ Jesus will confirm the lessons of the catechetical class and further the loyalty to the church of those who use them consistently.

We invoke the blessings of the Almighty on this precious undertaking.

R. NEUMANN.

CONTENTS

The Word of God	January 1– 7
The Ten Commandments — Introduction	January 8–14
The First Commandment	January 15–21
The Second Commandment	January 22–28
The Third Commandment	Jan. 29-Feb. 4
The Fourth Commandment	February 5–11
The Fifth Commandment	February 12–18
The Sixth Commandment	February 19–25
The Seventh Commandment	Feb. 26-March 3
The Eighth Commandment	March 4–10
The Ninth Commandment	March 11–17
The Tenth Commandment	March 18–24
The Conclusion	March 25–31
The Creed — The First Article	April 1–21
The Second Article	April 22-May 12
The Third Article	May 13-June 2
Prayer	June 3– 9
The Lord's Prayer — Introduction	June 10–11
The First Petition	June 12–16
The Second Petition	June 17–23
The Third Petition	June 24–30
The Fourth Petition	July 1– 7
The Fifth Petition	July 8–14
The Sixth Petition	July 15–21
The Seventh Petition	July 22–28
The Conclusion	July 29-Aug. 4
The Sacrament of Holy Baptism	August 5–18
The Confession	August 19–25
The Office of the Keys	August 26–31
Confirmation	September 1

The Sacrament of the Altar	September 2–15
The Seven Words from the Cross	September 16–22
The Beatitudes	Sept. 23-Oct. 1
Singing	October 2– 8
Christian Literature	October 9–15
Our Glorious Common Service	October 16–22
The Great I AMS	October 23–29
Overcoming	Oct. 30-Nov. 5
A Successful Life	November 6–12
Missions	November 13–19
Martin Luther and Our Generation	November 20–26
Stewardship	Nov. 27-Dec. 3
Feeding Christ's Lambs and Sheep	December 4–10
The Worship of God	December 11–17
The Ministry of Mercy	December 18–23
Jesus — Christmas	December 24–31

THINE FOREVER!

Thine forever! God of Love,
Hear us from Thy throne above;
Thine forever may we be
Here and in eternity.

Thine forever! Lord of Life,
Shield us through our earthly strife;
Thou, the Life, the Truth, the Way,
Guide us to the realms of day.

Thine forever! O how blest
They who find in Thee their rest!
Savior, Guardian, heavenly Friend,
O defend us to the end.

Thine forever! Shepherd, keep
These Thy frail and trembling sheep;
Safe alone beneath Thy care,
Let us all Thy goodness share.

Thine forever! Thou our Guide,
All our wants by Thee supplied,
All our sins by Thee forgiven,
Lead us, Lord, from earth to heaven. Amen.

MARY FOWLER MAUDE.

THE WORD OF GOD

Using the Word of God

Jan. 1

READ: Luke 4:16-30.
TEXT: And He opened the book and found. Luke 4:17.

❦

Today we are starting another year's journey in our life.

We want to start right, keep on going right, and end right. We want and need a reliable road map. We have it. The Bible, God's Word, is our road map for life. It is God's own map. It is the only absolutely true and accurate one.

It has been tested, tried, *used* by millions for centuries, and has always kept each one who truly followed it on the right road and brought him to the right destination. It will do the same for you.

However, we must read it, study it, and *follow* its directions just as given. It is not sufficient to have a Bible in the library or on the living-room table. We must have it in our head, our heart, and our life to do any good.

Open the Book. Read it. Meditate upon it. Put it into practice. With the help of God, *live* it. You will like the Bible more and more as you do these things. It grows on you.

Our Heavenly Father, I thank Thee for the Holy Bible, Thy Blessed Word, and for all the help which Thou givest me when I read it and meditate upon it. Lead me to want to read it more and to follow it better. In Jesus' name I pray. Amen.

THE WORD OF GOD

Jan. 2

Inspiration

READ: II Timothy 3:14-17.

TEXT: All Scripture is given by inspiration of God. II Timothy 3:17.

❖

"Holy men of God spake as they were moved by the Holy Ghost." We call this inspiration. It is this which makes the Bible different from all other books. It is the Word of God. Here we learn about God, about man, and about life. The knowledge contained in the Bible is not human wisdom. We call it revelation because God has revealed things which man could not otherwise learn. "My thoughts are not your thoughts," God says.

What does the Bible tell us that we could not learn by ourselves? It tells of God the Creator, and of the beginning and the end of all things. It teaches us about the kingdom of God and about God's love and His plan to make us His children through Jesus Christ.

The Bible is God's "street light" for us to walk by. It is God's "textbook" for us to study in the great school of life. It is God's "book of rules" for our play and our work. Whatever else we may be learning, let us learn from the Bible the truth about God and the Christian way of life.

O Holy Spirit, as Thou hast moved men to write these great truths, move me, I pray Thee, to love the Word of God and learn it. Amen.

THE WORD OF GOD
It is effective

Jan. 3

READ: II Peter 1:1-21.

TEXT: My word . . . shall not return unto Me void. Isaiah 55:11.

✠

How can I be *sure*? How can I be *sure* that God will hear me, answer me when I call, give me the peace I so desperately need, save me from my sins, and give me life eternal at last?

From countless souls the cry comes, the cry from the depths oftentimes of deep despair, the cry which can be answered only by Him who has the answer and knows how to give it. It is a cry which, while universal by virtue of its nature, is emphasized by the insecurity of an age where men and women have lost God. But, the way is not lost, nor is God's answer to seeking souls lost. His Word and promise stand *sure* though all other foundations be shaken.

His word is still His. It comes from God, and it is God's. God is not only yesterday's God. He is our God today, the same yesterday and forever. He gave His promise of salvation through His Son, and that promise stands for all who will believe. He speaks by the Holy Ghost, and the Holy Ghost still convicts and converts, counsels and comforts.

O God, help me to believe Thy promises and to accept Thy Word. I come to Thee in deep humility, praising Thee who dost forgive and forget, who dost save to the uttermost, and dost promise life and salvation to all who believe. Through Jesus Christ, our Lord. Amen.

THE WORD OF GOD

Jan. 4

It is right

READ: John 17:17-26.

TEXT: Thy Word is truth. John 17:17.

♣

There is a popular untruth which says, "It doesn't matter what you believe as long as you live right." You'd better not believe that, for it is false in any area of life. You can be a skillful driver of an automobile, but if you do not know where you are going you'll never arrive at your destination.

I once asked the superintendent of a hospital for mental diseases why there is an increase in patients who suffer mental disorders. He said: "Over seventy-five per cent of these people are here because they haven't been thinking right. Their thinking is twisted; therefore their lives are unbalanced."

What a wonderful thing it is for the Christian to have a guide for right thinking in God's Word. "Thy Word is Truth." Jesus is not only the Way but also the Truth. "Thou shalt love the Lord Thy God . . . with all thy mind."

Do you love Him that way? His Truth is right thinking and, therefore, right living.

Dear God, help me by Thy Holy Spirit to have a right judgment in all things and to find in Thy Holy Word the Truth about life, through Jesus Christ, my Lord. Amen.

THE WORD OF GOD

Its Power or Efficacy

Jan. 5

READ: Romans 1:1-17.

TEXT: The gospel . . . is the power of God unto salvation. Rom. 1:16.

✤

O blessed *Word*, all matchless Truth revealing,
Companion of this life, be thou to me!
By night, by day, sin's burdens come upon me stealing,
Thy trusty shield doth keep me free.

'Tis easy to go wrong. What we most need is definite direction as we journey along life's uncertain way. God has mercifully placed His signboard signals at the threatening crossroads to warn us of possible danger. His precious *Word*, daily read and carefully and prayerfully observed, will keep us from falling. With the trusting Psalmist let us boldly declare, "Thy *Word* is a lamp unto my feet, and a light unto my path." The little Catechism you faithfully studied should remain forever your happiest helper. Read it, study it over and over again! Treasure it as the second-best volume in your library! Its mighty foundation is the Book of books. *Christ*, the *Living Word*, is its beacon light, the guiding star of the ages.

Dear Father God, let me live as Jesus lived, faithful, loyal, loving, true. Make me humble and keep me so. Let Thy Spirit ever lead me to fulfill Thy sacred precepts, live and love Thy Holy Word, even unto the dawning of the perfect, promised day. Amen.

THE WORD OF GOD

Jan. 6

Read it daily

READ: John 5:39-47.

TEXT:. Search the Scriptures; for in them ye think ye have eternal life; and they are they which testify of Me. John 5:39.

✥

We are urged to *search* the Scriptures because they are the revealed will of God, and they contain all that we need to know concerning life here and hereafter. They are a gold mine of wisdom and truth whose treasures have never been exhausted by the most diligent and patient search.

When one wishes to know more about a given subject he reads books which deal with that subject. There are books of all kinds for those who would seek further knowledge, books on birds, flowers, music, art, sport, travel. Just so the Book of books is given us to tell us the way to life eternal.

It is reported that Abraham Lincoln said about a year before his death: "I am profitably engaged reading the Bible. Take all of this Book upon reason that you can, and the balance on faith, and you will live and die a better man." Yes, *search* the Scriptures, for they give the answer to all the problems of life, and in them we find eternal life.

Blessed Lord, give us a true eagerness to learn more about Thee and to find the truth that shall make us free. Assist, guide, and bless us as we search Thy Word that we, too, may find eternal life in Jesus Christ, our Lord. Amen.

THE WORD OF GOD
Believe it

READ: II Timothy 3:1-15.

TEXT: From a child thou hast known the Holy Scriptures, which are able to make thee wise unto salvation through faith which is in Christ Jesus. II Timothy 3:15.

Jan. 7

✧

What a privilege it is to have God's Word, to be able to read it, and thus to know His will for us! In this respect Christians are greatly blessed, for it is so easy to talk to God in prayer and then have Him talk to us through the reading of His Holy Word. Since you were a little child you have known something of this privilege. Your mother probably told you the most beautiful Bible stories even before you could read. When you started to Sunday school you learned more of them. In later years in Sunday school and in confirmation class you learned in addition the will of God for you. But none of us can be satisfied with that which he once learned. The strange thing about the Bible is that one must constantly keep reading and keep learning.

Dear Father in heaven, help us to read and study Thy Word faithfully and diligently. Help us to know Thee better and to love Thee more that in everything we do or say we may do it as those privileged to bear the high title of Christian. Do Thou mold our life that it may become a life of service to our fellow men and to Thy honor and Thy glory. Use us, we pray, and help us to have in our heart that peace that only Thou canst give. We ask it in Jesus' name. Amen.

THE TEN COMMANDMENTS — INTRODUCTION

Jan. 8

I am the Lord Thy God

The Conscience

READ: Romans 2:1-16.

TEXT: The work of the law is written in their hearts, their conscience also bearing witness. Romans 2:15.

✤

The moment Adam and Eve disobeyed God they were afraid and ashamed. That which makes men know they are doing wrong is the conscience. God gives this to every man. When men do not listen to conscience, it becomes darkened, and they do foolish and unclean things. Conscience no longer points out good and evil, right and wrong. That is why it was necessary for God to give the Ten Commandments, that we might know right from wrong.

The apostle Paul prays for some of the early Christians that "the eyes of their understanding might be enlightened; that they might know." So if conscience can be darkened it can be enlightened. It is a great thing to have a lively and an enlightened conscience. It is God's gift to you. It is the voice of God in your heart. Listen to it, and you will know what God wants you to do.

O God, who made man good, let me fear and love Thee above all things that I may have a conscience which warns me of evil and directs me toward the good, for Jesus' sake. Amen.

THE TEN COMMANDMENTS — INTRODUCTION

I am the Lord Thy God

Giving of the Law

Jan. 9

READ: Exodus 19:1-6.

TEXT: If ye will obey My voice indeed, and keep My covenant . . . ye shall be unto Me a kingdom of priests, and an holy nation. Exodus 19:5, 6.

♣

When Moses came down from Mt. Sinai, his face shone with a heavenly radiance. He had been in the solemn and holy presence of God. The Almighty had spoken to him. Indeed, the Lord had placed in his hands, for the lasting and uplifting spiritual direction of Israel, His own holy law. With this law God gave an explicit direction: "Obey My voice and keep My covenant."

It is no wonder Moses' face was agleam. He had been the instrument through whom God gave to Israel and the world His decree and His blessing.

Did God ever speak to you about His law? Of course He did. And each time He spoke He directed you to His covenant made with you. He asks you to take His law into your own heart. He wants you to remember how He made the law so much more effective by sending His Son to guide you into His eternal truth.

Gracious Lord, speak to me daily and tell me of Thy law. Make it clear to me and aid me in my study of Thy Truth, through Jesus, my High Priest and Savior. Amen.

THE TEN COMMANDMENTS — INTRODUCTION

Jan. 10

I am the Lord Thy God

The first table of the law

READ: Matthew 22:34-40.

TEXT: Thou shalt love the Lord thy God with all thy heart, and with all thy soul, and with all thy mind. Matthew 22:37.

♣

These words comprise the introduction to the simplest and yet the profoundest body of *laws* to be found anywhere. In them the Lord claims for Himself our exclusive worship. We are to love Him supremely (Matthew 22:37). More than father and mother, more than money and fame are we to love Him. This right He claims, first, because He has created us; second, because He has redeemed us; and third, because He continues to sanctify us, that is, keeps us in the true faith. "Ye are not your own; for ye were bought with a price; glorify God, therefore." Difficult, you say? Yes, indeed. Yet, how richly it pays to put God first in your life! Will you try to do that today? For a week? You will have a thrilling experience.

> The dearest idol I have known,
>   Whate'er that idol be,
> Help me to tear it from Thy throne
> **And worship only Thee. Amen.**

THE TEN COMMANDMENTS —
INTRODUCTION

I am the Lord Thy God

The second is like unto it

Jan. 11

READ: Luke 10:25-37.

TEXT: Thou shalt love thy neighbor as thyself. Matthew 22:39.

♣

According to the great word of the apostle Paul the substance of our Christian religion is faith, hope, and love. He was in no doubt as to which of these three was the greatest; it was love. We love God, our Father, because He first loved us. We shall not love our neighbor much until we love God first. But just as truly, it is idle for us to claim that we love God unless we show it by our love for others here on earth. That is the test and the proof.

When we love we serve and sacrifice. We are glad to do this for those we love. Their love for one another was a distinguishing mark of the early Christians. "Behold, how they love one another!" was the comment of outsiders. All things are possible to him who believes (faith); they are less difficult to him who hopes; they are easiest of all to him who loves. Love wins through!

O Lord, Thou who art perfect love, lead me to love and to serve others without thought of self but solely that it may do them good and glorify Thy name. Amen.

Jan. 12

THE TEN COMMANDMENTS — INTRODUCTION

I am the Lord Thy God

Taking heed to the law

READ: Exodus 19:7-13.

TEXT: Wherewithal shall a young man cleanse his way? By taking heed thereto according to Thy word. Psalm 119:9.

✦

Sometime in your life you may say to yourself, "Why should I heed any law but my own desire?" You will soon find that there are many restraints which prevent such wilful and selfish conduct. The law of God, the commands of parents, the rules of school and society, and the laws of the state; each has an authority to which you must give heed. Sometimes they do not agree. It would seem to be common sense to learn which is the highest authority.

God has not left us in doubt here. "I am the Lord thy God," He says. He made us, He knows what is best for us, and He has given a perfect law. But even the best of us sin so that we have the sense of uncleanness. Conscience makes us ask, "Wherewithal shall I cleanse my way?" It is good to know the answer to that question. "By taking heed thereto according to Thy Word." That means: "Watch your step. Fear God and keep the commandments."

O God, whose laws are perfect, and whose ways are right, lead me in a plain path all my days, through Jesus Christ. Amen.

THE TEN COMMANDMENTS — INTRODUCTION

I am the Lord Thy God

Beware of idols

Jan. 13

READ: Exodus 20:1-6.
TEXT: Little children, keep yourselves from idols. I John 5:21.

✢

There is but one God. Nothing can replace Him. Everything that is comes from Him. He can withhold, and He can give. The created thing cannot take the place of God, nor can we substitute the created for the Creator. To do so would bring disaster. We worship that which we love. If we love anything more than God we are idolaters. Then God has not the first place in our heart. Israel worshiped the golden calf. What do we worship and love more than God?

O worship the King, all glorious above,
And gratefully sing His wonderful love;
Our Shield and Defender, the Ancient of Days,
Pavilioned in splendor and girded with praise.

Dear God, let me love Thee with all my heart and mind. Give me the light and understanding that nothing can take Thy place in my love for Thee. Give me the strength to fight victoriously against all temptations to put idols in Thy place, that all the honor and the glory may be Thine. Amen.

THE TEN COMMANDMENTS — INTRODUCTION

Jan. 14

I am the Lord Thy God

Jesus, our perfect example in fulfilling the law

READ: Matthew 5:17-20.

TEXT: Think not that I am come to destroy the law, or the prophets; I am not come to destroy, but to fulfil. Matthew 5:17.

✤

Someone once said that Jesus was the only man who ever dared to live His life inside out. That is why God, who sees the heart, could say, "This is My beloved Son, in whom I am well pleased." This through-and-through righteousness, this perfect goodness, this doing always the things which pleased His Father, this was the fulfilling, the "filling full" of the law, so that Jesus "left us an example, that we should follow in His steps."

There is this wonderful thing about Christ's fulfilment of the law. He fulfilled it not only for Himself but for us also. He is our perfect example, but we are such poor imitators of Him. But if God finds us following in His steps He accepts us as righteous for Jesus' sake. So He is not only our example but our fulfilment and thus our Savior. So keep your eyes on Jesus, and He will bring you safely to heaven.

O God, grant that I may so follow Jesus as to grow to be a mature man after the likeness of Thy Son, Jesus Christ, in whom Thou art well pleased. Amen.

THE FIRST COMMANDMENT

Thou shalt have no other Gods before Me
Image worship forbidden

Jan. 15

READ: Isaiah 42:5-16.

TEXT: I am the Lord, that is My name; and My glory will I not give to another. Isaiah 42:8.

♣

As Christians, even though we acknowledge Christ to be our King, we live in a material world which requires our attention in order to have food, clothing, shelter, and the like. Our problem is to "render to Caesar" that only which belongs to him.

We also recognize certain aids to worship, that is, our altar, the cross, candles, and many other appointments. These are symbols to direct our attention to God. As such they have no power to confer any favor let alone accept worship. Whoever attributes power or expects a favor of them has forgotten God and has taken a place with the worshipers of Baal. "Little children, keep yourselves from idols."

To some people these aids to worship, or the state, or even self-love have become as great a hindrance to entering the kingdom of God as any graven image. "Thou shalt love the Lord thy God with all thine heart, and with all thy soul, and with all thy mind."

O God, if I have worshiped any material thing or money or pleasure or even my own self I ask Thy forgiveness. Holy Spirit, lead me into true love and devotion to Christ. Amen.

THE FIRST COMMANDMENT

Jan. 16

Thou shalt have no other gods before Me

Worship only Him

READ: Matthew 4:1-11.

TEXT: Thou shalt worship the Lord thy God, and Him only shalt thou serve. Matthew 4:10.

♣

To worship is to fear, love, *or* trust in something. To worship God is to fear, love, *and* trust in God above all things. Satan tempted Jesus, as he tempts us, to worship something other than God. Jesus was not deceived. He knew that God alone is great and good and worthy of our worship. To worship anything other than God, even something which is good, is idolatry and cannot bring the satisfaction and the blessing which come when we worship God.

We are unhappy and discontented when we let the lesser things have first place or try to divide our trust between God and other things. Jesus says, "No man can serve two masters." The first and great commandment is this, "Thou shalt love the Lord thy God with all thy heart." When God said, "Thou shalt worship the Lord thy God and Him only shalt thou serve," He gave us more than a commandment. He gave us the rule by which men can live happily and successfully. And God knows this is best for us because He made us.

O God, the Father Almighty, Maker of heaven and earth, let me fear, love, and trust in Thee above all things, that I may enjoy Thee forever. Amen.

THE FIRST COMMANDMENT

Thou shalt have no other gods before Me

Obey Him

Jan. 17

READ: Acts 5:29-40.
TEXT: We ought to obey God rather than men. Acts 5:29.

♣

All of us know what it means to *obey*. While it may often be a difficult task, yet we *obey* gladly when we know that He whom we are to obey is One who deserves our obedience. Martin Luther clearly proved to us how obedience to God is not only expected, but how that obedience brings its own personal reward. There is no one, no person, no power, no force greater than God. Peter and the apostles in their trying days as leaders in the early church quickly took up this command and in thought, word, and deed *obeyed* God first. My very first ideal in life must be so to live that my whole life will be a loving obedience to Him who so loved the world that He gave His only-begotten Son to be our Savior. There is no god like our God; let us follow Him in faithful, cheerful obedience.

Dear Heavenly Father, help me to be obedient to Thy command. Help me to obey Thee first of all. Help me to obey Thee in fervent love to Thee. In Jesus' name. Amen.

THE FIRST COMMANDMENT

Jan. 18

Thou shalt have no other gods before Me

Fear Him

READ: Ecclesiastes 12:1-14.
TEXT: Fear God, and keep His commandments. Ecclesiastes 12:13.

✤

Man is naturally religious. Many of his self-made gods terrorize him. *Our* God is holy and just. Before Him we should stand in awe. When the Bible speaks of "the *fear* of the Lord" it does not mean a quaking terror as a slave has for a cruel master but a childlike reverence that shrinks from doing wrong. True, we should *"fear* His wrath" when we have sinned. But our attitude should be one of respect that will cause us to honor, worship, and serve Him as our Father. Our *fear* must be like that of a child who hesitates to offend his father and desires to do his will. Joseph *feared* to sin because of his great respect for God's command and his reverence for God. When we thus think of fear we shall appreciate the statement: "The *fear* [reverence] of the Lord is the beginning of wisdom."

O God, teach us to know Thee as our Father, that we may stand in awe of Thee, hold Thee in reverence, respect Thy commandments, and worship Thee in spirit and in truth. Amen.

THE FIRST COMMANDMENT

Thou shalt have no other gods before Me

Love Him

Jan. 19

READ: I John 5.

TEXT: For this is the love of God, that we keep His commandments; and His commandments are not grievous. I John 5:3.

♣

To *love* God above all is the climax of a Christian life. Just to *love* God among others is a mental attitude; even a philosopher is able to bow his head before the almighty and wise Creator. But to *love* Him above all means a life surrendered to God.

No one is left in darkness concerning the will of God. It is given already in the Ten Commandments. His commandments are only the means of showing us the sort of life that is pleasing to Him. God does not make us servants who cannot do "otherwise." He is longing for *love* and our understanding of His plans for us just as our parents are happy when we thank them for their efforts at helping us to progress.

On the highway of the Christian life we realize that everything that is worth while is the free gift of a loving, heavenly Father. Realizing this, it is no longer a problem to *love* Him above all. It becomes a natural attitude of our heart.

Lead me, O Lord, in light; make out of my life a piece of crystal which reflects a Christian life and love for Thee for the glory of Thy name forever. Amen.

THE FIRST COMMANDMENT

Jan. 20

Thou shalt have no other gods before Me

Trust Him

READ: Proverbs 3:1-12.

TEXT: Trust in the Lord with all thine heart. Proverbs 3:5.

✤

Many millions of people in our land claim to be Christian because they believe in God, that is, they believe about God. They believe that God created the world, provides for all needs, and protects. They believe that Jesus was born in Bethlehem; that He suffered, died, and rose again. Even so do the devils — and tremble.

But the belief in God that is genuine is the *trusting*, confiding faith in God. We may believe in many doctors. We believe that they are good doctors. But we are willing that only one operate on us—we *trust* him.

"*Trust* in the Lord with all thine heart," says Solomon. A divided heart, a divided will bring no happiness and certainly not the calm and the abiding joy in Jesus. Daily and diligent study of the Scriptures creates a greater yearning for the magnanimous God and builds a will to obey and to serve. The incessant exercise of prayer sways our will to the Master, Jesus Christ. *Trust* in the Lord!

Merciful God and Father, Thou hast kindled the flame of faith in our heart. Enable us to place all our confidence in Thee, for Thou art trustworthy. Amen.

THE FIRST COMMANDMENT

Thou shalt have no other gods before Me

Jesus, our perfect example

Jan. 21

READ: John 4:31-38.

TEXT: Jesus saith unto them, My meat is to do the will of Him that sent Me, and to finish His work. John 4:34.

♣

Healthy bodies require nourishing food. Doctors prescribe certain foods for infants that they may grow strong. While we may show a preference for different kinds of food we realize that we must have sufficient quantities of those nutritious foods that build strong bodies. What we eat will show its value, not only in physical health, but in mental alertness and in our general outlook on life.

Observe that Jesus Christ emphasizes the spiritual food which always has first place in His life. "My meat is to do the will of Him that sent Me."

Only in humble obedience to His Father's will could He accomplish or finish "His work."

Our greatest blessing is to have this mind of Christ, to feed our eternal, priceless souls on His Word, gladly obey His will, and love Him as He loved us. Following His behests, devoting ourselves to His service are spiritual "calories" that sustain our souls.

Precious Lord and Savior, show us Thyself and give us willing, obedient hearts to live Thy Word and to love the Father through Thee, for Thy name's sake. Amen.

THE SECOND COMMANDMENT

Jan. 22

Thou shalt not take the name of the Lord thy God in vain

Do not curse or swear

READ: Leviticus 24:10-16.
TEXT: Bless and curse not. Romans 12:14.

♣

"Keep off the grass" seems to mean, "Step on." The "Fresh Paint" sign has many finger marks. It has always been that way. "Thou shalt not," under Satan's tempting power, led Eve and Adam to disobey God. Here is Law Two standing before man since Moses was with God on Sinai, saying in two words: "Swear not." Are you obeying? You have recently promised to serve the Lord in His church. His law is one. His name is the first name: "In the beginning, God." Lower it never. Would *you* let anyone ridicule, defame, slander, or curse your mother? Would you do it? God's name is higher and greater; praise Him. Curse Him never. A shot-down soldier managed to plant his flagstaff by his side and hold it to the breezes all day. When stretcher bearers found him, the wounded standard-bearer said proudly, "She never touched the ground." You will honor your Lord by keeping His name high and unsullied. Praise — swear never. Your honest words need no profane props.

God of love and law, Giver of patience and strength, for Jesus' sake help me to master doubt and indifference lest I think Thy name unworthy and profane Thine honor. Purify my heart and my lips that my speech may be pleasing to Thee. Amen.

THE SECOND COMMANDMENT

Thou shalt not take the name of the Lord thy God in vain

Do not conjure

Jan. 23

READ: I Samuel 28:1-25.

TEXT: Saul had put away those that had familiar spirits. I Samuel 28:3b.

✣

When we obey God we place ourselves at His disposal. To *conjure* means to try to bend God's will to meet our desires. This is a serious sin. God was good to Saul. And at first Saul was true to God and put away those who had familiar spirits (fortune-tellers and spiritualists). Later on, however, he deserted God and, instead of being sorry for his sins, he was determined to take things into his own hands. He called upon an evil spirit through the person of the witch of Endor. In the Second Commandment God warns us against such practices. He tells us what not to do and thereby implies what we should do. Luther states this message clearly, "We should so fear and love God that we will not . . . conjure . . . by His name." Let us thank God for these guiding words. The Christian will not patronize or put his faith in those who pretend to be able to work magic or "charms" by the use of God's name. God's own mysterious, yet loving way of working is sufficient for him.

We thank Thee, Heavenly Father, that Thou hast revealed Thy will in the commandments. Help us to avoid abusing Thy name and so to grow in love toward Thee that we shall sin less each day. Amen.

THE SECOND COMMANDMENT

Jan. 24

Thou shalt not take the name of the Lord thy God in vain

Do not lie or deceive

READ: Proverbs 19:1-16.

TEXT: He that speaketh lies shall not escape. Proverbs 19:5.

❖

To *lie* or *deceive* seems bad enough under any circumstances, but "in His name"—how awful that sounds! They *lie* in the name of God "who teach falsehood and error and yet declare that they are teaching God's Word." Lest we be misled by such teachers or become such teachers ourselves we cannot be satisfied with our present knowledge but must continue our study of God's Word.

To *deceive* by His name is "done by those who assume Christ's name, calling themselves Christians and yet are hypocrites and use their religion for a cloak." How many there are who do this!

"Lying" and "deceiving"—are these things really very serious? The Bible speaks of Satan himself as "the great deceiver." And it describes the eternal city, the "New Jerusalem," as the place where there shall be "no liars." May we ever keep our eyes on Jesus, our perfect pattern, who "left us an example that we should follow His steps."

"Who can understand his errors? Cleanse Thou me from secret faults. Keep back Thy servant from presumptuous sins; let them not have dominion over me. Then shall I be upright, and I shall be innocent of the great transgression." In Jesus' name. Amen.

THE SECOND COMMANDMENT

Thou shalt not take the name of the Lord thy God in vain

But call upon Him

Jan. 25

READ: Psalm 50:1-15.

TEXT: Call upon Me in the day of trouble, and I will deliver thee, and thou shalt glorify Me. Psalm 50:15.

♣

A group of boys and girls were having a good time bathing and swimming at a popular beach. There were much shouting and happy laughter. Playfully and thoughtlessly one of them yelled, "Help! Help!" The lifeguard came as fast as he could, and when he saw that no one was in danger he scolded them for calling for help.

Later in the day the lifeguard heard the same cry for help from another group, and when he arrived at the scene, it was just in time to save a struggling boy from drowning. How often thoughtless and inconsiderate people use God's name without reason or profit, calling God when they really do not want Him as in cursing and swearing! That is why He rebukes us and says, "He will not hold him guiltless that taketh His name in vain." But when we are in need we are to call Him. As the lifeguard, He will hear and come to our rescue.

Lord, Thy name is holy. Guard my tongue that I may not abuse Thy name. Help me to use it with reverence and devotion. For Jesus' sake. Amen.

THE SECOND COMMANDMENT

Jan. 26

Thou shalt not take the name of the Lord thy God in vain

Worship Him with prayer

READ: Psalm 95.

TEXT: O come, let us worship and bow down, let us kneel before the Lord our Maker. Psalm 95:6.

♣

In Millet's great painting, "The Angelus," two workers in the field are pictured. Having heard the sound of the evening bell coming from the village church, they have bowed their heads in worship, their implements of toil laid aside. This scene emphasizes the close relationship between work and worship which we find abundantly illustrated in the life of Jesus. As we read the Gospels we are so greatly impressed with the deeds of love and mercy which crowded His daily life that we are liable to overlook its devotional side. Very much of His time was given to prayer and worship. Before the day began and when it ended or in the midst of it He would go apart from the crowd and the voices and the duties that called Him to be at one with His Father. It was His custom to go to the synagogue on the Sabbath Day. There was something in public worship and prayer that even the Son of God thought important and worth while.

Dear Savior, as Thou didst teach Thy disciples to pray, teach Thou me. Grant me joy and blessing in my attendance at divine worship, and may I with my fellow Christians worship Thee in spirit and in truth. Amen.

THE SECOND COMMANDMENT

Thou shalt not take the name of the Lord thy God in vain

Worship Him with praise and thanksgiving

Jan. 27

READ: Psalm 29.

TEXT: Worship the Lord in the beauty of holiness. Psalm 29:3.

♣

"We should fear, love, and trust in God above all things," says Luther. This is worship. But they belong together, "fear and love and trust." If we only fear God, life becomes a tedious path that is fenced in by "thou shalt" and "thou shalt not."

But when we "fear, love, and trust" we can truly worship, and the name of God becomes a constant invitation to worship with "prayer, praise, and thanksgiving." Because God is just and good, and His name is holy, we call upon the name of the Lord in godly fear. We pray. Because God is merciful and kind and has loved us, we love Him and delight to do His will and give thanks to Him.

The Christian life can be a happy path with singing and pleasure and joy if we "fear, love, and trust in God above all things." Worship brings the fulfillment of the last verse of our Psalm, "The Lord will give strength unto His people; the Lord will bless His people with peace."

Let me fear Thee, O God, for Thy holiness, love Thee for Thy mercy, and trust Thee for Thy faithfulness, that I may worship Thee with prayer, praise, and thanksgiving. Amen.

THE SECOND COMMANDMENT

Jan. 28

Thou shalt not take the name of the Lord thy God in vain

Jesus, our perfect example

READ: John 17:1-16.

TEXT: I have manifested Thy name unto the men which Thou gavest Me. John 17:6.

✣

Every person has a name by which he is known to his fellows, but this name tells us nothing of the person's character. God has several names. These names not only tell us *who* He is, but they also tell us *what* He is. These names of God tell us that God is *love*, and He wants to do good things for men. Jesus showed us how we should use God's names to call on Him. There was a poor man who was both deaf and mute. Jesus taught him to pray to God and then healed him. There was a poor woman who had a wayward daughter. Jesus taught her to call on God and then made the daughter well. There were several people who were greatly troubled in mind because they had sinned. Jesus taught them to call on God and gave them peace of mind. Jesus taught us by His example to call on God in every need: when our body is sick, when our mind is anxious, when our conscience is troubled.

We thank Thee, dear Father in heaven, that Thou hast described Thyself to us by telling us Thy name. Teach us to come to Thee in every time of need with a firm faith in our heart that Thou wilt hear us and help us, for Jesus' sake. Amen.

THE THIRD COMMANDMENT

Remember the Sabbath day, to keep it holy
Rest and worship on the Lord's Day

Jan. 29

READ: Exodus 20:8-11.

TEXT: And God blessed the seventh day, and hallowed it, because that in it He rested from all His work. Genesis 2:3.

♣

The law of God decrees that one day in every week all men *must* cease their normal work and *must* worship Him.

For a sound body, a normal nervous constitution, and peace of soul we need this day of rest and change. The adage coined by the wisdom of the ages might be paraphrased thus:

> "All work and no rest
> Makes wrecks of the best."

So our Father has commanded this "way of life."

Furthermore, Christians have discovered that there is no activity more refreshing and re-creative than worshiping God in the services of His house.

And so it is a matter of common sense that we observe this practice that we worship our Creator and Redeemer on the Lord's Day and refrain from every activity and recreation that interferes with worship and health.

Blessed Lord Jesus who hast promised, "I will give thee rest," enable us to do our work faithfully and to enjoy our rest peacefully, worshiping Thee here and hereafter. Amen.

THE THIRD COMMANDMENT

Jan. 30

Remember the Sabbath day, to keep it holy
Deem His Word holy

READ: I Samuel 3.
TEXT: Speak, Lord, Thy servant heareth. I Samuel 3:10.

✣

What a fine boy Samuel was! When God spoke to him in the Temple, he was there ready to hear what he said.

How does God speak to us today? Through His Word. When the pastor reads from the Bible and explains what he has read he is speaking the words of God.

When we listen carefully and take part in the service, our life is blessed and helped. For the Word of God and the Sacraments are means of grace—channels through which God's love and power flow into our life. No wonder young people, kneeling at the altar on their confirmation day, promise to "be instant in the use of the means of grace!"

Are *you* in God's house every Sunday? Remember, the best way to keep the Third Commandment is to give heed to God's Word and "willingly hear and learn it."

God, our Father, help us to love Thy house and Thy Holy Word. Brighten our life with the sunshine of the gospel that we may be Thy glad people. For Jesus' sake. Amen.

THE THIRD COMMANDMENT

Remember the Sabbath day, to keep it holy
Gladly hear His Word

Jan. 31

READ: Luke 10:38-42.

TEXT: Blessed are they that hear the Word of God, and keep it. Luke 11:23.

❖

As Christians we must frankly face the fact that Jesus did not keep the Sabbath after the manner of the religious leaders of His day. He had a better way—God's own way. Love was the keynote to His life and His work. He faithfully attended the services of the synagogue and heard the Scriptures. But because He loved His fellow men as He loved the Father He also never missed an opportunity to do them good. And when this opportunity presented itself on the Sabbath Day, He was not restrained by a superstitious or legalistic attitude toward the day. He blessed His fellow men with healing even though it offended the Pharisees.

If our use of the Sabbath Day is wholesome and helpful, we shall keep it in the spirit of love. Our love for God will cause us to use the day to hear His Word. Our love for our fellow men will lead us to spend some of the day calling on sick friends and bringing them His message and Christian cheer.

O Holy Spirit, give me the understanding which led our blessed Lord to use the Sabbath as He did and teach me to use the Lord's Day in the same loving way. In Jesus' name. Amen.

THE THIRD COMMANDMENT

Feb. 1

Remember the Sabbath day, to keep it holy
Gladly learn His Word

READ: Ecclesiastes 5:1-7.

TEXT: For whatsoever things were written aforetime were written for our learning. Romans 15:4.

✤

God gave us His holy Word to cleanse our heart, enlighten our mind, and strengthen our life. Through the Word we learn about His wrath against sin. We learn also about His love and His mercy and His forgiveness of those who humbly confess their sins and who look to Him in faith. Through the Word the Holy Spirit comes to make us patient and enduring, to comfort and sustain us in the struggle of life and to inspire us with hope and courage. "Ye shall know the truth, and the truth shall make you free."

All of life is a learning process. Young people especially are happy to learn. Are we letting God's Word be central in our curriculum? It is life and light and joy and peace. It gives us the fellowship of prophets and apostles. It reveals to us Christ in all the riches of His grace.

What a privilege to go to church! What a joy to hear and to learn God's Word! What blessings are ours through the gospel!

Heavenly Father, we thank Thee for Thy holy Word. Implant it anew in our heart that we may learn to love Thee as we ought to love, for Christ's sake. Amen.

THE THIRD COMMANDMENT

Remember the Sabbath day, to keep it holy
Gladly go to church

Feb. 2

READ: Psalm 122.
TEXT: Not forsaking the assembling of ourselves together. Hebrews 10:25.

✣

Dr. Simon Peter Long, an eminent Lutheran pastor, said it was his custom when he observed any of his confirmed young people becoming irregular in church attendance to send for them and inquire what they had been doing that was not right. He insisted that wrongdoing made them dislike church-going. If we find that we do not care about going to church we ought to ask ourselves why. It is a sign that the soul is sick, and that we are afraid to go to the doctor.

It will help, too, if we think of this and of all commandments of God not as the arbitrary rules of a hard master, which we must obey or suffer a penalty, whether we like to obey or not. They are rather the loving instruction and counsel of an all-wise God, who made us, and who knows what is best for us. He knows that Christian fellowship, public worship, the confession of sins, and reverent hearing of His Word are best for His children and make for happiness and contentment. Let us gladly go to church.

O God, send forth Thy light and Thy truth. Let them lead me to Thy holy place, where I may find joy and gladness. Amen.

THE THIRD COMMANDMENT

Feb. 3

Remember the Sabbath day, to keep it holy

Gladly do His Word

READ: James 1:21-27.

TEXT: Be ye doers of the word, and not hearers only. James 1:22.

✣

Pretty words may sound attractive, and they may fool some people, but they do not fool God. Our blessed Savior expects more from Christians than mere profession of Christianity and outward appearance. In spiritual matters as well as in secular affairs it is true, "Actions speak louder than words." One who truly believes in Jesus recognizes Him as a man of action, as One who obeyed the will of God in every detail. "I came down from heaven, not to do Mine own will, but the will of Him that sent Me." The disciple must be like his Master. As the great apostle Paul said: "Let this mind be in you, which was also in Christ Jesus." Let us be attentive, devout hearers of the Word of God, but let us also be *consecrated* doers of His will. Doing of the Word of God in faith and in trust carries with it a glorious promise: "Be thou faithful unto death, and I will give thee a crown of life."

Blessed Lord Jesus, help me daily to follow in Thy footsteps as a doer of the Word of God. Take my life and let it be consecrated, Lord, to Thee. Amen.

THE THIRD COMMANDMENT

Remember the Sabbath day, to keep it holy
Jesus, our perfect example

Feb. 4

READ: Luke 4:16-30.

TEXT: Jesus entered, as His custom was, into the synagogue on the Sabbath Day. Luke 4:16.

♣

During the course of His preaching tour in Galilee, Jesus came to His home town, Nazareth, and, as His custom was, He entered the synagogue on the Sabbath Day. Beautiful custom! We look upon Him as a blessed example worthy of imitation.

Jesus' parents had taken Him to the synagogue regularly. Never did He forget the day when as a boy of twelve He was permitted to attend the Temple services in Jerusalem. On the Sabbath Day He was a regular worshiper in the synagogue, and for the festival days He did not fail to journey to Jerusalem to worship in the Temple.

As a child of Jesus, baptized into His name and confirmed at His altar, should you not follow His example and be a regular worshiper at divine services?

Jesus has a blessing in store for you at every service. As His custom was, so you should attend divine services regularly that God may speak to you, and you to Him, that you together with other Christians may share His fellowship there.

We thank Thee, Lord Jesus, for the privilege we have of worshiping Thee in Thy sanctuary. We would draw nigh to Thee; come Thou to us and bless us. Amen.

THE FOURTH COMMANDMENT

Feb. 5

Honor thy father and thy mother

Obedience to parents and superiors

READ: Leviticus 19:1-3.

TEXT: The eye that mocketh at his father, and despiseth to obey his mother, the ravens of the valley shall pick it out, and the young eagles shall eat it. Proverbs 30:17.

✤

Other commandments tell us what we must not do. This one tells us one thing that we must do. It is God who speaks and not man: therefore we must heed or suffer His displeasure. We learn to honor and revere God by honoring our parents. They are responsible to Him for our training and development; we owe them our obedience. God promises a rich reward to those who obey, but of those who refuse to bestow such honor the "good eye" shall be plucked out, and they shall lose sight of all that is beautiful and worth while, for they have lost sight of God.

Why does God demand *obedience*? He seeks your good. He wants you to be happy. "If they obey and serve Him, they shall spend their days in prosperity, and their years in pleasure." *Obedience* gives life. Disobedience brings death. It is yours to choose. Choose life. Begin by obeying your parents.

Father, help me to obey Thy commands, for I would be like Jesus, who was obedient even to the death on the cross. Help me at all times to say, "Thy will be done in me." Amen.

THE FOURTH COMMANDMENT

Honor thy father and thy mother

Honor, serve, obey, love, and esteem them

Feb. 6

READ: Ephesians 6:1-10.
TEXT: Children, obey your parents in all things.
Colossians 3:20.

❖

The Fourth Commandment is the first commandment in the second table of the law. Our parents are God's representatives whom we should honor and acknowledge and thereby honor God. If we remember this we shall naturally not disrespect but honor, serve, obey, love, and esteem them as long as we live. We can never repay the sacrifices they endured for us, but let us realize that, next to God, they are our greatest possession. If we honor them we shall obey them both in spirit and in action. This commandment contains not only a promise of a reward but also a threat of punishment if we disobey our parents and superiors. Can you imagine a young man saying to his mother: "Mother, you can go to hell. I'll never darken this door again"? We know of one who did; and he left, slamming the door. Within three weeks his crushed and mangled body was brought from the coal mine through that same door.

Dear heavenly Father, help us to honor and obey our parents in all things, for this is pleasing to Thee. Let us live the Christian life so that Thou mightest be pleased with us. We ask it in the name of Jesus. Amen.

THE FOURTH COMMANDMENT

Feb. 7

Honor thy father and thy mother

Obedience to masters

READ: Colossians 3:20-25.

TEXT: Obey in all things your masters according to the flesh. Colossians 3:22.

♣

Dr. Martin Luther once wrote a tract called, *Christian Liberty*. His two propositions were: I. A Christian man is the most free lord of all and subject to none. II. A Christian man is the most dutiful servant of all and subject to everyone.

We thank God that there is no longer human slavery among us. But as men become free from slavery and the bondage of sin and enter into the glorious liberty of the sons of God they discover that they want to serve. The democratic system is built upon the idea of the willing service of free men. The president is the servant of the American people. We are servants of the state and owe allegiance and obedience to it. We owe honest service to our employers, and we owe to every man respect, courtesy, kindness, and service. It is the sign of true Christians "to live," as St. Paul says, "as free men; but to live as the servants of God."

O God, make me, indeed, a son of God and therefore free that I may humble myself to be a servant of all after the pattern of Thine only Son, our Lord Jesus Christ, and for His sake. Amen.

THE FOURTH COMMANDMENT

Honor thy father and thy mother

Obedience to church

Feb. 8

READ: Hebrews 13:17-25.

TEXT: Obey them that have the rule over you. Hebrews 13:17.

♣

Look! A two-headed calf! What a freak!

Obedience is to keep us from becoming freaks in our relationships to God and to man. Christ as head of His church rules me out as another head of the church. Man, holding a God-appointed position of leadership, makes it impossible for me to hold that position at the same time. No normal being has two heads. A home, a congregation, a church school, a league, or any other group cannot prosper with two heads.

Obedience, strange to say, tends toward happiness and freedom. Disobedience results in a bad, troubled conscience and makes restrictions necessary.

A Christian finding life healthier and happier, due to obeying God's will, understands that he cannot engage in the Father's business effectively if he does not obey those whom God has placed over him. Our church merits our faithful, conscientious obedience to its direction and cooperation in its work.

I would labor effectively in Thy kingdom, dear Jesus. Give me grace obediently to take my place lest I prove to be a hindrance rather than a help. Amen.

THE FOURTH COMMANDMENT

Feb. 9

Honor thy father and thy mother

Obedience to the state

READ: Romans 13:1-10.

TEXT: Let every soul be subject unto the higher powers. Romans 13:1.

♣

Our God is a God of order. He governs all creation by laws He has established in the moral as well as in the physical realm.

The law which our God has established in the moral realm, in so far as it pertains to our citizenship on earth, is expressed in the Fourth Commandment. This commandment binds us as Christians to obedience and subjection to the powers that be, that is, our national, state, and community government. Submission to and conscientious administration of authority are a vital Christian duty. When St. Paul declares, "Let every soul be in subjection to the higher powers," he is speaking as a spokesman for God, and in this world of ours where so much delegated power is abused it is necessary for us Christians carefully to weigh our duty of citizenship lest we sin against God and against our fellow men. The best sort of patriotism is a Christian duty.

Lord Jesus, Thou who hast so humbly subjected Thyself to the powers in this world as the Son of man, guide us in our efforts to keep Thy commands with regard to obedience to all authority. Amen.

THE FOURTH COMMANDMENT

Honor thy father and thy mother
Obedience to God

Feb. 10

READ: Acts 5:17-32.
TEXT: We must obey God rather than men. Acts 5:29.

✣

"Obedience" is not a very popular term with most of us. It sounds kind of dull and childish, and we prefer to think that we've outgrown the obligation to be "obedient." But the time never arrives when we can afford to forget what God expects of us, and the first thing is obedience. We must obey Him and His will rather than anyone else.

What does that have to do with our parents? God has given them to us and us to them. And He has given them supervision over our life—to train and guide and counsel us and provide for our other needs. They are responsible to Him for their parental faithfulness, and we, in turn, learn obedience to Him through our loving obedience to our parents. So God has wisely said, "Honor thy father and thy mother that it may be well with thee, and thou mayest live long upon the earth."

Someone has said, "Wicked men obey from fear: good men from love." It is the latter kind of obedience that God desires. And that begins "at home."

O God, teach us true obedience. Grant us the will to obey. Fill us with Thy divine love that obedience to Thee and our parents may become more and more complete. In Jesus' name. Amen.

THE FOURTH COMMANDMENT

Feb. 11

Honor thy father and thy mother

Jesus, our perfect example in obedience

READ: Luke 2:42-52.

TEXT: And He went down with them . . . and was subject unto them. Luke 2:51.

♣

The life of our Lord Jesus on earth was one of submission to the will of His Father in heaven. One of the outstanding characteristics of His redemptive work was obedience. Yet in His human relationships He also showed the proper regard and respect for the wishes of those whom God placed over Him. Of Him we read as a dutiful child, "And went down with them, and came to Nazareth, and was subject unto them."

Here the Lord gives us a perfect example of obedience to the will of His parents. He did not think Himself above them or their equal. He always did what pleased them. It must be very displeasing to the Lord Jesus when in our day so many boys and girls snub, hurt, and offend their parents by unkind and flippant words, or when they disregard their wishes entirely. As obedient children let us follow His noble example.

Dear Lord Jesus, help us to be obedient children. Make us kind and devoted. Give us a dutiful heart that is willing to serve Thee and our dear parents. Amen.

THE FIFTH COMMANDMENT

Thou shalt not kill

Do your neighbor no bodily harm

Feb. 12

READ: I John 3.

TEXT: Whosoever hateth his brother is a murderer. I John 3:15.

✤

Surely, we say, we have not sinned against this commandment! We have not killed anyone! May we never! For God alone gives life; He alone may take it.

The Fifth Commandment, however, forbids more than murder. God commands us through it "not to do our neighbor any bodily harm or injury" and "to assist and comfort our neighbor in danger and want." Thus, as in every commandment, He forbids us to hate and commands us to love. Only by so doing shall we be able to fulfill His will.

Have you ever, in a moment of anger, hoped that something should happen to someone, or wished him bad luck?

"Whosoever hateth his brother is a murderer." Hate is sin and leads to ever more and more sin. But if the Lord Jesus dwells in our heart by faith, sin will die, there will be no more room for hate; and our love will help us more and more to keep this and all the commandments of God.

Dear Lord Jesus, who didst give Thy life in love for us, help us to love others as Thou dost love us, that we may be a blessing to our fellow men, never harm, but ever help them. Amen.

THE FIFTH COMMANDMENT

Feb. 13

Thou shalt not kill
Nor cause him any suffering

READ: Genesis 4:1-16.

TEXT: For in the image of God created He man. Genesis 9:6.

♣

In Noah mankind made a new start. The old generation was washed away; the new mankind was about to launch forth. One of the sins on account of which the previous generation was destroyed was violence; in God's plan for man *violence* has no place. God Himself does not act in unprovoked violence. He created man in His own image, which is to be kept inviolate. Man shall not lift up his hand against his brother, thereby to deface that image.

There is much suffering in the world and will be while the world stands. Much of it is the result of carelessness and indifference toward the welfare of others. When a motorist's "driving through" a stop sign or traffic light results in the injury of others, he violates this commandment. The Christian will try to avoid either deliberately or accidentally bringing suffering to his fellow men. They are all God's creatures, precious in His sight. The Christian owes them his concern, his brotherly interest and kindness.

O God, our Father, who didst create us brothers and sisters, fill us with love for each other; strengthen us in deeds of brotherly love; let us ever live as Thy children in Jesus Christ. Amen.

THE FIFTH COMMANDMENT

Thou shalt not kill

But help and befriend him in every time of need

Feb. 14

READ: Matthew 7:1-12.

TEXT: Whatsoever ye would that men would do to you, do ye even so to them. Matthew 7:12.

✣

Luther always points out that each commandment means not only, "Thou shalt not," but also, "Thou shalt." So in this commandment it is not enough not to kill. We keep the commandment only when we preserve life and help and befriend anyone in need. As a Christian I do not wish to kill or hurt or harm another. But I am just as guilty when I refuse help to them or fail to relieve their distress.

Who is my neighbor? Whom should I help? Jesus answered that question in the parable of the Good Samaritan. There is no one in all the world, far or near, to whom I should not be a neighbor.

Again let us think of the commandment as the loving counsel of the all-wise Maker and Father, who loves us all. God knows that if men refrained from war and killing and rather helped and befriended each other, this would make for pleasant homes, good communities, and a peaceful world. This is the Golden Rule. This is the mind of Christ.

O God, who art gracious and full of compassion, and whose will it is that none should perish by the act of another, let me have the mind of Christ that I may be a friend to all the children of men. Amen.

THE FIFTH COMMANDMENT

Feb. 15

Thou shalt not kill
Concerning capital punishment

READ: Genesis 9:1-7.

TEXT: Whoso sheddeth man's blood, by man shall his blood be shed. Genesis 9:6.

♣

You have just read God's law which is the foundation for what we call "capital punishment." God spoke these words to Noah and his family, the only people left after the Great Flood. At the very beginning of a new generation of men this law was laid down as a protection to human life. "I will hold men accountable for one another's life," God has said.

Whenever the capital-punishment argument comes up, God's Word must be final for the Christian, no matter how sentimental he may become over executions of criminals. God, who has made men, claims the sole sovereignty over their life. To established government and its official courts alone, says Paul in Romans 13, has God delegated the right to carry out this law. We must respect His wisdom in this divine appointment. When government demands the life of a wilful murderer it is acting in God's name in the interest of society and the prevention of crime.

Eternal and wise God, help me always to accept Thy Word as the final truth in regulating the affairs of all men and give me a holy respect for the great value Thou dost place upon one's life. For Jesus' sake. Amen.

THE FIFTH COMMANDMENT

Thou shalt not kill

Concerning war

Feb. 16

READ: I Chronicles 5:11-22.

TEXT: For there fell down many slain, because the war was of God. I Chronicles 5:22.

✤

The Fifth Commandment teaches, "Thou shalt not kill." In time of war especially the question often arises: "Is it not a sin against the Fifth Commandment to go to war?" Many have answered yes and become conscientious objectors. Are they right?

Let us look at the Scriptures and the Confessions of our church. Christ tells us that there shall be wars and rumors of wars to the end of time. As long as Satan is in the world and evil in the hearts of men, war will come. We cannot, therefore, evade its consequences but must share its responsibilities.

As for the individual, the Augsburg Confession teaches that the Christian may serve as a soldier, and it is his duty as a citizen to take up arms when it is in defense of his country. If, however, he is convinced in his conscience that his country is in the wrong, it is his God-given privilege to refuse to bear arms.

Father Almighty, we thank Thee that in our country we may worship Thee according to Thy Word and the dictates of our conscience. Give us peace, peace in our land, peace in our heart, through Jesus Christ, our Lord. Amen.

THE FIFTH COMMANDMENT

Feb. 17

Thou shalt not kill

Concerning suicide

READ: Romans 13:10-14.
TEXT: Do thyself no harm. Acts 16:28.

✣

Have you ever been completely discouraged? Did the thought ever come to you that life was not worth living? Perhaps sickness, failures, and disappointments of various kinds gave you a feeling of, "What's the use!" Then you have been face to face with your life's worst enemy.

Self-murder, whether by slow degree through a life in vice, where drunkenness, gluttony, and sex indulgence hold sway, or by a direct act of suicide, is a most hideous sin which dishonors the Father who created us, deprives the Son and the Holy Spirit of their mission of salvation and sanctification, and ushers the perpetrator into a hopeless eternity. Concerning the mentally unbalanced, we have no answer; God alone can judge responsibility. As for ourselves, life is not ours but God's; we dare not take it but must preserve it.

O Lord, teach me to realize the value of my temporal life. Help me to be grateful to the Giver of that life and to know my Savior, through whom alone I can be more than victorous in all temptations, trials, and discouragements. Amen.

THE FIFTH COMMANDMENT

Thou shalt not kill

Jesus, the Good Samaritan

Feb. 18

READ: Luke 10:25-37.

TEXT: When he saw him, he had compassion on him. Luke 10:33.

❧

Through the Fifth Commandment the Lord, our God, would protect and preserve life. He would protect and preserve plant life and animal life, but He is especially concerned about human life. It is our best earthly possession, and it is true that a man will give all he has for his life. A redeemed and sanctified life has remarkable possibilities, hence we must never abuse our life, but we must aim to preserve it.

Jesus gave us the story about the man who fell among the thieves. We find three classes of men represented in this story: there are those who beat him up; those who passed him up; and the one who picked him up, the Good Samaritan. Jesus is our Good Samaritan, for He gave Himself into death in order that we might have life, and have it more abundantly. He is our perfect example in saving life, and since He has loved us so wonderfully, we should also love Him and our fellow man.

Eternal Father in heaven, help us by Thy grace to understand the value of life. Forgive us where we have failed in our love to Thee and our fellow men. Help us to follow the example of our Lord Jesus Christ and to be good Samaritans while we live. Amen.

THE SIXTH COMMANDMENT

Feb. 19

Thou shalt not commit adultery

Lead a chaste and pure life

READ: I Corinthians 3:16-23.

TEXT: Blessed are the pure in heart: for they shall see God. Matthew 5:8.

♣

Blessed, that is, happy are the pure in heart. The inefficiency, the bitterness, the frustration which mar so many lives and enfeeble everyone at times are due to the fact that our heart and our mind become clouded, our purposes confused, our personalities divided, and consequently the whole quality of our being is depressed. When dirt gets into the carburetor of the motor, it misses fire. When the eyes of the mind are blinded by passion or hatred or avarice or pride, we no longer see God. The sun goes out. To "see God" is to live in harmony with the best of which we are capable. It is to be true to the ideal with all one's heart and mind and senses functioning for that "best" which ever stirs deep within the heart of man, too often only as a wistful dream. The pure in heart are the blessed company who possess the undivided mind and the clean spirit.

Dear Lord, since with Thee all things are possible and without Thee all life becomes distracted and futile, send, we beseech Thee, Thy Holy Spirit to purify and cleanse our heart and our mind so that we may be wholly Thine and rejoice in Thy power and presence, for Jesus' sake. Amen.

THE SIXTH COMMANDMENT

Thou shalt not commit adultery

Husband and wife each love and honor the other

Feb. 20

READ: Ephesians 5:22, 23.
TEXT: Wives, submit yourselves unto your own husbands.... Husbands, love your wives. Colossians 3:18, 19.

♣

The Fifth Commandment requires a right attitude of respect, courtesy, and kindness toward everybody. The Sixth Commandment concerns two people who in marriage come apart from all others, and who must have a special love and honor toward each other. God appointed it so and said, "A man shall leave his father and mother and be joined to his wife, and they shall be one flesh."

This commandment is God's prescription for human happiness in the home. Husband and wife must have right attitudes toward each other, each knowing his or her proper place as "is fit in the Lord." In a Christian home godly living, personal humility, unselfish conduct, family worship, church attendance, and the establishment of Jesus Christ as the Head of the house will enable husband and wife to keep the marriage vow to "love, honor, and cherish until death."

O God, who hast ordained marriage, grant that when we enter upon this holy estate we may find grace to live in constant fidelity and true affection toward each other, that we may find true happiness here and entrance into the home eternal. Amen.

THE SIXTH COMMANDMENT

Feb. 21

Thou shalt not commit adultery

Marriage is honorable

READ: Galatians 5:19-21.
TEXT: Marriage is honorable in all. Hebrews 13:4.

✣

Life at its best is always a partnership. As children we first see it in our own homes where father and mother in sincere, godly love toil together for us. We then form a divine partnership with God in our confirmation promises which are sacred and become more meaningful with the years. And as we have grown in our home and in our church in the fear and the love of God we have been preparing to join our heart in the sanctity of marriage. It is a blessed experience when a fine Christian young man and a lovely Christian young woman bind their hearts in unstained love. We know they are truly no more just two personalities but one unit, a partnership. And we know also that what God has joined together must remain sacred in the sight of men. These splendid young people have made a covenant in Christ which will spell *home, happiness, and peace.*

Dear gracious God, we thank Thee that Thou didst establish marriage for man's welfare and happiness. Keep us pure, clean, and holy in life now that we may become fit husbands and wives and establish homes that will be pleasing to Thee. Amen.

THE SIXTH COMMANDMENT

Thou shalt not commit adultery

Concerning divorce

Feb. 22

READ: Matthew 19:3-9.

TEXT: What God hath joined together let not man put asunder. Matthew 19:6.

❖

One day a man and his wife, following an argument, decided to part ways, to get a divorce. Their pastor asked them to listen to the words of the wedding service which he had used when they were united in marriage. After hearing the solemn words, they asked, "Did we really promise to walk down life's pathway, 'forsaking all others, keep thee only unto her (him) as long as ye both shall live,' and 'I plight thee my troth till death do us part' "? They decided not to be divorced.

In the wedding service you have the will of God for marriage. There you learn that divorce—every divorce—involves sin and so is contrary to His will. The Bible recognizes divorce only where one of the partners has broken the marriage vows either by violating the Sixth Commandment or by deliberately deserting the other. The innocent party is thereby released from that marital obligation and may in the course of time remarry.

Lord Jesus, bless the holy ordinance of marriage. Strengthen all Christian husbands and wives in constant fidelity and true affection toward each other until death do them part. Amen.

THE SIXTH COMMANDMENT

Feb. 23

Thou shalt not commit adultery

Concerning adultery

READ: Matthew 5:27-32.

TEXT: Whosoever looketh upon a woman to lust after her hath committed adultery with her already in his heart. Matthew 5:28.

♣

Our Lord Jesus was concerned about our eyes when He mentioned the Sixth Commandment in the Sermon on the Mount. If you can keep your eyes from breaking the Sixth Commandment you will have no difficulty with the other members of your body. Train your eyes to enjoy the good. Read only that which is uplifting and clean and wholesome. Avoid the company of those who speak unclean language and tell filthy stories. Cultivate acquaintance with the boys and the girls of the best Christian character. Ask your Savior, the Lord Jesus, to go with you, and you will preserve your soul. Do not worry if an evil thought does come into your mind. These are temptations. Luther has wisely said, "You cannot keep all evil thoughts from your mind any more than you can keep birds from flying over your head, but you can keep the birds from building nests in your hair." So you can avoid those places, that company, those books and magazines which suggest evil thoughts. Your Lord and Savior will help you.

"Create in me a clean heart, O God, and renew a right spirit within me." Amen.

THE SIXTH COMMANDMENT

Thou shalt not commit adultery
God instituted marriage

Feb. 24

READ: Genesis 2:18-25.

TEXT: It is not good that man should be alone, I will make a help meet for him. Genesis 2:18.

♣

God is all-wise and good. He saw that it was not good for man to be alone. God made a companion for the man. It was woman.

Then God married the man and the woman. They were now to be one in everything. They were also to provide a home for the children God would give them.

God says that a husband and a wife must love one another and be faithful one to the other. When they are married they promise each other that they will be faithful unto death. God gave us the Sixth Commandment to protect the home. By this He shows us that marriage is serious.

We can prepare now for the home God will give to us. We are to be clean and pure in body, mind, and soul. There must be no unclean habits, words, or thoughts in the life of God's child. Jesus said, "Blessed are the pure in heart, for they shall see God." Only Jesus can make us and keep us truly clean and pure.

Dear Jesus, we thank Thee for home. Cleanse my mind and soul every day so that I may be pure in heart and clean in body. In Jesus' name. Amen.

THE SIXTH COMMANDMENT

Feb. 25

Thou shalt not commit adultery

Jesus sanctified marriage

READ: John 2:1-11.

TEXT: There was a marriage in Cana of Galilee . . . and Jesus also was bidden . . . to the marriage. John 2:1, 2.

✣

Those who invited Jesus to the wedding in Cana of Galilee were wise. Without Him they would have missed a great blessing. Jesus sanctified their marriage. Jesus ought to be invited to every wedding. We may invite Him by having our pastor read the marriage service so that the vows may be made under the church's blessing, with sincere and reverent minds.

Jesus wants to stay in every home. We may keep Him by having a family altar, that is, by reading God's Word, each one for himself and all together as a family group, thinking carefully what the Word teaches and asking God's help to do it. Where Jesus stays He prompts everyone to fear God and to try always to please Him. He helps parents and children to love and to respect one another and to be pure in thoughts and words and deeds. Where Jesus stays, God's blessings abound.

Lord Jesus, come to our home and stay there so that we may always be clean and upright in heart and in life. Amen.

THE SEVENTH COMMANDMENT

Thou shalt not steal

Do not rob your neighbor

Feb. 26

READ: Proverbs 30:7-9.
TEXT: Let him that stole, steal no more. Ephesians 4:28.

✣

A thief never prospers. Sooner or later his sin will catch up with him. Not only does that which he steals dwindle away, but society puts a mark upon him. People will not trust him because he does not respect the difference between "mine and thine." In every prison and reformatory a path has been worn into solid stone floors by the feet of thousands of dishonest people. It is like the rut of a sinful life which may have begun by stealing just one cent and then led to larger thefts which brought the woe to them of which Jeremiah writes. The demand for honesty of heart and life is made not only by society. It comes from God. It is necessary to happiness and respect. We should be honest with God and return to Him gifts of thanksgiving of that with which He has entrusted us.

Dear heavenly Father, Thou givest gifts to all. Help me to be honest in all my dealings with others and share with the unfortunate. In gratitude to Thee lead me to give of what is mine for the service of Thy church, for Jesus' sake. Amen.

THE SEVENTH COMMANDMENT

Feb. 27

Thou shalt not steal

Do not defraud your neighbor

READ: I Thessalonians 4:1-12.

TEXT: For this is the will of God ... that no man go beyond and defraud his brother in any matter. I Thessalonians 4:3-6.

❧

Stealing is a very dangerous sin and a very common one, when we see it in all its forms. Luther stresses "unfair dealing and fraudulent means." In the Old Testament we read of one who said, "I saw, I coveted, I took." Sin, when it comes to us in the form of temptation, first asks for tolerance, it then seeks equality, and it finally assumes mastery. It is said that the "little foxes spoil the vines." Little sins lead to great sins. Cheating in business, driving sharp bargains are the fraudulent practices that are the same as stealing. They are void of godliness and are due to another sin, that of covetousness. The fact is that all sins are related and every one is bad. Moreover, if we commit one sin we are "guilty of the whole law." Hopeless, indeed, would be the state of the sinner were it not for the fact that "we have redemption through His blood, the forgiveness of sins, according to the riches of His grace," Ephesians 1:7.

Father, give us a pure heart that our hands may be clean. Take away all selfishness and increase in us a growing desire to give rather than to receive. Let Jesus rule our life. Amen.

THE SEVENTH COMMANDMENT

Thou shalt not steal

Protect your neighbor's property

Feb. 28

READ: Luke 16:1-12.

TEXT: Therefore, all things whatsoever ye would that men should do to you, do ye even so to them. Matthew 7:12.

❖

Love makes the world go 'round. That was settled for all time and under all circumstances when Jesus told the story of the Good Samaritan.

How timely this story today, which illustrates the Golden Rule and in general is so little and so superficially regarded in our time! Instead of following the Golden Rule we have rather adopted the rule of gold. But God's rule, God's commandment requires going out of our way to protect our neighbor's property, whether it means returning his lost wallet or taking his schoolbooks in out of the rain or helping with his chores when he is sick. It is in such "everyday" things that we prove the sincerity of our Christianity.

Dear Lord, help us to have the vision of the Master as we look upon the great living, moving body of the peoples of the earth and make us charitable and patient and broad-minded in our relations to them; and may we have the mind and the spirit of the great and Good Samaritan, even Jesus, the Righteous One. Amen.

THE SEVENTH COMMANDMENT

Feb. 29

Thou shalt not steal

Earn your living by honest work.

READ: II Thessalonians 3:10-18.

TEXT: If any will not work, neither let him eat. R. V. II Thessalonians 3:10.

♣

Have you ever heard anyone say: "The world owes me a living. Some have more. I do not have my share. Therefore, I have a right to my share. And since they do not willingly give me my share, therefore, I have the right to take what is coming to me. I have the right to take from others in any way possible or convenient that which in reality should be mine"?

Thus would Satan seek to lure, ensnare, and destroy the souls of men. The old evil foe who means us deadly woe is not satisfied with halfway measures. He is not satisfied unless we do his bidding and are completely subject to him. Scripture says: "Recompense to no man evil for evil. Provide things honest in the sight of all men," Romans 12:17. That means doing honest work, and doing it honestly, not just in order to get paid, but to make a satisfying contribution to the welfare and the happiness of other people.

Dear heavenly Father, bless the labor of my hands. Help me at all times to be honest in thoughts, words, and deeds so that my soul may bless Thee here in time and in eternity forever. Amen.

THE SEVENTH COMMANDMENT

Thou shalt not steal

Cheating and gambling are wrong

March 1

READ: Genesis 3:14-19.

TEXT: In the sweat of thy face shalt thou eat bread. Genesis 3:19.

♣

God has provided us with physical equipment such as the members of the body, the senses, and the mental faculties. They may be trained and used to provide a living for ourselves and those who depend on us.

This is God's way of "keeping us going." It is the "sweaty work way." Some folks call it the "hard way" because of the work connected with it. On that account it is not agreeable; some folks do not like to work. They are afraid of anything that is hard. The important fact, however, is that it is God's way. That is the way in which God wants us to earn a living.

Because some folks want the "easy way" they have invented other ways of getting a living: cheating and gambling. It is the "easy way," man's way, and it is contrary to God's way and will. Better to follow God's way even if it is the hard way. Then you know you are right.

Help me to discover my physical and my mental powers and to develop them. Give me opportunity to work. Give me courage to withstand the trend of the times and not to follow the "easy way." Amen.

THE SEVENTH COMMANDMENT

March 2

Thou shalt not steal

Be faithful in your work

READ: Luke 16:1-12.

TEXT: It is required in stewards that a man be found faithful. I Corinthians 4:2.

♣

We are all stewards, that is, keepers and users of things and abilities which have been given us, and for whose use we are responsible.

The employer is a steward and should pay honest wages. The worker is a steward and should give an honest day's service. Disputes and difficulties between labor and management arise because men are not being good stewards of wages or time. God gave us the Seventh Commandment to teach us that honesty is the basis of good-will and understanding.

We are all stewards also in the use of our money, time, and strength for the care of the poor and needy and for the Lord's work.

To have a good conscience, the blessing of God, and the confidence and respect of my fellow men I must do my chores willingly, my school lessons faithfully, my work honestly, my thinking rightly, my giving generously, and I must do all "heartily, as unto the Lord."

O God, who looketh upon the heart, help me to be honest in my work and faithful in all things, that, being a good steward, I may find favor with Thee and with all men. Through Jesus Christ, the Faithful. Amen.

THE SEVENTH COMMANDMENT

Thou shalt not steal

Jesus, our perfect example

March 3

READ: II Corinthians 8:1-9.

TEXT: Though He was rich, yet for your sakes He became poor, that ye through His poverty might become rich. II Corinthians 8:9.

♣

The desire to get rich is universal. Almost everything we do, from choosing friends to selecting courses of study, is motivated by this desire. Even our religious life is thought of largely in terms of what we can get out of it. The fact is that all of us are so deeply lost in this desire for personal gain that we look upon any kind of "profit motive" as something to be preserved at all costs.

But now look at Jesus! How unselfishly He lived! How completely He lived for the enrichment of others! He was willing even to become poor in order to make others rich. This, writes Paul, is your perfect example. God has made you rich in Christ in order that you might enrich others. To aspire to anything less is to rob both God and your neighbor.

O God, send us Thy Holy Spirit that we might be given power to live completely for Thee and for our neighbor. Amen.

THE EIGHTH COMMANDMENT

March 4

Thou shalt not bear false witness against thy neighbor

Do not deceitfully belie, betray, backbite, nor slander your neighbor

READ: Ephesians 4:25-32.

TEXT: Putting away lying, speak every man truth with his neighbor. Ephesians 4:25.

♣

An old story tells us that a king once asked of the wise men of Greece to bring him the best and the worst part of the sacrifice. Shortly after the wise man sent the tongue of a sacrificed animal to the king. Thus the wise man indicated that the tongue may be the best or the worst part. It depends upon the use made of it. The New Testament writer James compares the tongue to the little helm that steers great ships. But it is also the most dangerous member in the human body which can create untold misery and wretchedness. Our good name and character may be defamed and wrecked by the tongue that peddles rumors among men. The tongue creates wars which throw nations and the world into chaos. God gave us our tongue to speak truthfully and to glorify His name in everything we say.

Heavenly Father, cleanse our heart from evil that our speech may be clean and pure. Help us to glorify Thee in everything we say and do. For Jesus' sake. Amen.

THE EIGHTH COMMANDMENT

Thou shalt not bear false witness against thy neighbor

Speak well of your neighbor

READ: I Samuel 19:1-7.

TEXT: And Jonathan spake good of David unto Saul, his father. I Samuel 19:4.

♣

Jonathan's friendship for David is proverbial. By speaking well of him, Jonathan saved his life. He was an athletic lad, a courageous youth, and a fearless warrior. Yet he performed the greatest service to David simply by speaking good of him. Thus Jonathan proved his friendship.

Opportunities to do likewise present themselves constantly. A life may be saved by kind words but ruined just as effectively by a slanderous tongue. When Diogenes was asked, "What is that beast, the bite of which is most dangerous?" he replied, "Of wild beasts, the bite of the slanderer; and of the tame beasts, that of the flatterer."

Jesus is man's best friend. He never debased Himself by flattering anyone, yet even on the cross He spoke good of His enemies, saying, "Father, forgive them, for they know not what they do."

"Oh! many a shaft at random sent finds mark the author little meant; and many a word at random spoken may soothe or wound a heart that's broken" (Scott).

O God, for Jesus' sake, keep my tongue from evil and my lips from speaking guile. Amen.

THE EIGHTH COMMANDMENT

March 6

Thou shalt not bear false witness against thy neighbor

Gossiping is wrong

READ: James 4:1-11.
TEXT: Speak not evil, one of another. James 4:11.

✤

My mother always taught us children that, when we could not speak well of others, we should say nothing. Keep silent. This, she explained, "would enable us to discover some good in everyone that we could talk about." "Never," said she, "say anything behind another's back that you would not cheerfully say to his face. It is easier to besmirch a character than to help build it."

Character is priceless in God's sight, and the evil we may speak of another reveals what manner of person we are in God's sight. Our Lord always spoke against the evil that would destroy men's souls, but He never went about spreading evil reports about others. Follow Him in this.

The writer James writes: "If any man among you seem to be religious, and bridleth not his tongue but deceiveth his own heart, this man's religion is vain," James 1:26. Out of the heart the mouth speaketh. So keep thy heart with all diligence, for out of it are the issues of life.

Let the words of my mouth and the meditations of my heart be acceptable in Thy sight, O Lord, my Teacher and Savior. Amen.

THE EIGHTH COMMANDMENT

Thou shalt not bear false witness against thy neighbor

Lying in business is wrong

March 7

READ: John 8:33-44.

TEXT: He [Satan] is a liar, and the father of it. John 8:44.

♣

In doing business people are oftentimes tempted to lie. In advertising, in recommending their goods they do not always strictly adhere to the truth. Some think a man cannot be successful in business if he would tell nothing but the truth.

But lying is from the devil, of whom Jesus says, "He is a liar, and the father of it." Even if one should suceed in obtaining a temporary and material advantage by lying he can never enjoy his success as a blessing but has polluted his conscience by commiting a sin against God.

God is truth, and He wants His children to walk in truth. If God wants to bless us with material gifts He is able to accomplish His will without our sinful meddling. If we do the will of God and sin not, He will in the end have everything turn out well, and we can really enjoy His blessings.

Lord, enlighten my heart to see that nothing can be a blessing for me if it is obtained by sin. Help me to tell the truth in all things. Amen.

THE EIGHTH COMMANDMENT

March 8

Thou shalt not bear false witness against thy neighbor
"White lies" (social lying)

READ: Revelation 21:1-8.

TEXT: Deliver my soul, O Lord, from lying lips, and from a deceitful tongue. Psalm 120:2.

✣

We often speak less or other than the truth, especially in our social and our business life. The truth is often harsh and offends men. The untruth, we think, is kinder. We call these "white lies" and dismiss them as necessary and harmless.

How can we as Christians reconcile truth with kindness so that we shall always speak truth with our neighbor?

First, let us not deceive ourselves. "God looketh upon the heart." He despises a lying tongue. He desires the love of truth in the heart so that truth may be upon our lips.

Then we ought not to invite or expect unmerited praise and flattery and thus tempt others to speak untruths to us. And we must be so true and loving and kind in our own manner and speech that truth from our lips will not offend.

It is not easy. This commandment is most frequently broken. We need to pray daily for guidance and help in our speech.

O God, who lovest truth and hatest deceit, so direct my thought to love the truth that I may keep my tongue from evil and my lips from speaking guile, after the pattern of my Lord Jesus Christ. Amen.

THE EIGHTH COMMANDMENT

Thou shalt not bear false witness against thy neighbor

Lying in politics is wrong

March 9

READ: Proverbs 14:22-35.

TEXT: Righteousness exalteth a nation, but sin is a reproach to any people. Proverbs 14:34.

✤

The Eighth Commandment forbids lying and deceit in every form. There is no such thing as a respectable "white lie" or an honorable shady business deal. God condemns all kinds of deceit from the least to the greatest. Absolute truthfulness is one of the foundation stones on which our country and its institutions are built. If the citizens of a nation lose confidence in their leaders; if they question the honesty and the integrity of those in authority—that nation is headed for a fall. Lying in politics is just as wrong and as contemptible in the sight of God as are deceit and dishonesty between individuals. The whole nation, yes, the whole world is held together by trust in the word of man to man. If that trust is lost, if we begin to question the honesty of our fellow men, if such mistrust spreads, the foundation of community life has begun to crumble. May we take heed when God says, "Speak ye every man the truth to his neighbor," Zechariah 8:16.

Our heavenly Father, Thou God of righteousness and truth, cleanse my sinful heart of all dishonesty and deceit. Help me to be honest and truthful in motive, thought, word, and deed. For Jesus' sake. Amen.

THE EIGHTH COMMANDMENT

March 10

Thou shalt not bear false witness against thy neighbor

Jesus, our perfect example

READ: Matthew 11:7-19.

TEXT: There hath not risen a greater than John the Baptist. Matthew 11:11.

✣

What's in a name? What about my reputation? How do you rate among your fellows? Important questions! Certainly, these things God binds up with the Eighth Commandment. We dare not ignore them. Jesus Himself thought and spoke well of His fellows. Of John the Baptist He said, "There hath not risen a greater than he." A worthy example for us to follow.

Being constructive is better, for obedience to this commandment affects us as well. We avoid the feeling of meanness which develops when we tell tales about others. We enjoy our associations and our friendships much more, for intimacy is quite impossible when we speak ill of people behind their backs. We do others a good turn when we stress the good qualities in them whenever we can instead of the unsatisfactory ones. We are being helpful when we try to find the good and further that good which is in others.

O God, make Thy truth to shine about and within us so that we may know Thy will more clearly and understand how earnestly Thy love desires us to walk according to Thy divine purposes. We ask this in the name of Christ. Amen.

THE NINTH COMMANDMENT

Thou shalt not covet thy neighbor's house

Do not seek by craftiness to gain possession

March 11

READ: Luke 12:13-21.

TEXT: Take heed, and beware of covetousness.
Luke 12:15.

✤

God tells us in the Ninth Commandment how to live at peace with our neighbors. "Do not covet," He says. To covet is to want something so badly that we are unhappy unless we get it or are willing to use dishonorable means to obtain possession.

We may rightly admire all good and beautiful things belonging to our neighbors, but we should not be sly and crafty and deceitful and scheme to get what we want without our neighbor's consent.

Covetousness is a sin of the heart; sometimes it's hidden from men, but "out of the heart are the issues of life." Covetousness is idolatry.

Covetousness makes for unhappy relations and distrust among neighbors because the greedy heart is never satisfied. We should remember the words of Jesus, "Take heed and beware of covetousness . . . for a man's life consists not in the abundance of the things he possesses."

O God, who hast promised us all that we need for this body and life, deliver me, I pray Thee, from the unhappiness of covetousness and teach me the joy of helping others. Amen.

THE NINTH COMMANDMENT

March 12

Thou shalt not covet thy neighbor's house

Do not obtain anything under pretense of a legal right

READ: I Kings 21:1-24.

TEXT: Woe unto you . . . for ye devour widows' houses. Matthew 23:14.

♣

Law-abiding citizens, yet thieves! That's what Jesus called these Pharisees. For though they held closely to the letter of the law they knew the law's loopholes, and so by clever crookedness they had succeeded in gobbling up the property of widows and orphans. These poor souls, without the wisdom or wealth to defend themselves, fell easy prey to the religious shysters.

Perhaps we face the same opportunities. By craft and trickery we could obtain possession of what rightfully belongs to someone else. Perhaps the other party is uneducated, gullible, trusting. It would be easy to cheat such a one.

God maintains but one standard: absolute honesty at all times. Dishonesty is sin even where the law is slack about it. We should keep a close watch over our actions so that our life may be as upright and as honest as Christ expects us to be. When we resist the temptation to covet we also outlaw such dishonest and mean practices.

Dear Lord Jesus, let not the lust for wealth lure us into ways of crookedness. Make us worthy of the trust and confidence placed in us. In Thine own name. Amen.

THE NINTH COMMANDMENT

Thou shalt not covet thy neighbor's house

Assist and serve your neighbor

March 13

READ: Genesis 14:13-24.

TEXT: Look not every man on his own things, but every man also on the things of others. Philippians 2:4.

♣

Abraham was a good neighbor. He brought all his resources to aid his neighbors. The priest and the Levite in the parable of the Good Samaritan were not good neighbors. They did not attack or wound the traveller, but neither did they help him. People of a community often prove good neighbors when they gather to do the work of a sick or injured man or help the family in need.

They are good neighbors who look not only to their own interest but also to the interest of others.

Young people can be good neighbors, too. There are always opportunities for the young and the strong to do service for the sick or aged or weak. It is not enough to refrain from damaging their property. We obey this commandment only when, with the spirit of Christ, we help them in every time of need.

O God, who art a Friend to all men, give me a heart that is friendly to all so that I may serve as a neighbor and thus fulfil the law of Christ. Amen.

March 14

THE NINTH COMMANDMENT

Thou shalt not covet thy neighbor's house

Guard against the love of money

READ: Luke 6:24-38.

TEXT: The love of money is the root of all evil.
I Timothy 6:10.

♣

In our social order everyone has to have some money. There is nothing wrong with money itself or with having money. What is wrong is what people do with money and their attitude toward it. The Bible speaks truth when it says, "The love of money is the root of all evil."

When Judas came to the chief priests, seeking an opportunity to betray Jesus, his question was, "What will you give me?" We know there were other motives connected with what Judas did, but he loved money, and he was given his blood money; in the end, however, it so burned his fingers that he threw it down in the Temple and went and hanged himself. So has the love of money brought about the spiritual downfall of many.

Let us try with the help of God to keep a Christian attitude in the acquiring and the use of money so that we may be good stewards of these material things which the Lord entrusts temporarily to our care.

Give me the grace, O Lord, to use my possessions as Thou wouldst have me use them. Help me to remember that I must someday give account to Thee of what I have done with my money. Amen.

THE NINTH COMMANDMENT

Thou shalt not covet thy neighbor's house

Be content with what you have

March 15

READ: Genesis 25:29-34.

TEXT: But godliness with contentment is great gain. I Timothy 6:6.

♣

The gain of godliness is a good conscience. The gain of a good conscience is contentment. Covetousness and discontent are teammates. The covetousness of Jacob robbed him of contentment. The covetousness of Judas led him to betray his Lord and resulted in such discontent that he went and hanged himself.

Few gain real contentment in this life because they want so many things beyond their actual needs. Obedient children and godly men and humble and unselfish Christian believers can have rich contentment even if they are poor in this world's goods.

Yet possessors of wealth may have contentment, too. It was not his possession but his covetousness which made the rich young ruler so discontented. Our Lord Jesus, born in poverty and possessing nothing, had the great contentment of the knowledge of God's love because, He said, "I do always the things that please My Father." We can have that contentment, and that is the great gain of life.

O most merciful God, give us grace by Thy Holy Spirit to be content with what we have, believing that our heavenly Father knows what things we have need of and will provide for us our daily bread. Amen.

THE NINTH COMMANDMENT

March 16

Thou shalt not covet thy neighbor's house

Pray for neither poverty nor riches

READ: Proverbs 30:1-9.

TEXT: Give me neither poverty nor riches. Proverbs 30:8.

♣

This was the devout desire of one concerned with the progress of grace in his humble soul. He wanted nothing in life that would hinder his spiritual growth. He feared that wealth would incline him to deny God, and that poverty might lead to acts of dishonesty.

Sin does not always involve open wickedness. Temptation may arise from some unwholesome attitude of mind. In particular it is a common habit to crave certain possessions or positions, to become positively unhappy without them, and to envy those who do have them. There is no notion more foolish than the idea that happiness depends on material things.

The life of moderate means is always the best. It is the atmosphere in which the great men of the world have lived. Believe that God knows what is best for you and be satisfied in Him. With Christ all things are yours.

Dear heavenly Father, help me to be satisfied with the life which Thou hast ordained for me and to covet earnestly the best gifts which are wrought by Thy Spirit. Amen.

THE NINTH COMMANDMENT

Thou shalt not covet thy neighbor's house
Jesus, our perfect example

March 17

READ: Matthew 8:18-22.

TEXT: The foxes have holes, and the birds of the air have nests: but the Son of man hath not where to lay His head. Matthew 8:20.

✣

Jesus was not complaining when He said that He had not where to lay His head. He was not afraid that night would overtake Him without shelter and protection. He was certain that God would provide a bed for Him in a home which belonged to someone else, or if He had to sleep outside under the canopy of heaven, God would shelter Him there. Without God a house cannot provide security, but with God there are shelter and protection even if you have no home. His ways of providing vary, but His faithfulness toward all His creatures never varies. It embraces you also. If, in His wisdom God has seen fit to make your portion of goods smaller than your neighbor's, do not complain, do not envy him, do not covet his inheritance or home. God means to show you that He can and will provide even if you have not where to lay your head.

Dear Father in heaven, Thou hast created me and hast determined my portion of goods. Grant that I may ever receive it with thanksgiving and be content therewith. Amen.

THE TENTH COMMANDMENT

March 18

Thou shalt not covet thy neighbor's wife, nor his manservant, nor his maidservant, nor his cattle, nor anything that is thy neighbor's

READ: Matthew 14:1-12.

TEXT: Thou shalt not covet thy neighbor's wife. Exodus 20:17.

✣

Men may covet other things besides money or possessions. A man may covet his neighbor's wife or a wife some other's husband. That is the ugly sin called lust, and Jesus says that, even when it is only in the heart, it is adultery.

This covetousness often results in the breaking of a home by divorce, and this is contrary to the will and the purpose of God.

In this commandment God further provides for the happiness of His children by safeguarding marriage, which is a relationship between two people only. Lust is an enemy of that happiness in the home. We are living in a day when divorce is regarded lightly, and there are many broken homes. The reason is to be found in covetous and unclean hearts and disregard of God's holy laws. Clean hearts and true love are the best defense against broken homes. The daily prayer of husband and wife should be, "Create in me a clean heart, O God."

O God, who hast given this commandment for the enlightening of my eyes, let my hands be clear and my heart pure that our home may receive Thy blessing, for Jesus' sake. Amen.

THE TENTH COMMANDMENT

Thou shalt not covet thy neighbor's wife, nor his manservant, nor his maidservant, nor his cattle, nor anything that is thy neighbor's

March 19

Do not entice away your neighbor's servants

READ: Romans 13:8-14.
TEXT: Love worketh no ill to his neighbor. Romans 13:10.

✣

A few years ago one of our "wartime" problems was the fact that industries with "cost plus" war contracts from the United States government and, therefore, not limited by wage rates were hiring the employees away from companies with closed contracts accepted on the basis of wage rates which could not be raised.

Industry has long been taking people away from the farms and from domestic service by the lure of larger wages or what look like larger wages to the workers. People of wealth are still said to hire one another's servants away from them. The times change, but the problems do not. It may be that the day will come when all will receive the same wage for their work and all be content in their work. What would ever cause such a day to come? The Scriptures and the Catechism say that love would—that love would prompt us not to entice our neighbor's servants away from him but help him to hold them.

Father, convert our heart by leaving no other desire than Christ therein that all the issues of our life may be fashioned by His love for men. Amen.

THE TENTH COMMANDMENT

March 20

Thou shalt not covet thy neighbor's wife, nor his manservant, nor his maidservant, nor his cattle, nor anything that is thy neighbor's

Do not entice away your neighbor's cattle or anything that is his

READ: Exodus 10:24-26.

TEXT: Let no man seek his own, but every man another's wealth. I Corinthians 10:24.

♣

The sinful desire of coveting, wanting what is not yours to the extent of taking it by dishonest means, leads not only to injury to your neighbor but to a contamination of your own soul. Neither man nor child can walk with God or have the Holy Spirit dwelling in his heart and his life who takes what is not his own or what has not been freely given to him by another. Covetousness strikes deeper than stealing! It is the root within the heart that eventually causes men to break all of the commandments.

A sure way to keep this commandment is always to obey Paul's command to the Corinthian Christians, "Let no man seek his own, but each his neighbor's good." "Forget self and think of others as Jesus did, 'I came not to be ministered unto, but to minister.'" Levison said, "He who does nothing for his community and neighbor is 'just no good.'"

Forgive, O Lord, my failure to do the hard right and the sin of doing the easy wrong. Help me to look to Thee for all things needful in this life. Amen.

THE TENTH COMMANDMENT

Thou shalt not covet thy neighbor's wife, nor his manservant, nor his maidservant, nor his cattle, nor anything that is thy neighbor's

March 21

Seek to have them remain and discharge their duty to him

READ: Romans 15:1-7.

TEXT: I beseech thee for my son Onesimus . . . whom I have sent again. Philemon 10-12.

✣

Reading between the lines of the letter of Paul to Philemon, we may imagine a fascinating story. Paul was preaching at Rome. Among those who listened from time to time was a man by the name of Onesimus. Soon the story of Jesus had so gripped his heart that he came oftener to hear the thrilling message of a Savior for all. The day came when he told the apostle that he also wanted to be a Christian.

He was baptized and became an active member of the church. Paul found that he could make good use of him in his Christian ministry.

Onesimus, however, was a runaway slave. Did that matter? Certainly. The Roman law had no pardon for runaway slaves. As much as Paul needed his services he urged him to return voluntarily to his old master, Philemon, commending him to his good graces. For Paul his own conscience and doing "the right thing" were the most important matters.

Lord, make me faithful in every task and let me be an incentive to others to follow in Thy footsteps. In Jesus' name. Amen.

THE TENTH COMMANDMENT

March 22

Thou shalt not covet thy neighbor's wife, nor his manservant, nor his maidservant, nor his cattle, nor anything that is thy neighbor's

Concerning original sin

READ: II Samuel 15.

TEXT: As by one man sin entered into the world, and death by sin; and so death passed upon all men, for that all have sinned. Romans 5:12.

✤

Many years ago a very rich man built for his family a palace that in luxury and in beauty excelled many of the great castles of the old world.

Two months after he moved into this palatial home his only son died of a lingering fever. During the years that followed the palace was occupied by other families. Yet ill health and death visited each of them. After a long and determined search an old open sewer was found beneath the foundations of the house. All through the years it had poured poison into the walls of that beautiful home and brought death to its occupants.

Just so operates *original sin,* the secret poison that lurks in every human life. If it is not overcome it will bring eternal death to everyone.

Heavenly Father, we thank Thee that in Christ our sin is forgiven; grant us the needed help and courage to continue overcoming sin in our own life so that we may escape condemnation and obtain eternal life. Through Jesus Christ, our Redeemer. Amen.

THE TENTH COMMANDMENT

Thou shalt not covet thy neighbor's wife, nor his manservant, nor his maidservant, nor his cattle, nor anything that is thy neighbor's

Concerning actual sin

March 23

READ: Matthew 15:10-20.

TEXT: Out of the heart proceed evil thoughts. Matthew 15:19.

✣

Covetousness is the desire to have what God denies or to do what God forbids. It flourishes on the falsehood that "forbidden fruits are the sweetest." It lurks in the innermost recesses of the heart. If conquered for a season, like the demon of the parable, it returns with sevenfold strength. One must ever be on guard against it. That is why we have the double warning of Commandments Nine and Ten. Here is the secret part of every actual sin. When Satan tempted Eve in Eden he first of all aroused in her the desire to eat of the fruit of the forbidden tree. Thus he continues his wily ways in our day. The opposite of covetousness is contentment. Truly, "Godliness with contentment is great gain." Beautifully does the apostle Paul become our example saying, "I have learned in whatsoever state I am therewith to be content."

Dear heavenly Father, give me the strength of Thy Spirit constantly to conquer and rule the desires of my heart, knowing that "he that ruleth his own heart is mightier than he that taketh a city." Amen.

THE TENTH COMMANDMENT

March 24

Thou shalt not covet thy neighbor's wife, nor his manservant, nor his maidservant, nor his cattle, nor anything that is thy neighbor's

Jesus, our perfect example

READ: Romans 10:1-9.

TEXT: Be ye followers of God as dear children. Ephesians 5:1.

✣

The word "followers" here signifies "imitators." As children of God we are to imitate, i. e., copy the life of Jesus. This may confuse or even frighten us because Jesus lived a perfect life. We may learn to write by having a perfect sample set before us that we copy over and over. The copy we make never becomes perfect. But in time it comes to tell the same thing as the original. So Jesus is our perfect example; He did not covet. We can be only imitators of Him. We cannot live a perfect life as He did. But by obedience to His Spirit, by His grace, and by diligent service on our part, our life will speak more and more the Christian message to those about us.

> "Walk in the light! and thine shall be
> A path though thorny, bright;
> For God by grace shall dwell in thee,
> And God Himself is light."

Almighty God, who hast given us Jesus, Thine only-begotten Son, to be our example of a godly life, grant to us grace that we may daily endeavor to follow the blessed steps of His holy life. Amen.

THE TEN COMMANDMENTS — CONCLUSION

March 25

I the Lord thy God am a jealous God

God threatens to punish all who transgress these commandments

READ: Romans 6:1-14.

TEXT: The wages of sin is death; but the gift of God is eternal life through Jesus Christ, our Lord. Romans 6:23.

♣

God asks us to obey Him; to keep His commandments. The commandments are for our good. Because God loves us He guides and directs us into that which is right.

It is iniquitous and perverse to disobey Him. He becomes a jealous lover and will surely punish us for our sins. We are told, "The wages of sin is death." Because of disobedience we deserve death.

But "God promises grace and every blessing to all who keep His commandments." We must finish that verse in Romans—the wages of sin is death, "but the gift of God is eternal life through Jesus Christ our Lord." We deserve the wages, but in God's love for Jesus' sake, who died for us, He gives the gift—eternal life. Wages are paid, gifts are gratis.

Dear Lord, we deserve nothing. Yet Thou hast given us so much, all things and life eternal through Jesus Christ. Wilt Thou accept our profound gratitude? Continue to be merciful unto us and bless us. Amen.

March 26

THE TEN COMMANDMENTS — CONCLUSION

*I the Lord thy God am a jealous God
We should therefore fear His wrath*

READ: Romans 6:15-23.

TEXT: Fear not them which kill the body, but are not able to kill the soul; but rather fear Him which is able to destroy both soul and body in hell. Matthew 10:28.

✤

We have been learning that we should fear, love, and trust in God above all things. What is this fear?

It is not fear of things which can hurt or harm the body; fear of sickness, pain, death, or the devil. None of these things, not even the devil, can kill the soul. "Why fear them?" Jesus asks.

It is rather fear of this sort, that we know God not only as the holy and just One who will punish sin, but because we know Him as the loving Father who forgives sin and offers us life and salvation through Jesus Christ. When we have faith and love we fear only lest we displease our heavenly Father. This fear of the Lord is the beginning of wisdom. It is good for the soul, it cleanses the heart. It brings us to life eternal. "Hear the conclusion of the whole matter. Fear God and keep His commandments."

O God, who art greatly to be feared, loved, and trusted above all things, teach me Thy way and train my heart to fear unfaithfulness to Thee. Amen.

THE TEN COMMANDMENTS — CONCLUSION

March 27

Visiting the iniquity of the fathers upon the children unto the third and fourth generation of them that hate Me

We should in no way disobey His commandments

READ: Exodus 24:1-8.

TEXT: All that the Lord hath said we will do, and be obedient. Exodus 24:7.

♣

One of the great gifts and blessings of God, our Father, is the freedom of the will, the ability to make our own decisions and to choose our own way of life. Since, however, we are sinful and our judgment is imperfect we need the commandments of God to guide us in the use of our will. Christ, who said, "I do not Mine own will, but the will of My Father," is our perfect example.

We should, therefore, obey the commandments, not because we feel that we must or are afraid not to obey them, but because we love them for what they are, namely, kindly guideposts to direct us as children of God in the Christian way of life.

We should, therefore, in no way disobey His commandments lest we lose His promise, "He will show mercy to thousands of them that love Him and keep His commandments."

O God, our Father, give us the wisdom to understand, the grace to love, and the will to obey Thy commandments. Through Jesus Christ, Thy Son, our Lord. Amen.

THE TEN COMMANDMENTS — CONCLUSION

March 28

Visiting the iniquity of the fathers upon the children unto the third and fourth generation of them that hate Me

He promises grace to those who keep His commandments

READ: Titus 2.

TEXT: For the grace of God that bringeth salvation hath appeared to all men. Titus 2:11.

✣

A life dedicated to God is the best investment in the world. It pays big dividends. God promises vast treasures of grace and untold blessings to all who walk in His ways.

"Jehovah knoweth the way of the righteous, but the way of the wicked shall perish." Wise old David opens his heart to us as he meditates upon the eternal truth, which many years later Paul expresses in the words, "The wages of sin is death, the gift of God is eternal life." They knew from personal experience the terrifying wages of sin as well as the glorious fruit of righteousness. Yes and so Peter and Paul, the thief on the cross, and all God-fearing people of every age knew, even as you and I know, what blessings of love, joy, peace, goodness, and unfailing help our Father in heaven sends those who love and serve Him here below.

Dear Father, help me to do the right and to shun the wrong. Place within my heart a burning desire for the wonderful blessings promised me through my Savior. Amen.

THE TEN COMMANDMENTS — CONCLUSION

And showing mercy unto thousands of them that love Me and keep My commandments

He blesses all who keep His commandments

March 29

READ: Ephesians 1:1-14.

TEXT: Blessed be the God . . . who hath blessed us with all spiritual blessings in heavenly places in Christ. Ephesians 1:3.

✣

Have you ever doubted that it actually pays to keep God's commandments? You have seen your worldly friends "getting away with things"; perhaps they have even seemed more popular than you because they winked at some of God's commandments. But here your Catechism holds forth this promise without any "ifs or ands." Well may you wonder if that is actually true. Look carefully at today's Bible verse. It is Paul writing. Paul's life had been a hard life. He was imprisoned, shipwrecked, hated, and finally even killed because of his love and his zeal for the true God. He certainly tried to keep God's commandments. Yet Paul here blesses God "because He hath blessed us."

Dear Lord, I must confess before Thee that often I have not kept Thy commandments as I should or even could. Yet do Thou, for the sake of Thy dear Son Jesus, give me joy in keeping them. Give me true enjoyment of all the spiritual blessings that are mine through faith in Christ. Amen.

March 30

THE TEN COMMANDMENTS — CONCLUSION

And showing mercy unto thousands of them that love
Me and keep My commandments

We should therefore love Him, trust in Him, and gladly
keep His commandments

READ: I John 5:1-13.

TEXT: I delight in the law of God after the inward man. Romans 7:22.

✤

Have you ever travelled without a map or clear directions and ended up in a country lane or dead-end street?

Many men miss the way to happiness; they stray from the narrow path that has at its end a straight gate through which the traveller can enter into life. Many never find that path at all. Paul was guided into it as you were guided into it in the catechetical class. Paul was glad, grateful, overjoyed, "I delight in the law of God after the inward man." It was no gloomy task; the law of God in our heart leads us into the joy of life with Almighty God. That delight will help us to keep travelling it, refusing the bypaths that beckon into wrong. We are going to live with God in Christ Jesus!

Dear God, Father of our Lord Jesus Christ, I thank Thee for Thy guidance. May the inspiration of Thy love ring joyous notes in my heart until I can hear the glad bells of heaven at the end of the road, the beginning of life. Amen.

THE TEN COMMANDMENTS — CONCLUSION

Jesus, our perfect example in obedience to the Ten Commandments

March 31

READ: Philippians 2:5.

TEXT: He humbled Himself, and became obedient unto death, even the death of the cross. Philippians 2: 8, 9.

✣

God places a very high value on obedience. It is one of the most priceless gifts which we can bring to Him. "Behold, to obey is better than sacrifice, and to hearken than the fat of rams," I Samuel 15:22.

This is also a very difficult gift to bring unto God. There is an inbred spirit in us, our old nature, which dislikes very much to do the will of God. In fact, this unwilling spirit would rather do anything else than to obey God. It is only when our heart has experienced a transformation by the power of God's grace that obedience is a delight.

Even Jesus, God's own Son, had to learn obedience (Hebrews 5:8). "Though He was a Son, yet learned He obedience by the things which He suffered; and having been made perfect, He became unto all them that obey Him the author of eternal salvation," Hebrews 5:8, 9.

Lord, make me an obedient child of Thine. Take from my heart every trace of unwillingness and help me find joy in doing Thy will and in keeping Thy commandments. For only in so doing can I remain a true child of Thine. Amen.

THE CREED — THE FIRST ARTICLE
Of creation

April 1

READ: Genesis 1:1-10.
TEXT: In the beginning God created. Genesis 1:1.

✿

Even since childhood days, when life began to unfold its many mysteries, we have asked the questions, "Where did this earth come from" and, "Who made the universe?" Different answers have been given, but there is but one answer that satisfies the soul of a Christian. "In the beginning God created the heaven and the earth."

It is the mark of an unintelligent man to say that this world came by chance or by the blind process of materialistic evolution. The best men of science who look beyond test tube and microscope agree that it can't be explained without God. His own record tells us that God created this universe with His mighty word. God's word is dynamic. He said, "Let there be light, and there was light." He said, "Let there be a firmament," and the beautiful dome of heaven appeared. He said, "Let the waters be gathered, and the dry land appear," and they did so. And God saw that it was good.

Almighty God, our dear heavenly Father, we thank Thee for Thyself and for Thy power and for the wonders of Thy creation. And we pray Thee to send forth Thy light into our heart so that we may at all times praise Thee with our lips and glorify Thee with our life. We ask it in Jesus' name. Amen.

THE CREED — THE FIRST ARTICLE
Of creation

April 2

READ: Genesis 1:11-13.

TEXT: And God said, Let the earth bring forth grass, the herb yielding seed, and the fruit tree yielding fruit after his kind. Genesis 1:11.

♣

On the third day of creation God provided the earth with trees, plants, herbs, and grass. How dusty, drab, and dirty the world would be without them! Their beauty alone adds much pleasure to our life.

The grass, plants, herbs, and trees were provided to give us much more than pleasure. God intended that they should serve us in our needs. From them we receive food, clothing, medicine, and shelter.

And notice how He provided that all future generations should also enjoy them—He endowed each form of plant life with the capacity to reproduce, each "after his kind." There is the amazing miracle of life reproduction which we see going on around us all the time.

To know that our God provided all this for us should make us happy and glad. This knowledge, however, should also remind us to make grateful and intelligent use of these gifts of God.

Father Almighty, we thank Thee for all the living things in the world which Thou hast provided for our use and enjoyment. Help us to be truly grateful for these gifts and benefits. In Jesus' name. Amen.

THE CREED — THE FIRST ARTICLE
Of creation

April 3

READ: Genesis 1:14-19.

TEXT: And God said, Let there be lights in the firmament. Genesis 1:14.

✤

"The heavens declare the glory of God, and the firmament showeth His handiwork." How marvellous and great are the works of God as revealed in the firmament or heavens! We pause in silent awe and adoration as we think, "Yet God is greater than all this."

God has provided light and life for the earth in a wonderful way. We know that light is necessary for plant life and animal life. Now God is light, but light that cannot be approached. "Our God is a consuming fire," before whose glory the brightest flash of an atomic explosion is as a dim candle in the noonday sun. This original light must be "stepped down" until it is suitable for life. So God fixed the sun in our heavens to give light in proper proportion. It is inspiring to think that God, who is light and the source of life, has made the sun to bring light and life to the earth and to us.

Jesus is the "Light of the world, and the light in Him is the life of men," that is, of their souls. He is the Sun of righteousness. We should praise God for the light which streams from His creation and for the light which enlightens our souls in Jesus Christ.

O God, in whom is no darkness at all, let me walk in the light as Thou art in the light that I may have fellowship with Thee and with Jesus Christ, my Lord. Amen.

THE CREED — THE FIRST ARTICLE

Of creation

It didn't just happen

April 4

READ: Genesis 1:20-23.

TEXT: And God created great whales . . . and every winged fowl . . . and God saw that it was good. Genesis 1:21.

✤

Two men were arguing about the beginning of things. The first man, a Christian, said that God created all things. The second, an agnostic, said that everything just happened. They parted, and the Christian conceived an idea. He made a beautiful miniature house with windows, doors, chimney, and all. Later his agnostic friend came to visit him. The visitor's first words after seeing the work of art were, "Who made it?" The Christian replied, "It just happened." The visitor again asked the same question and received the same answer. Becoming almost angry, he asked what his friend was driving at. The Christian then said calmly: "My friend, you deem it silly for me to say that this simple little house just happened. How then can you say that the world just happened, the world with its sun, moon, stars, trees, grasses, animals, birds, fish, and the crown of all, man?"

Father in heaven, we know that all things were made by Thee. Help men everywhere to acknowledge Thy creative, sustaining, and redeeming power. In Jesus' name. Amen.

THE CREED — THE FIRST ARTICLE

April 5

Of creation

READ: Genesis 1:24, 25.

TEXT: And God made the beast of the earth . . . and cattle. Genesis 1:25.

✤

Have you ever tried to imagine how different this world would be if there were no animals? If there were no horses, cows, and sheep, no chickens, no wild animals, no birds, and no fish, our whole mode of living would be altered. Then we should not have many of the things we use in our daily life, especially in the area of clothing and food; then we should have to be vegetarians. But God wished to give us an abundant life and, therefore, He created the animals of which the above Scripture passage speaks. How thankful we should be that God created animals for us!

Let this word from the Holy Scripture also remind you again that GOD is the Creator of everything. Some would-be wise people try to leave God out of the picture when they explain the origin of living creatures. But if you do not accept God's explanation you simply have no answer to the question concerning the origin of all things, including the animal world.

Dear Father in heaven, how infinitely great are Thy power, wisdom, and glory manifested in the creating of the great variety of animals! Give us grateful hearts for the grace of their existence. Amen.

THE CREED — THE FIRST ARTICLE
Of creation

April 6

READ: Genesis 1:26-31.
TEXT: God created man in His own image. Genesis 1:27.

✣

As the marvellous crowning act of creation God made man in His own image. Man is not an animal which knows neither right nor wrong; he is not a machine whose action is unthinking and unfeeling; he is not a stone which neither thinks, feels, nor acts.

Man is a person, made in the likeness of God, a being who, like God, can think, and feel, and act.

In the beginning this image of God, this personality which is man, was created in righteousness and true holiness. Man was good. Then temptation came, the cunning serpent deceived, and man acted wilfully, disobediently. His thought, love, and action became sinful. The image of God still remained, but marred, defaced, and ruined by sin.

Jesus Christ came that we might see what Godlikeness is, and He has power to restore that image in us so that we become new creatures, again "created after God in righteousness and true holiness." This I should desire with all my heart.

O Most Holy Creator, who madest me in Thy likeness, let me yield my heart unto Jesus Christ that He may work His perfect work in me and by Thy Holy Spirit re-create me after His likeness. Amen.

THE CREED — THE FIRST ARTICLE

Of creation

April 7

READ: Genesis 2:1-3.

TEXT: God blessed the seventh day, and sanctified it. Genesis 2:3.

✤

On the sixth day creation was completed. The seventh day God rested from His creative activity. And He forever after designated that day as one of rest for man.

What a boon the day of rest! Oh, the depth of wisdom that lies in this arrangement! "Six days shalt thou labor." The seventh is the Lord's day. On this day no work shall be done. In God's economy one day of rest is necessary for the building up of our physical energies, for the deepening of our spiritual life, for the enlarging of our social interests and the discharging of our duties to our fellow men. This is truly the Lord's day. It belongs to Him. When we dedicate it to Him, He in turn pours out such blessings upon us that the days following become easier to live in, and our work is easier to do. The wisdom of God gave this day. Let not the foolishness of man overrule this wisdom!

Father, Thou hast dedicated this day to us, for in Thy wisdom Thou knowest that we need rest. Help us to find our rest in Thee through worship, meditation, and joyful living. In Jesus' name. Amen.

THE CREED — THE FIRST ARTICLE

He gives me food and raiment

April 8

READ: Genesis 2:4-7.
TEXT: And Thou givest them their meat in due season. Psalm 145:15.

✤

We of America have become accustomed to sitting down to tables loaded with tasty, wholesome, and nourishing food. We grow strong in body and are enabled to live active, useful, and helpful lives. We wear clothing that adorns our bodies and makes them more attractive and at the same time protects them from the cold and the heat. We are so accustomed to God's providence that we take it for granted or claim personal credit for it. How many of us pause in gratitude as we realize that all these gifts come to us through the goodness of our heavenly Father? How many of us pause to thank Him each day for His love and His faithfulness which are so beautifully expressed in His bountiful provision?

Certainly we should pause to thank Him in prayers of gratitude and in our manner of life. As His children we show our gratitude by employing these gifts to their intended use, to strengthen us so that we may always serve Him joyfully and faithfully in His church.

Father in heaven, we thank Thee for Thy faithfulness. We pray that we may be faithful in using the gifts of Thy bounty in serving Thee throughout all the days of our life. Amen.

THE CREED — THE FIRST ARTICLE

April 9

He gives me home and family

READ: Genesis 2:18-25.

TEXT: Every good gift and every perfect gift is from above. James 1:17.

♣

"Count your blessings, Name them one by one, See what God hath done."

High up in the list of blessings for which you are indebted to God are your home and family. Through them and your Christian parents God has given you an honorable heritage. He supplies you with earth's dearest friends; He has given you a steadfast faith in the Father who cares; the Redeemer who saves; the Holy Spirit who guides; He has imparted to you unfailing love in the home and grounded you in the sure hope of a better life to come.

What return are you making? Must it be said of you, "Home is the place where we are treated best and grumble most"? Are you propagating home's blessings by your spirit, words, and deeds? Do you respect your loved ones and "honor thy father and thy mother that thy days may be long (another gift of God) upon the land which the Lord Thy God giveth Thee"?

Gracious Father, I thank Thee for my home and my loved ones. Continue to bless us all, abide with us, make us Thine, and use us in Thy kingdom, for Jesus' sake. Amen.

THE CREED — THE FIRST ARTICLE

He gives me all my possessions

April 10

READ: Genesis 12:1-5.

TEXT: All the land which thou seest, to thee will I give it. Genesis 13:15.

❧

The sacredness of property rights is a principle inherent in religion. In Genesis 13:15 God said to Abraham, "All the land which thou seest, to thee will I give it." And thus God's seal was placed on the rights of a man to own and possess his house and his lands.

As Christians we are not only not to take property from others unlawfully, but we are to help and protect our fellow men in the keeping of their property. Not only property rights but our possessions, all of them, come from God to us. He is the rightful owner, and we are but stewards of His to use His property for the happiness and the welfare of ourselves and our fellow men. I can fulfill my responsibilities as a Christian, either to God or man, only when I use all that I possess to the glory of God and the good of man.

Our Father in heaven, we give Thee thanks for all things which we possess. They are the gifts of Thy bountiful hands. Help us to use these gifts in such a manner that Thy name may be glorious among men and Thy kingdom advanced on earth. We ask it through Thy blessed Son, our Lord and Savior. Amen.

THE CREED — THE FIRST ARTICLE

April 11

He daily provides abundantly for all my needs

READ: Matthew 6:24-34.

TEXT: Thou openest Thine hand, and satisfiest the desire of every living thing. Psalm 145:16.

✣

What a really satisfying thing it is for mother, when preparing dinner, to be able to step into the well-filled fruit cellar and take down several cans of the many good things stored there and prepare them for the dinner she must serve! So also is God's forethought for us, He who is the Creator and Provider of all things has ready for us all that we need.

His hand is never empty but filled with the best things we might want. Nor is God a miserly giver; His gifts are abundant and satisfying. They are really good for us when He gives them. Oh, perhaps they do not satisfy our foolish whims, but He does give us all that we need.

Among the many things for which we may depend unfailingly on God is the bread of life, His Word. We too often overlook this. God's Word must always be regarded in the light of the Savior's words, "Man shall not live by bread alone, but by every word which proceedeth out of the mouth of God."

O God, the Giver of all good things, who lovest us and art ready to give out of Thine abundance all that is good for us, grant us also a rich supply of Thy Holy Word to keep us in the faith of our Savior and Redeemer Jesus Christ. Amen.

THE CREED — THE FIRST ARTICLE

He protects me from all danger

April 12

READ: Acts 27:23-44.

TEXT: The angel of the Lord encampeth round about them that fear Him, and delivereth them. Psalm 34:7.

♣

It is so easy to forget that our life is beset by many and great dangers to both body and soul. Those responsible for public safety caution and warn us by proper safety signs and signals. In spite of these precautions we are not safe, however conscientiously we observe them. How blessed, then, to know the Lord is our protector. He knows our dangers best and has the power to protect us. Because we are His children, His eyes are ever over us that danger cannot permanently hurt us. His ear is open to our prayer. His shadow hides us so that the wicked one cannot harm us. His angels are 'round about us to keep us in the right and narrow way. Yes, we are safe if we commit ourselves, body and soul, into the gracious keeping of the Almighty.

Almighty God, who knowest us to be set in the midst of so many and great dangers, grant us Thy protection that we may live in safety for which we praise Thee with grateful heart. Amen.

THE CREED — THE FIRST ARTICLE

April 13

He guards and keeps me from all evil

READ: Psalm 23.
TEXT: There shall no evil befall thee. Psalm 91:10.

✣

How encouraging is the knowledge that God watches over His children! Were it not for His watchful care, we should fall before many spiritual enemies and might suffer much physical harm.

There is much evil around us of which we are not aware. "Surely He shall deliver thee from the snare of the fowler," Ps. 91:3. The fowler's snare lies hidden from the eye. It is carefully covered to catch the unsuspecting victim. So the wiles of Satan are often laid in secret places. We cannot see them. Our adversary is skilful in the use of camouflage. Though a wolf at heart, he often appears in sheep's clothing. Against his deception and trickery only God can save us. He sees the dangers to our soul and guards us against them.

Then there are dangers which we can see but which we cannot overcome with our own strength. When these temptations appear, we have a right to send for help. We may ask God to deliver us. He will always come to take up the fight against the enemy of our soul. "There shall no evil befall thee."

We thank Thee, O God, that Thou dost show concern for us. Help us when we are tempted and tested always to turn to Thee for help. We want to put our hands in Thine and know that Thou art with us. Amen.

THE CREED — THE FIRST ARTICLE

Trust in the Lord

READ: Psalm 27.

TEXT: Your faith should not stand in the wisdom of men, but in the power of God. I Corinthians 2:5.

April 14

♣

There comes a time in the life and the experience of all young people when they learn that not everyone is to be trusted. They discover that father and mother make mistakes; that their companions may deceive them; that the world is filled with wicked men who have evil designs against them; and that their own heart and mind are not reliable.

To learn that men are not to be trusted is part of the lesson of learning that God alone is faithful, and that I can and must trust in Him for wisdom, guidance, and help. We can depend on God.

"The Lord is the strength of my life. Of whom shall I be afraid? When my father and my mother forsake me, then the Lord will take me up. He shall set me up upon a rock."

Where do we learn this? From the Word of God. We can believe that. Believing, we shall find that it is good to "wait on the Lord, for He shall bring it to pass." "The Lord will deliver the righteous, because they trust in Him."

Heavenly Father, who changest not nor failest, grant that our trust in Thee may be as a sure foundation so that we may endure all the storms and trials of life even unto the end, through Jesus Christ, the Faithful. Amen.

THE CREED — THE FIRST ARTICLE

April 15

He cares for me

READ: Genesis 32:9-12.

TEXT: As a father pitieth his children, so the Lord pitieth them that fear Him. Psalm 103:13.

✣

A man whose heart had been deeply touched by the death of a friend expressed the desire to begin the Christian life and told his pastor so. "There's just one thing that makes me hesitate," he added, "I'm afraid that I can't hold out. You know where I work there are some very rough fellows. I don't believe there is a real Christian in the crowd." For an answer the pastor reached down and lifted a flower from a vase on the table. "Do you see this flower, Arthur? It grows in the mud and slime of a marsh. Yet see how clean and spotless it is. That is because God kept it, and He can keep you, too." It ought to be enough for every Christian just to know he is in God's keeping.

God has been depicted in many ways by many different religions. But Christianity is unique in this respect. It is the only religion that depicts God as a Father who is interested in His children.

O God, our heavenly Father, increase our faith in Thee. Keep us in joy and in sorrow close to Thee. May we always live obedient to Thy will so that when the strains of life become tense, the consciousness of this Father-and-child relationship may bring comfort and help. Amen.

THE CREED — THE FIRST ARTICLE

He does this without any merit or worthiness in me

April 16

READ: Luke 15:11-24.

TEXT: I am not worthy of the least of all the mercies, and of all the truth, which Thou hast showed unto Thy servant. Genesis 32:10.

✤

Like Jacob of old, each one of us today must realize that, while God cares for us like a father for his children, we are not worthy of this loving care. We do not deserve even the least, the smallest of God's mercies. We have not earned one single blessing from God even though He has showered us with them like rain from heaven. We have not merited the tiniest particle of truth and grace by anything we have done or can do.

Why is this so? It is because of our sins and our sinfulness. It is because we have broken God's laws. And lawbreakers deserve nothing but punishment. Yet because God is love He cares for us and gives us His blessings. He does this for Jesus' sake, and because we believe in the Savior. What a wonderful God is our God!

O God, help me to see how unworthy I am of Thy care. Help me to repent of my sinfulness and to live according to Thy will. In Jesus' name. Amen.

THE CREED — THE FIRST ARTICLE

April 17

For all which I am in duty bound to thank Him

READ: Psalm 100.

TEXT: O give thanks unto the Lord, for He is good; for His mercy endureth forever. Psalm 107:1.

✤

Our heavenly Father is, indeed, a great God. Not only has He made the universe, the sun, moon, stars, and the earth on which we live, but also everything that is in it. We ourselves are the highest of God's creatures because God has made us in His own likeness, our bodies from the dust of the earth and our souls by His own breath.

How wonderfully God controls the laws of nature, how kindly He cares for the tiniest of His creatures! The very hairs of our heads are numbered, the Bible says, and even the sparrows do not fall without God's knowledge. He sends His rain in due season and warm sunshine to ripen the grain so there is food for man and beast.

We should be most ungrateful to forget the God who made us and provides so well for us. "O give thanks unto the Lord, for He is good; for His mercy endureth forever."

Dear heavenly Father, make us thankful for our many blessings. Teach us to share them with others who are in need, and who do not know Thee. We ask this in Jesus' name. Amen.

THE CREED — THE FIRST ARTICLE

I am in duty bound to praise Him

April 18

READ: Psalm 103.

TEXT: Bless the Lord, O my soul, and forget not all His benefits. Psalm 103:2.

♣

How can I praise God acceptably. The Psalmist David asked, "What shall I render unto the Lord for all His benefits toward me?" He answers (Psalm 116:12-19):

"I will take the cup of salvation." God offers this to us freely. It is great praise and pleasing to God to accept it by believing on the Lord Jesus Christ.

"I will call upon the name of the Lord." I will pray. I will ask for more. It is praise so to believe in God who wants to give blessings as to desire and to ask again and again. "Ask, and it shall be given."

"I will go to church." "I will pay my vows now in the presence of all the people." I have promised to be faithful in the use of the means of grace. To be faithful is to praise.

"I will give." "I will offer the sacrifices of thanksgiving." To give, not meanly, but willingly, thankfully, trusting the Lord to provide for my needs: this is the proof of sincere praise.

O God, who art glorious in all Thy works and ways and worthy of the highest praise, open Thou my lips so that I may utter praises and direct my life that it may glorify Thee. Amen.

THE CREED — THE FIRST ARTICLE

April 19

I am in duty bound to serve Him

READ: Mark 14:3-9.

TEXT: As for me and my house, we will serve the Lord. Joshua 24:15.

✣

To serve God gladly is a beautiful quality in Christian life. Every Christian should try to develop it. God can be served in many ways, but perhaps the most pleasing service we can offer Him is to establish a right relation to the home and the church. The home should be regulated by certain laws of God. Daily devotion, daily prayer are one of the regulations that must always be in order. The spirit of love and obedience is another one that must be in evidence. The Christian home should have a good, a godly influence. The world about us needs that godly influence more than anything else. Joshua knew that when he said, "As for me and my house, we will serve the Lord." A proper relation to the church is another way to serve. Here it means, first of all, a regular attendance which encourages others to keep the Lord's Day holy. But God has also assigned certain tasks to the church. A Christian will always be interested and active in these projects.

Dear God, make us ever mindful and willing to serve Thee. Show us where service is needed and let us never be found indifferent to that call. Make us true servants in the home and in Thy kingdom, the church. Amen.

THE CREED — THE FIRST ARTICLE

I am in duty bound to obey Him

April 20

READ: Joshua 24:14-25.
TEXT: Obey My voice, and I will be your God.
Jeremiah 7:23.

♣

The chief lesson taught us in The Fourth Commandment is to obey our parents in the Lord. How necessary and meaningful this is; and what wonderful promises are forthcoming! "That it may be well with thee, and thou mayest live long on the earth." If these blessings come to us as a reward for faithful obedience to our parents, how much greater blessings will come to us if we obey God! We read in our text, "Obey My voice, and I will be your God." This literally means that in obedience to Him who loves us we become the sons of God. As sons of God we become heirs of His salvation perfected in Christ Jesus. This, in turn, means blessings on earth and blessings for all eternity.

Gracious Father in heaven, give me ears to hear Thy voice and a heart that is responsive to Thy will. Amen.

THE CREED — THE FIRST ARTICLE

The mercies of God

April 21

READ: Luke 17:11-19.

TEXT: I am not worthy of the least of all the mercies. Genesis 32:10.

♣

God's goodness and His gifts are too often taken for granted. Yet when one stops to think deeply, how numerous and inexhaustible they are—numerous as the sand of the sea and inexhaustible as a fountain!

To mention but a few: think of the beauties of the earth, the glories of the heaven, the sweetness of home and friendship; also the preciousness of forgiveness of sins, of salvation and eternal life. Always where there is a true appreciation of God's great kindness and His lavish gifts, there is a deep sense of unworthiness. Certainly they were not earned nor deserved. Like Jacob of old, there is a cry that bursts from our heart, "I am not worthy, not worthy." Only out of such a humble spirit can there be born a truly grateful heart, our hands lifted up in a sincere prayer of *thanksgiving* and our life directed in lines of *thanksliving*.

Dear heavenly Father, help me to understand that Thy mercies are always greater than I deserve and more than I need. Give me a trusting and a grateful heart; I ask it in Jesus' name. Amen.

THE CREED — THE SECOND ARTICLE

Of redemption

Conceived by the Holy Ghost

April 22

READ: Matthew 1:18-25.

TEXT: God sent forth His Son, made of a woman. Galatians 4:4.

♣

You and I, as all men since Adam, have had human fathers and mothers. But when God would send His Son into the world to redeem the world, a great miracle happened. For while Jesus Christ was born of a woman as all men have been He was not born of a human father but by the will of God and of the Holy Ghost.

Here, indeed, is a great marvel and a mystery. A marvel that God should find one so holy, so humble, and so submissive as the Virgin Mary who was chosen to bring God incarnate into the world! And a mystery as to the person of Jesus Christ, who is both Son of God and Son of man! I cannot know all that this means. I only know that God said of Jesus Christ, "This is My beloved Son, hear ye Him."

If we so believe we shall find that Jesus Christ is both Lord and Savior because He is the Son of God, and our brother and companion because He is the Son of man. "Thanks be unto God for His unspeakable gift."

O God, the Father of my Lord Jesus Christ, let Thy Holy Spirit enlighten my heart that believing I may obtain eternal life through Jesus Christ, Thy Son. Amen.

THE CREED — THE SECOND ARTICLE

April 23

Born of the Virgin Mary

READ: Isaiah 7:14-16.

TEXT: And wrapped Him in swaddling clothes, and laid Him in a manger. Luke 2:7.

✤

We bow in reverence and awe before this mystery. Here is our faith: that the Christ of glory, Son of the Father, God of God, is also man, "born of the Virgin Mary." Our faith is not founded upon the miracle of the virgin birth but upon the Virgin-born. It is the one who came into the world and not the manner of His coming that determines our convictions. Learn to call Jesus Lord and you will not stumble at His birth.

For see: Jesus did not become God's Son at Bethlehem or at Calvary or on Easter. He brought His eternal sonship with Him to Bethlehem. Thus God identified Himself with men.

Have you identified yourself with this God-man? Let Jesus become your King and Lord, your Savior and your Friend. Yes your Brother! "Born of the Virgin Mary" means that we can know God, see Him face to face, walk by His side, and be strengthened by His pierced hand.

O Christ, Thou didst humble Thyself to be born of a virgin in order that Thou mightest redeem all men. Make us humble, reverent, faithful, for Thy sake. Amen.

THE CREED — THE SECOND ARTICLE

Suffered under Pontius Pilate

April 24

READ: Matthew 27:1-25.
TEXT: The Son of man must suffer many things. Luke 9:22.

✤

Jesus suffered under Pontius Pilate. St. Paul suffered under Nero, and Martin Niemoeller suffered under Hitler. And so the roll call might go on. Millions would speak for our generation; voices out of Poland, Norway, Russia, Germany, Greece, England, America, saying, "We know what suffering is!" Some men suffer for their own sins while millions are made to agonize for the sins of others.

Wherever the blood of these folks runs red today, there Jesus' heart is bleeding in the agony of it. For as a young man this strong Son of God suffered unto the cross. The awful load He carried along that cruel road running out to Calvary was not the wooden cross that crushed Him to the earth nor any guilt of His own but the heaped-up sin of the world. Because of our transgressions He had to "suffer many things," and "by His stripes we are healed."

Our heavenly Father, we thank Thee for Him who suffered under Pontius Pilate. Grant us a right understanding of His suffering in our behalf. Give us courage to resist evil. Enable us to endure humiliation and pain for righteousness' sake. Amen.

THE CREED — THE SECOND ARTICLE

He was crucified

April 25

READ: Matthew 27:29-38.

TEXT: Then delivered he Him . . . to be crucified. John 19:16.

♣

Pontius Pilate pronounced these fateful words on the first Good Friday, "To the cross with thee!" He had spoken those same words many times. As a rule, they were addressed to the worst criminals and enemies of society. Now, against his better judgment, he condemns Jesus, the Innocent, to death with these words.

The cross, once a symbol of hate and despair, has become a symbol of love and hope. Because Jesus was there crucified, the cross has become an ornament in our churches. The cross reminds us that we are saved through the suffering and the death of our Redeemer. The cross always appears foolish and offensive to the unbeliever. But to us it is a powerful magnet, a beacon light, a refuge through all of life.

Hold Thou Thy cross before my closing eyes;
Shine through the gloom and point me to the skies.
Heaven's morning breaks and earth's vain shadows flee;
In life, in death, O Lord, abide with me. Amen.

THE CREED — THE SECOND ARTICLE

Dead and buried; He descended into hell

April 26

READ: Matthew 27:57-61.

TEXT: He bowed His head, and gave up the ghost. John 19:30.

✣

As the Son of God, Jesus need never have known suffering and death. "He was crowned with glory and honor." As the God-man He shared and knew all the experiences of the children of men. "He tasted death for every man." He did this voluntarily, for He said: "No man taketh My life from Me. I lay it down of Myself."

Jesus came to die because we have to die. He went even farther than death. He went beyond, He descended into hell, where a place is prepared for unbelievers and unrepentant sinners. There He proclaimed His victory over sin and Satan. Then He arose from the dead and says to us, "I died; and behold I am alive forevermore, and I have the keys of death and hades."

I can be sure that Jesus knows all my experiences and can help me when tempted. He is "able to save to the uttermost them that call upon His name." "I will believe that Jesus Christ, true God, and also true man, is my Lord, who has redeemed me."

O Lord Jesus Christ, who hast died for me, help me to believe in Thee so that after I have suffered here I may share Thine eternal glory at the right hand of the majesty on high. Amen.

THE CREED — THE SECOND ARTICLE

April 27

The third day He rose again from the dead

READ: Matthew 28:1-8.
TEXT: The third day He shall rise again. Mark 10:34.

✤

Among the hundreds of Bible prophecies miraculously fulfilled this is the most wonderful, "He shall rise again." Truly the keystone doctrine in God's Word!

Early in the morning the friends of Jesus with singing souls repeated the wonderful Easter tidings told them by the angels. "Early in the morning our song shall rise to Thee." You, early in the morning of your life, young friends of the Savior, strong in faith, with Christian song in your souls, you ought to go and tell others the glorious news.

Christ is risen indeed! It's a proved fact; a thrilling theme; a glorious truth that all believers should boldly affirm to His glory. Never allow unbelievers or doubting Thomases to shake your Bible faith.

You're a co-heir with the risen Christ unto eternal life. He will give strength to rise over sin and temptation, ever to live for Him with victory songs in your heart.

I know that my Redeemer lives,
What comfort this sweet sentence gives!
Living and loving Friend, keep me in the Christian faith.
Help me to live for Thee. Amen.

THE CREED — THE SECOND ARTICLE

Jesus as Judge

April 28

READ: II Corinthians 5:1-10.

TEXT: For we must all appear before the judgment seat of Christ. II Corinthians 5:10.

✣

This verse of Scripture may be either a source of dread or a source of comfort to us, depending on whether or not we have a saving faith in Christ. It reminds us of the certainty that, whoever we are, we must stand before the judgment seat of Christ. All must appear there. The assurance that the Judge will deal righteously with us, for Christ Himself will sit upon the judgment seat, is of little comfort to one who knows that he is guilty. Our comfort lies in the fact that we shall be judged by One who has already paid the penalty for our sins and so removed our transgressions from us. If we are living in active, loving trust in Him and by His power we need have no fears. Our life of faith in Christ whereby we are accounted righteous gives us the courage needed to face that day.

We thank Thee, O God, for the assurance which Thou hast given to us that we shall be judged, not on the basis of our deeds or personal merit, but that we shall be accounted righteous through a living faith in Christ who gave Himself for us. Amen.

THE CREED — THE SECOND ARTICLE

April 29

He has redeemed me a lost and condemned creature

READ: Galatians 3:1-13.

TEXT: Christ hath redeemed us from the curse of the law. Galatians 3:13.

♣

When Christ died on Calvary's cross He purchased our freedom from the condemnation of the law. He removed our curse by taking it upon Himself. We were acquitted. The resulting freedom brings to the believing soul an assurance of forgiveness of sin and an escape from the dominion and the power of Satan. It moves the heart to an expression of "love, joy, peace, good temper, kindliness, generosity, fidelity, gentleness, and self-control" in all our relations with our fellow men. It opens the understanding to an appreciation of God's will and purpose in our life. It makes possible an acceptance of all the blessings of Christ's gospel of redemptive love.

This freedom offers a wonderful challenge and a responsibility to young people. Will you accept that challenge and find your greatest happiness in a loving and obedient doing of the Lord's gracious will to His glory and to the building of a character pleasing unto Him?

Dear heavenly Father, we thank Thee for our precious liberty in Christ Jesus. We beseech Thee to keep us steadfast in our faith and in our loyalty and devotion to Thee, for Jesus' sake. Amen.

THE CREED — THE SECOND ARTICLE

He has bought me

April 30

READ: I Corinthians 6:15-20.

TEXT: For ye are bought with a price. I Corinthians 6:20.

♣

Salvation is the free gift of God to those who have faith in Jesus Christ, but our redemption cost much. All the gold and the silver in the whole world, all the vast material resources of the earth would not be enough to pay the price of a soul.

What was that tremendous price? It cost God His only Son whom He gave for us all. It cost Jesus His very life which He so willingly and gladly sacrificed for you and for me. He paid the supreme price by giving His own holy and precious blood to cleanse us from all sin.

Imagine yourself in the wretched condition of a slave bought by some kind, loving master who immediately sets you free. We were slaves to sin, but Christ has purchased us and made us free. Should we not then thank, love, praise, and serve Him each and every day of our life?

Dear Savior, who hast bought us with Thine own precious blood and delivered us from sin, help us ever to live a life of sincere gratitude and obedient service. Amen.

THE CREED — THE SECOND ARTICLE

May 1

He has freed me from all sins, from death and the power of the devil

READ: Matthew 18:23-27.

TEXT: Stand fast, therefore, in the liberty wherewith Christ hath made us free. Galatians 5:1.

✣

Isn't it great to be an American! No king, no dictator to order my life; no master whose will I, as a slave, must do without protest; no one to fear lest I be jailed or beaten or killed! I'm a free man!

Isn't it great to be a Christian! No fear of punishment for sinful habits that crop out in spite of my striving to live as God desires; no fear that, when the grave closes over me, I shall suffer unending misery; no bondage to "the flesh" that causes shame and heartaches; no slavery to the will and control of Satan! I am free to enjoy the good things that God has placed in the world for me. Free to laugh and sing and love, because Jesus paid the price of all sin and set me free forever.

To keep this freedom by His help I'll try always to grow in love to Him, talk often with Him, and study His Word that I may better learn His will. I want to keep this happy freedom which He has given me.

Dear Father, help me ever as Thy child to guard the freedom our blessed Savior, by His suffering, hath obtained for me. Keep warm my love for Thee. Give me ever a desire to obey Thy holy will, through the same Jesus Christ, my Lord. Amen.

THE CREED — THE SECOND ARTICLE

Not with silver and gold, but with His holy and precious blood, and with His innocent sufferings and death

May 2

READ: Hebrews 9:24-28.

TEXT: Ye were redeemed not . . . with silver or gold . . . but with precious blood. I Peter 1:18, 19.

✤

Great sums of money have been paid out by relatives and friends to purchase the freedom of a kidnapped person. Humanitarians of former years often spent large sums to buy slaves and then set them free. Such sacrifices are small compared to what Jesus paid for our redemption. He laid down His life and shed His blood for us. This ransom paid by Christ cannot be measured in terms of money, for money can never redeem souls from the power of sin, death, and the devil. One drop of Christ's blood is worth more than all the riches of this world because He is the spotless Lamb of God, the Son of the Highest. He had no sin to atone for, but He suffered the utmost for us guilty sinners. Truly, "we are bought with a price."

O Christ, Thou spotless Lamb of God, I can never thank Thee enough for my redemption for which Thou hast paid such a high price. Cleanse me, Lord, and make me pure. Amen.

THE CREED — THE SECOND ARTICLE

May 3

That I might be His own

READ: John 17:6-17.

TEXT: Neither shall any man pluck them out of My hand. John 10:28.

✦

Jesus, the Good Shepherd, saw me, His lost sheep. He felt very sorry for me. He left His Father's house and came to earth. He looked for me until He found me. He brought me home again. Now I belong to Him.

Think what it cost Him to find me. He left all the privileges of heaven behind Him. He gave up for a while His crown, His throne, His power, and His right to rule and reign. He accepted the limitations of humanity and was born, grew up, and underwent the experiences of other men. But beyond that, He suffered unjust persecution and death. All this He endured in order to become the Good Shepherd; in order that He might reach out to me and bring me home again. And now I am His. I am secure in His care and protection. I can face any threat or temptation knowing He is ready and able to sustain me and ward off danger. With Him I am secure.

Jesus, Thou art the Good Shepherd. Thou didst lay down Thy life for the sheep. O Lord, I thank Thee that Thou hast purchased me with Thine own blood and hast made me Thine. Let me be always true to Thee. In Thy name I ask it. Amen.

THE CREED — THE SECOND ARTICLE

Live under Him in His kingdom

May 4

READ: John 18:36-40.
TEXT: For me to live is Christ. Philippians 1:21.

♣

An anchor for the soul is needed "in order that I might be His, live under Him in His kingdom, and serve Him in everlasting righteousness."

There are so many temptations to live for money or pleasure that it is a glorious achievement to be able to say, "For me to live is Christ."

The temper and the contrariness of children confirm what God's Word teaches, that we are "shapen in iniquity and conceived in sin." The heartaches and the distresses of life prove the unhappy lot of unredeemed mankind. Life must be turned inside out and exposed to the "Sun of Righteousness" that sin may no longer have dominion over us. Then we come under the loving dominion, the benevolent sovereignty of Christ.

The prodigal son went from home to live for the fun that money could buy. When his pockets were empty, his life was empty, and he asked: "For me to live is—is what? Why, nothing! Hired servants of my father have more. I am unworthy. I will arise and go to my father." He could now see his father's kindness in the light of Christ and love.

Dear Lord Jesus, help me not to stray in disobedience, but may I accept Thy authority over my life and ever live with Thee and for Thee. Amen.

THE CREED — THE SECOND ARTICLE

May 5

Serve Him in everlasting righteousness, innocence, and blessedness

READ: Luke 1:68-75.

TEXT: But ye are a chosen generation, a royal priesthood, an holy nation, a peculiar people; that ye should show forth the praises of Him who hath called you out of darkness into His marvellous light. I Peter 2:9.

✤

Nobility in the eyes of the world came to those who by chance and circumstance had royal blood in their veins. Seldom could any other hope to share the advantages afforded royalty although occasionally some humble peasant could be dubbed a knight for some daring deed or heroic achievement.

As God's children, however, we share in a nobility that raises us far above the royal families of the monarchs of the earth. We are called to *serve* no mere earthly king but the Lord of heaven, to whom all authority on earth and in heaven has been given. Ours is a privilege that comes regardless of circumstances, or station in this life, however lowly. Through faith in Christ we are set free from the bondage of the earth to serve Him.

Dear Lord Jesus, as knights of old pledged allegiance to their lords and lived in their service, so I would pledge anew to Thee this day my allegiance and seek Thy grace and strength to serve Thee faithfully in word and in deed. Amen.

THE CREED — THE SECOND ARTICLE

The person of Christ
Christ, the Lamb of God

May 6

READ: Isaiah 53:3-7.

TEXT: Behold the Lamb of God which taketh away the sin of the world. John 1:29.

✤

An eminent churchman once said, "Our great security against sin lies in our being shocked at it," for sin has been and is the world's chief problem. We all have to face it and wrestle with it.

The sinfulness of sin cannot be exaggerated; its penalty no man can pay; its burden no man can carry. That is why Christ made His advent in human flesh. "He was wounded for our transgressions and bruised for our iniquities." "The Lord hath laid on Him the iniquity of us all." Your sin and mine and every man's, they were all laid upon Jesus Christ. And when He bore them He fulfilled the Old Testament symbol of the lamb sacrificed on the altar as an offering for sin.

Our hope is Christ. He is the Physician with the healing medicine. He is the Holy One who has unlocked the gate of heaven. He is the Redeemer who has sacrificed Himself to take away the guilt and the power of sin. By His grace we are saved.

O most merciful God, who knowest the temptations which beset us, have mercy upon us and help us. Cleanse us from all unrighteousness and lead us into the more abundant life. Through Christ we ask it. Amen.

THE CREED — THE SECOND ARTICLE

May 7

The person of Christ

Christ, the Messiah

READ: John 1:35-42.
TEXT: We have found the Messias. John 1:41.

♣

Christ IS the Messiah. He came to be our PROPHET, revealing Himself as Redeemer according to the gospel; He became our PRIEST, to offer Himself as sacrifice. He now is our KING, ruling, directing, protecting us. John the Baptist pointed out this Christ to Andrew and John. Andrew heard, and his brother Peter was informed. Your pastor taught you of the Messiah. Have you told others? We must never hoard the good news. We do not have Him to keep for ourselves. We now live in Him, and we must share Him with others. Our Christianity must be more than an ornament. It must be an *active* thing. God loved us and gave His Son. The Son loved us and gave Himself. We promised allegiance at confirmation. We are now bound to say to the world, "He is mine, and I now give Him also to be thine."

God, we thank Thee for Thine unspeakable gift. In the measure that grace has flowed to us, so may we also tell to others. We ask in the Messiah's name. Amen.

THE CREED — THE SECOND ARTICLE

The person of Christ
Christ, our Mediator

May 8

READ: I Timothy 2:1-6.
TEXT: There is one God and one mediator. I Timothy 2:5.

♣

Most of us have no trouble in understanding Jesus from the standpoint of His being a good and righteous man. But when it comes to knowing what Jesus means to and for ME: well, that is different. Christ as Mediator is one of those different aspects. Many of us are *interMEDIATES*. We are "between" the "kid age" and the grown-up age. So, too, Jesus is standing between us and God. God has asked that we do His will. We know that we do not always do it. For this we are sorry. Jesus, in effect, says to God: "These boys and girls love Me, they believe in Me. They are sorry for their evil deeds. So take My love and let it be for them before Thee." Are you sorry? Do you love Jesus? Then Christ is YOUR Mediator, too! The only hard part of all this is REALLY ACTING ON IT AND USING CHRIST'S MEDIATION.

Dear Lord Jesus, whom now I know as Mediator, help me by Thy good spirit so that each day I may be truly sorry for my evil deeds and be glad in Thy loving care for me. Amen.

THE CREED — THE SECOND ARTICLE

May 9

The person of Christ
Christ, the Prophet

READ: Deuteronomy 18:15-22.
TEXT: Of a truth, this is the prophet. John 7:40.

♣

Truly Christ is the Prophet of God. He is the God-sent Messenger to men. He is the utterance, the expression, the oracle and voice of God through whom He makes known His holy and righteous will in the law and His good and gracious will in the gospel. He is the revealer of God to man, the discloser of the mind, will, and heart of God toward man. He is the One who unveils the character and the disposition of the heavenly Father, lays open God's heart of love toward sinners, makes manifest His desire, His willingness, His ability and trustworthiness to save them. It is He who offers, gives, and bequeaths to them the grace of God, the forgiveness of sin, peace, pardon, and perfect righteousness as well as life eternal and salvation everlasting. He is God's own and only Son, the Spirit-filled Messiah, all-knowing and all-truthful, the unerring teacher of truth.

Lord Jesus, help us with all our heart to listen to Thy voice, to read and to hear Thy holy Word, to believe every statement, to trust every promise, to heed every warning, to obey every commandment and to appropriate every privilege and blessing Thou extendest for time and for eternity. Amen.

THE CREED — THE SECOND ARTICLE

The person of Christ
Christ, the High Priest

May 10

READ: Hebrews 8:1-6.

TEXT: We have a great high priest . . . Jesus, the Son of God. Hebrews 4:14.

✤

Two brothers grew up together. Although both of them had the same training, one became a lawyer and the other a criminal. Three times the criminal was brought into court, and each time his brother pleaded his cause, and he was released. The lawyer became a judge. Once more the criminal was brought to court, but this time his brother said: "I am sorry. This time I cannot plead your case. Arise, and receive your sentence."

So Christ, our High Priest, is continually pleading for us. We should, indeed, be lost if He did not intercede for us. Our Savior is truly our High Priest. He was the Anointed of God, the Holy Spirit dwelling in Him. He purchased our salvation on the cross. He arose from the dead and ascended into heaven. There He intercedes in our behalf. Let us accept Him as our High Priest, so we shall not have to stand before Him and receive our sentence from Him as a Judge.

Dear Savior, I thank Thee that Thou hast become my High Priest. Plead for me so that I may share the salvation which Thou hast purchased for me with Thy precious blood. Amen.

THE CREED — THE SECOND ARTICLE

May 11

The person of Christ
Christ, the King

READ: Matthew 21:1-11.

TEXT: He shall show, who is the blessed and only Potentate, the King of kings, and Lord of Lords. I Timothy 6:15.

✣

Prophet, Priest, King. How often we hear these words used in connection with Christ and His work! He is the true Prophet to reveal to us the whole will of God. He is the true Priest to intercede for us at the throne of grace and to atone for our sins once and for all by His sacrificial death. He is our King to reign forever and ever. He reigns over us in the kingdom of power, of grace, and of glory.

Today we can say, "Behold thy King." Today we can sing, "And He shall reign forever and ever." In a world of hatred and bloodshed our King still reigns. His kingdom is in the hearts of believing men. In those hearts He abides and operates. His kingdom shall have no end. His followers are heart-touched and spirit-guided.

Is He your King? Does He reign and rule in your heart to comfort, strengthen, guide, and stay you?

Heavenly Father, teach us to realize more and more that we have a King of kings. May this King rule in our heart and our life day by day. We ask in His own precious name. Amen.

THE CREED — THE SECOND ARTICLE

The person of Christ
Christ, both our Lord and God

May 12

READ: John 20:24-29.

TEXT: And Thomas answered, My Lord and my God. John 20:28.

✤

To know truly who and what Jesus is, and what He is to us is the full catechism of life. Thomas had been a humble, loyal learner for three years, a faithful disciple, indeed. He gladly accepted Jesus as his Lord, and this means his Teacher and Master. He lived obediently according to what he had learned. When the risen Christ came to His own in the upper room to declare to them the new truth of His life after death, Thomas was not present. When he heard his friends' account of Jesus' resurrection he could not believe. He demanded special proof for himself. This Jesus returned to give, and Thomas understood it. If he had stopped learning about Jesus he would not have been a true Christian. He could have told others about Jesus only as Master and Lord. But when Jesus stood before him to be seen and heard and touched, Thomas learned that He was more than any man's Lord or Leader ever had been. He learned that Jesus was also God.

O blessed Christ of God and very God, lead me into such earnest, active living that I may learn the new truths that are taught in obedience and in service, for Thy dear name's sake. Amen.

THE CREED — THE THIRD ARTICLE

Of Sanctification

I believe in the Holy Ghost

May 13

READ: Acts 2:1-18.

TEXT: I will pray the Father, and He shall give you another Comforter, that He may abide with you forever; even the Spirit of truth. John 14: 16, 17.

♣

"How often have I wished for someone to be with me! I want him to stand by me."

Polish your lamp, my young friend. Look! Here is the One who remains a friend when other friends are few. He will love you when other love is lacking. He helps you to speak well. He trusts you although others taunt. When examinations are here, He helps you to remember. When life is filled with choices, He says, "This way" or, "That road." Do you really wish for someone to be with you always? Read the Scripture text again.

His name is Comforter. He is the Holy Ghost. You can count upon Him always. Here is the coming true of your wish. The Holy Ghost is God. God is with you always. Love Him and His Word. Keep His commandments. You will never wish for a better helper.

Renew Thyself in me, O Holy Ghost. Strengthen me with Thy many gifts. Increase within me the will to walk with Thee as faithful friend and loving doer. Amen.

THE CREED — THE THIRD ARTICLE

I believe in the Holy Christian Church

May 14

READ: Matthew 16:13-20.

TEXT: Upon this rock I will build My church, and the gates of hell [Hades] shall not prevail against it. Matthew 16:18.

✣

In this day of world conflict Americans are supporting and aiding their government in many unusual ways. The spirit of national patriotism is on the march. We are happy to say, "I am an American." It is altogether fitting and proper that we should feel this way.

We should also remember that the Holy Christian Church, the agency established by God to further His kingdom among men and the most important "task-force" in our world is also on the march. There is no end to spiritual strife. Problems that require divine guidance for solution are always with us. But our spiritual "patriotism" shows us where our duty lies. We are not only happy to say, "I am a Christian." We must also take a firm stand in defense of what is right, good, and true. May we honestly dedicate and rededicate ourselves to the unfinished work of the Holy Christian Church.

Eternal Father, give us courage, fortitude, and vision to be on "active duty" in the battle of love; make clear to us our duty in Thy Holy Christian Church. Amen.

THE CREED — THE THIRD ARTICLE

May 15

I believe in the communion of saints

READ: Hebrews 12:1-11.

TEXT: Now therefore ye are no more strangers and foreigners, but fellow citizens with the saints. Ephesians 2:19.

✣

You are glad you are a citizen of your nation—not a stranger in the land, nor a foreigner. You are glad that you "belong." Just so, because of your faith in Jesus Christ you are a fellow citizen of His kingdom, you belong to the world-wide communion or fellowship of believers, you are one of God's children. And if you are His you are growing as a Christian, you are letting Him make you a better person, you are now one of the multitude of Christian "saints." You are glad are you not that you are united with those whom God has called all through the ages; one with Abraham, Moses, Daniel; with the apostles; with St. Paul; with Luther; with the missionaries of the cross and with all the heroes of the gospel? You are now a member of the church, united with all who accept Jesus as their Savior and Lord and who seek to please Him in their daily life. You are one of those today on whom Jesus depends to serve Him.

O Christ, Thou Head of the church, in whom are united all of Thy believing followers as citizens of Thy everlasting kingdom, grant unto us to trust Thee always, to follow Thee faithfully, and to serve Thee loyally, for Thy name's sake. Amen.

THE CREED — THE THIRD ARTICLE

I believe in the forgiveness of sins

May 16

READ: John 20:19-23.

TEXT: Blessed is he whose transgression is forgiven, whose sin is covered. Psalm 32:1.

❧

When we disobey our parents we are ashamed and afraid and uncomfortable in their presence. Things can be made right only if we come and say, "I am sorry, please forgive me." We do this because we believe that they love us and want to forgive us.

Sin and disobedience of God's law separate us from God, and conscience makes us ashamed and afraid. It is a great consolation to assert in our Creed, "I believe in the forgiveness of sins." We believe that because God's Word declares that "if we confess our sins, He is faithful and just to forgive our sins."

Jesus Christ, the Head of the church, gave this authority to the church to announce and declare this forgiveness to repentant sinners when He said, "Whosoever sins ye forgive, they are forgiven."

The church thus becomes the more precious to us as we believe that "in the Christian Church He daily and richly forgives me and all believers all our sins."

O Holy Spirit, grant that I may eagerly return when I have sinned, believing in the love of God the Father, who is ready always to forgive my sins, through Jesus Christ, my Lord. Amen.

THE CREED — THE THIRD ARTICLE

May 17

I believe in the resurrection of the body

READ: John 11:39-46.

TEXT: They taught the people, and preached through Jesus the resurrection from the dead. Acts 4:2.

✤

The doctrine of the resurrection of the body is one of the most distinctive and clear teachings of Scripture. Many religions and philosophers have taught the immortality of the soul, that is, ongoing existence in a spirit state after death. But God promises us a future as total personalities, body and soul. That does not seem reasonable to the human, so-called scientific mind. But it is the great hope and assurance of the believing Christian. It takes the gloom out of life and makes life truly worth living. Death is not the end of life. On the last day our body shall be raised and reunited with the soul. Being born of the Spirit, the Scriptures are our supreme authority. We have the clear teaching of Christ and His apostles. We have the historic fact of Christ's resurrection which the world cannot deny. Nothing shall rob us of the comforting truth, "Because Christ lives, we shall live also."

Heavenly Father, grant us Thy Spirit's grace, that we may continually hold fast to our faith in the resurrection. Grant, dear Lord, that our resurrection be a resurrection unto life. Amen.

THE CREED — THE THIRD ARTICLE

I believe in the life everlasting

May 18

READ: John 5:39-47.

TEXT: For this is the will of Him that sent Me, that every one which . . . believeth on Him, may have everlasting life. John 6:40.

♣

The story of creation clearly shows the difference between the creation of man and the universe as such. In creation God was satisfied to use His powerful Word: He spoke, and things came into being. With man it was different, "God formed man of the dust of the ground and breathed into his nostrils the breath of life, and man became a living soul."

Man was not created to die; he carries within him a living soul, the breath of God which cannot die.

The death of Christ would have no meaning at all except for this fact; the work of the Christian Church has as its sole object the salvation of souls to have them share everlasting life, eternal at-homeness with God.

And God has made it possible for sinful man to attain this blessed state: Christ is the Savior of all, but faith, simple, pure, and strong is necessary.

Heavenly Father, I thank Thee for my faith in Jesus which assures me of life everlasting. Keep and preserve to me by Thy Holy Spirit this simple faith, through Jesus Christ, my Savior. Amen.

THE CREED — THE THIRD ARTICLE

Bringing forth the fruits of the Spirit

May 19

READ: Galatians 5:19-26.

TEXT: The fruit of the Spirit is love, joy, peace, longsuffering, gentleness, goodness, faith, meekness, temperance. Galatians 5:22, 23.

✤

When a man who owns an orchard has carefully planted and cared for his trees he expects in proper season fruits from his labors. God provides soil, sunshine, and rain. Fruits appear. Man rejoices and thanks God for His providence.

The Christian life is somewhat like that. When a young Christian is really a disciple of Christ and permits God's Holy Spirit to work carefully, patiently, and persistently in his life, fruits will appear in the form of a quality of life which differs essentially from non-Christian and unholy living.

Notice, too, how much like the life of Christ is this new kind of life. Christ was in a unique way loving, joyful, peaceful, humble, patient, good, full of faith and self-control. The Christian's goal in life is to become like Christ. The fruits St. Paul speaks of indicate our growth in the Christian life if we possess them.

Lord, let me daily so walk in fellowship with my Redeemer that the Holy Spirit may bring fruits of Christlikeness into my life, making it rich, full, beautiful, and holy. Amen.

THE CREED — THE THIRD ARTICLE

I cannot by my own reason or strength believe in Jesus Christ

May 20

READ: I Corinthians 2:11-16.

TEXT: The natural man receiveth not the things of the Spirit of God. I Corinthians 2:14.

♣

Pride in our own ability and confidence in our own self are a part of our human nature. We thrill to the words, "I am the captain of my soul; I am the master of my fate." In our relation to God even we are apt to be self-righteous; the demands of God, however, are more than surface goodness and outward service. The divine command reads, "Thou shalt love the Lord, thy God, with all thy heart and with all thy soul and with all thy mind and with all thy strength." If we are honest with ourselves we know that this is beyond our ability. "The mind of the flesh is enmity against God." If we are to become the children of God and live in a way pleasing to Him, it must come about by the work of the Holy Spirit in our heart and our life. We must surrender our life to Christ and trust Him alone for our righteousness and salvation. "Blessed are they who hunger and thirst after righteousness, for they shall be filled."

Keep us humble, O God, and help us to seek Thee only as our refuge from sin and temptation. Give us the faith in Thee as a loving Savior who will never fail us. Amen.

THE CREED — THE THIRD ARTICLE

May 21

I cannot by my own reason or strength come to Him

READ: John 6:32-44.

TEXT: No man can come to Me, except the Father ... draw him. John 6:44.

✣

Faith in oneself is necessary for getting on in life. Yet no one can really succeed in life without a faith in a great personality outside of himself. Study the life of Jesus and note the emphasis He places on the Father. "I and the Father are one," was the urge that compelled Him on His earthly mission. The overwhelming sense of the presence of God puts many "musts" into His whole life. Study His prayer life and the secret of His power is revealed. He lived by the strength God gives to the trusting soul. The Father was the magnetic lure ever present in the years of His earthly ministry. He was God-sent and God-led. We who follow Him can succeed only by letting God in His own way of faith bring us to Him. Our soul is restless in a confused world until we are connected by God with the unfailing source of spiritual power ever available in Himself.

Dear Father, I put my trust in Thee. Draw me ever closer to Thee. Thou hast called me and empowered me to live in Christ. Keep me in the faith. Amen.

THE CREED — THE THIRD ARTICLE

The Holy Ghost has called me by the gospel

May 22

READ: II Thessalonians 2:13-17.

TEXT: God called you by our gospel. II Thessalonians 2:14.

✣

Gospel means good news. The good news is that Jesus Christ died on the cross for my sins so that, if I accept this fact and believe it and confess my sins to God, I shall receive forgiveness and be able to live forever. This is good news indeed.

There are various ways by which this good news is presented to us. God calls us or invites us to come to Him by means of the *written* Word which is the good news of life and forgiveness we can read about in the Bible.

He calls us by means of the *spoken* Word which is the good news of life and forgiveness we and other Christians can hear with our ears and tell to others with our voices.

He also calls us by means of the *visible* Word which is the good news of life and forgiveness that baptism and the Lord's Supper bring us.

The world needs this good news. Let us daily pray God that we might accept His invitation and then be instruments through whom others are given that invitation.

Dear Father in heaven, we thank Thee for the good news of forgiveness and life. May we personally heed Thy invitation to us and also be instruments to bring this message of Thine to others. Amen.

THE CREED — THE THIRD ARTICLE

May 23

The Holy Ghost enlightens me with His gifts

READ: II Corinthians 4:1-6.

TEXT: It is God . . . who shined in our hearts, to give the light of the knowledge of the glory of God in the face of Jesus Christ. II Corinthians 4:6.

✤

An ancient legend has it that a father discovered an ointment with which to bring the dead back to life. Carefully he instructed his son how to apply this ointment. The father died. The son took the ointment from the shelf and according to instructions poured a third over the corpse of his father. The father opened his eyes. When the son poured the second portion over his father, the father sat up in bed. That so surprised the son that he dropped the third portion. Immediately it evaporated, and the father relapsed into death.

This illustrates a spiritual truth. God the Father created and preserves us, the Son redeemed us, but only through the Holy Spirit can we appropriate the blessings of the Father and the Son. The Spirit enlightens us. He convinces us of our sinfulness and of the need of a Savior. And He continues to teach us as Christians so that more and more we understand what previously puzzled us.

We beseech Thee, Almighty God, let our souls be lighted by Thy Spirit so that, being filled as lamps by the divine gift, we may shine as lights in a dark and evil world; through Christ Jesus, our Lord. Amen.

THE CREED — THE THIRD ARTICLE

The Holy Ghost sanctifies me

May 24

READ: I Corinthians 6:1-11.

TEXT: But ye are washed, but ye are sanctified, but ye are justified in the name of the Lord Jesus, and by the Spirit of our God. I Corinthians 6:11.

✤

As confirmed Christians you have become different from those who have not accepted Jesus as Savior and Lord. You are "in the world," yes; but "not of the world." You are to "walk circumspectly," as St. Paul says. So as Christians it is your duty and privilege to flee sinful lusts, desires, and actions. Why?

First, because you have been *baptized* into Christ and the Christian faith, and you have promised to put off all filthiness of the flesh and the spirit.

Second, because you are *sanctified,* set apart, separated from earthly things and connected with spiritual things, joined to the living God.

Third, because you are *justified.* Your sins and guilt have been blotted out through Jesus Christ.

Fourth, because the *Spirit of God,* having produced this change, would continue His work of grace until finally, at the ned of this life, you are "remodelled" into the complete likeness of Christ.

O God, our heavenly Father, who doeth all things well, we beseech Thee that we may so receive and use Thy means of grace, Thy Word and the Holy Sacraments, that we may be kept by Thy divine power, and may be wholly sanctified through the Holy Spirit. Amen.

THE CREED — THE THIRD ARTICLE

May 25

The Holy Ghost preserves me in the one true faith

READ: II Timothy 4:1-18.

TEXT: The Lord . . . will preserve me unto His heavenly kingdom. II Timothy 4:18.

✣

Not only does the Holy Ghost create in me true faith in Christ Jesus, my Lord and Redeemer, but He also *preserves* me in this faith; He keeps my faith alive, healthy, active. We may admire a new garment, book, or automobile, but if such articles are not properly cared for they soon look old and dilapidated.

Nothing could be more beautiful than a group of young people before God's altar on confirmation day. How sincere they appear to be! How "their hearts burn within them!" Yet, they need to be *preserved* in this fervent faith, when doubts arise, enthusiasm dwindles, and love cools. They have "begun to build," they have received some of the benefits as citizens of God's kingdom, but only God the Holy Ghost can *preserve* them in the grace of their baptismal covenant.

Gracious Lord and heavenly Father, I thank Thee that by Thy Holy Spirit Thou dost enable me to believe in Jesus Christ as my Lord and Savior. O Holy Spirit, wilt Thou keep me a healthy, active Christian that by Thy grace I may remain loyal to the end of my life and thus share the glories of Thine eternal kingdom. This I ask in Jesus' name. Amen.

THE CREED — THE THIRD ARTICLE

The Holy Ghost transforms me from glory to glory

May 26

READ: II Corinthians 3:11-18.

TEXT: But we all . . . are transformed into the same image from glory to glory, even as by the Spirit of the Lord. II Corinthians 3:18.

✣

How may I experience such a transformation? In Ephesians 3:17, Paul prays "that Christ may dwell in your hearts by faith." The word "dwell" is from a Greek word made up of two words, one meaning, "to live," the other meaning, "down." Paul prays that our Lord may live in our heart as His home. He is already in us, but His desire is to settle down and feel at home in every thought, word, and deed.

It is one thing to be in a person's home but quite another to feel completely at home there. Does He have free access to all parts of your heart and your life? When this is true, you will be "transformed into the same image from glory to glory, even as by the Spirit of the Lord." You will develop into a spiritual adult.

Dear Lord Jesus, I know that Thou dost dwell in my heart by faith, but I pray that I may also have the grace to make Thee feel at home at all times and in all places and so may continue to grow from year to year. Amen.

THE CREED — THE THIRD ARTICLE

May 27

The Holy Ghost calls, gathers, enlightens, and sanctifies the whole Christian Church on earth

READ: Ephesians 5:20-27.

TEXT: Christ also loved the church, and gave Himself for it; that He might sanctify and cleanse it with the washing of water by the word. Ephesians 5:25, 26.

♣

It has been said that "a good man is one, no matter how bad, who is growing better." That is what St. Paul meant when he addressed the church at Corinth as "them that are called to be saints."

Jesus Christ loved the church because it is made up of those who have come to Him to be delivered from their sins and who want to be better men and women.

Think of the whole church, then, as all the believers in the world, whom the Holy Ghost calls and gathers, sinners as they are, to be enlightened and sanctified and to become one "glorious church, holy and without blemish."

We ought then to love the church since Christ loved it and gave Himself for it, that is, for you and for me.

Savior, if of Zion's city, I through grace a member am,
Let the world deride or pity, I will glory in Thy name.

Holy Spirit, let me find in the church of the living God help to become better continually through the Word and the sacraments and the grace of our Lord Jesus Christ. Amen.

THE CREED — THE THIRD ARTICLE

The Holy Ghost preserves it (the church) in union with Jesus Christ in the one true faith

May 28

READ: Ephesians 4:1-6.

TEXT: Endeavoring to keep the unity of the Spirit in the bonds of peace. Ephesians 4:3.

✤

You are now a professing Christian, a member of the church. As such you are faced with added responsibilities. One of these is to help "keep the unity of the Spirit in the bond of peace." This can be accomplished only by the help and the guidance of the Holy Spirit. He makes us aware that the universal church is one because it is united in a single faith in and relation to Jesus Christ. As members we must constantly strive toward understanding and helpfulness among God's people. Young people do have a part in the promotion of harmony in the church. Their influence can help or hinder. Some do little more than to criticize while others lend themselves in the spirit of love, endeavoring to be helpful. Nothing is needed more in the church today than a determined resolution among the youth to help "keep the unity of the Spirit in the bond of peace." Let the Holy Spirit use you.

Dear heavenly Father, if it please Thee to use me, take me and fill my life with the power of Thy Spirit. Let my influence help the cause of understanding and harmony and peace among the members of the church. Amen.

THE CREED — THE THIRD ARTICLE

May 29

The Holy Ghost daily forgives abundantly all my sins

READ: I John 1:1-10.

TEXT: If we confess our sins, He is faithful and just to forgive us our sins. I John 1:9.

✤

As Christians, reclaimed by God's Spirit, we have the new life of Christ in us urging us toward the things that please God. We also have within us a rebellious human nature with its sinful impulses, and we live in the midst of a sinful world. Besides, in our ignorance we commit many sins, thinking we are doing good; as Luther says, "We sin much every day."

We are like children coming in to mother from their work or play all tousled and dirty and perhaps bruised from contacts with the world. They need to be bathed and reclothed. Mother is more anxious and concerned to have them clean than they are. So the Holy Spirit is anxious to have us cleansed from the grime and poison of our sins and waits anxiously to have us come to Him for the washing and cleansing. Are we aware of our needs? Are we penitent for our failings? Do we "make a clean breast" of our wrongs in our prayers? Then He will cleanse us.

Spirit of Holiness, who forgivest the sins of them that come to Thee in penitence, look mercifully upon me, begrimed with the sins of another day. I would be clean as God wants me. "Wash me, and I shall be whiter than snow." Amen.

THE CREED — THE THIRD ARTICLE

The Holy Ghost at the last day will raise up me and all the dead

Our final victory

May 30

READ: Revelation 21:1-7.

TEXT: All that are in the graves shall hear His voice, and shall come forth. John 5:28, 29.

♣

As I write these words I am looking out of my study window. The leaves are falling. Soon the cold winds of winter will sweep across our Kansas prairies and will carry them. Where? To me all this is but a symbol of the fact that each one of us will fall only too soon. Perhaps in the past few years your own brother or uncle or a very close friend has fallen on some field of battle, far from friends, home, or loved ones. But there is One who is very near to the Christian, who meets that crisis in life for him.

Martin Luther, looking out of his window on a world torn by trouble just like ours, wrote on the Third Article of our Creed, "In the last day He will raise up me and all the dead." What a joy that is to each of us now to know that for the Christian death is not the end, but the very beginning! The grave does not have the final word; the final word is Christ's, and it is "resurrection," "victory."

Dear Master, help us to be confident now and to attain finally that victory, and unto Thee be all the glory now and forever. Amen.

THE CREED — THE THIRD ARTICLE

May 31

The Holy Ghost will grant everlasting life to me

READ: Revelation 22:1-7.

TEXT: He that believeth on the Son hath everlasting life. John 3:36.

✤

When Jesus said, "Ye must be born again," He spoke of the beginning of a new life in us, an everlasting life. What does this mean?

Let us think of our entire life as a journey. We begin it as the driver of our own car, our own body. Then one day we meet Jesus, and He says, "Let me drive." So we change drivers. That is what happens when we are born again. We are then like St. Paul who said, "I live, yet not I, but Christ liveth in me."

That may occur in our infancy; or it may come later in our remembered experience. But it must happen if we are to have life.

So we journey on. We have a new life but must still use the same old body for a while. It gets older and more and more infirm until it just quits. It is ready for the graveyard. We call this death.

But if we have been given over to Christ, even if the body dies we go right on living—living this everlasting life which God gives through the work of His Spirit to those who believe on His Son.

O God, grant me grace by Thy Holy Spirit to give over the control of my life to Jesus Christ that I may live godly here in time and in heaven forever. For His name's sake. Amen.

THE CREED — THE THIRD ARTICLE

The Holy Ghost gives me the power to prove the spirits

READ: Acts 1:1-13.

TEXT: Try the spirits, whether they are of God. I John 4:1.

June 1

❦

You, as a recent confirmand, are in process of "moving up" into higher departments of learning. Grade school gives way to high school, and the latter may be followed by college or the university. Each successive step is a challenge to your faith. Strange teachings, new fellowships, deeper reading, laboratory experiences widen the outreach of your mind. Some young people are easily upset. Their faith wavers. Doubts attack them, and they begin to ask more often, "What is truth?"

Here is a helpful answer: your Bible, your pastor, your church with its solid confessions, and above all —your Christ says, "Prove the spirits, test the teachings." Do they harmonize with God's Word? "Come unto Me," says the Savior. "Come and see!" "Prove all things, and hold fast to that which is good." This type of test appeals to youth. It is scientific. It is Scriptural. It is common sense, and if the teaching is of God it will always stand the test.

Lord God, grant me the willingness, the courage, the understanding to test all knowledge under the standard of Thy truth and to accept only that which is pleasing to Thee. Amen.

THE CREED — THE THIRD ARTICLE

June 2

The Holy Spirit gives me more abundant life

READ: John 10:1-10.

TEXT: I am come that they might have life, and that they might have it more abundantly. John 10:10.

♣

Jesus is the Good Shepherd. He wants to feed and shelter us, lead and protect us, and give us a free and abundant life. There are some Christians who do not seem to believe that but are fearful, unhappy, long-faced folks who neither enjoy life nor want others to enjoy it. Poor souls, how empty is their life!

Jesus came to put abundance into our life. By the Holy Spirit He can fill our soul with so many beautiful things: gratitude, faith, love, strength, zeal, good-will, peace, kindness, happiness, and hope. Such abundant lives overflow with blessings for others.

Some most abundant lives have been lived by suffering, bed-ridden saints, poverty-stricken, handicapped, crippled, or blind. Helen Keller, though she was blind and deaf, lived a life of such abundance that she became a blessing to the world. Rich souls, how abundant is their life!

Only Jesus Christ, through the Holy Spirit, can give us this power of abundant living. Ask for it.

O God, who hast given Jesus Christ to be our Good Shepherd, give me power by Thy Holy Spirit to live like Him that others may be blessed by my abundance. Amen.

PRAYER

Jesus teaches us to pray

June 3

READ: Matthew 26:36-46.

TEXT: Lord, teach us to pray, as John also taught his disciples. Luke 11:1.

✤

Some men pray only when they are in danger or need. Others pray because they fear, love, and trust in God. In prayer they draw near to God, and God draws near to them.

Jesus prayed because He loved the Father and knew that the Father loved Him. They loved to talk with each other. God wants us to feel like that.

His disciples were impressed by Christ's habit of prayer and asked Him to teach them to pray. John the Baptist, they said, had taught his disciples to pray. So Jesus taught them the prayer we call the Lord's Prayer. "Our Father which art in heaven; hallowed be Thy name; Thy kingdom come, Thy will be done, on earth as it is in heaven. Give us this day our daily bread; and forgive us our trespasses, as we forgive those who trespass against us. Lead us not into temptation, but deliver us from evil. For Thine is the kingdom, and the power, and the glory, Amen."

In a way similar to this, thoughtfully and sincerely, we should pray every day.

Lord, teach us to pray as Thou didst teach Thy disciples to pray that we may ask of God with all cheerfulness and confidence as dear children ask of their dear father. Amen.

PRAYER

June 4

Pray humbly as the publican

READ: Luke 18:10-14.

TEXT: The sacrifices of God are a broken spirit; a broken and a contrite heart, O God, Thou wilt not despise. Psalm 51:17.

♣

How dare a man boast before God? God knows our inmost thoughts. Even should a man be very good, there is enough of evil in him to bring him under the condemnation of the law. How foolish in the sight of God must the Pharisee have seemed!

With what tenderness must God have looked upon this publican, who stood afar off, with bowed head and downcast eyes, and who prayed simply, humbly, "God, be merciful to me, a sinner."

That is the best way to pray, for God knows what we need before we ask Him and better than we ourselves know. And God answers prayer, not because we are good, but only because He is merciful. God's mercy includes everything, and "a broken and a contrite heart He will not despise."

> With broken heart and contrite sigh,
> A trembling sinner, Lord, I cry;
> Thy pardoning grace is rich and free:
> O God, be merciful to me.

O Almighty and Holy God, whose mercy is from everlasting to everlasting, teach me to approach Thee humbly that my prayer may be heard always. Through Jesus Christ I pray this. Amen.

PRAYER

Pray regularly, as Daniel did

June 5

READ: Daniel 6:10-23.

TEXT: Daniel . . . kneeled upon his knees three times a day, and prayed, and gave thanks before his God, as he did aforetime. Daniel 6:10.

✣

Praying was dangerous Daniel learned! It meant defiance of the evil around him; loss of favor with the king; and probable death. But Daniel knew it was far more dangerous *not* to pray. To stop praying would take away his contact with his heavenly King; it would force him to stand alone against the hate of his enemies; and it would dispel the effectiveness of that power which protected him later from the lions. Daniel knew the danger of praying, but he knew the *disaster* of not praying!

Praying is dangerous today! Young people know it sometimes invites the scorn of others, and it always leads into potentially dangerous action for Christ if we pray, "Not my will but Thine be done." Yet youth prays, for youth is not afraid of danger if God is there to guide, encourage, and strengthen. Youth fears only the disaster of having that contact with Him severed.

Heavenly Father, may I lose all fear of man and his scorn or hate by always keeping bright my blessed fellowship with Thee, through Jesus Christ, my Lord. Amen.

PRAYER

June 6

Pray apart, as Jesus did
Prayer — the secret closet

READ: Matthew 14:22-33.

TEXT: Jesus went up into a mountain apart to pray. Matthew 14:23.

✠

Alone with God, in the secret place of the Most High! Enter into your quiet place and close the door, shutting out from you the world with its noise and business and shutting you in with God. That is what you do when you enter a public telephone booth. You close the door, shutting out the noise so that your friend may hear you, and you may hear your friend. Prayer is a two-way conversation with God in a quiet place.

A canalboat enters the lock. The gate is closed behind it. Then the gate at the farther end is opened. The boat rises to a higher level and then continues on its journey. So when we enter our prayer closet, our quiet place, we shut the door behind us. Then heaven's door opens, and God comes in "our souls to greet, and glory crowns the mercy seat."

Heavenly Father, help me through fervent prayer to attain to ever-higher levels of spiritual experience and holy living so as to please Thee in all things. In Jesus' name. Amen.

PRAYER

Pray when in trouble

June 7

READ: Exodus 14:13-31.

TEXT: Call upon Me in the day of trouble, and I will deliver thee, and thou shalt glorify Me. Psalm 50:15.

✤

No person is exempt from trouble. This includes every one of us. In your youth, when responsibilities are few, you may believe that the burdens and the trials of which you have heard will not befall you. But all too soon you will be confronted with trials of all kinds, and you will not be able to carry them. As a child of God you will in full confidence go to your heavenly Father and pour out your heart to Him. You will not dictate to Him as to how He will deliver you; that will be left to Him. God has His own way of delivering us when in trouble as He did St. Paul. He takes away our burden, answering the last petition of the Lord's Prayer, "Deliver us from evil!" To show your gratitude, thank God for His interest in you. Remember the ten lepers who were healed; only one returned to thank Jesus. In the day of trouble let not the fires on your altar go out!

Dear Father in heaven, Thou knowest our burdens and trials better than we do. Wilt Thou enable us to carry successfully all these burdens of life. Grant us a full measure of faith to trust Thee at all times and never doubt Thy guiding hand. May the trials of life teach us to pray more fervently, for Jesus' sake. Amen.

PRAYER

Pray without ceasing

June 8

READ: Luke 18:1-8.
TEXT: Pray without ceasing. I Thessalonians 5:17.

♣

A servant girl was once asked if she knew what it meant to "pray without ceasing." "O yes," she replied. "When I awake I thank God for the morning light and pray that Jesus, the Light of the world, may shine in my heart. When I prepare the meals I pray that God will feed us with the bread of life. When I wash the dishes I pray that God will wash all uncleanness from my heart. And so through the day I pray. O yes, I know what it is to pray without ceasing."

There was once a humble worker in a French monastery, named Brother Lawrence, who practiced the "presence of God." He thought of God as being present every moment, in every task, and that he could talk with God.

Such a life is prayer in itself, prayer without ceasing. By thinking thus, by praying thus, we come to love more deeply the time devoted to public worship and prayer.

We thank and praise Thee, dear heavenly Father, for Thy loving-kindness expressed in this admonition. Help us to realize more fully our constant need of Thy sustaining grace and Thy willingness to hear our prayers. Unto the end that we may remain faithful unto death endow us with a greater measure of the Spirit of prayer. Amen.

PRAYER

Pray in Jesus' name

June 9

READ: John 16:16-27.

TEXT: Whatsoever ye shall ask the Father in My name, He will give it you. John 16:23.

♣

Not a magic password or the mysterious "open sesame" from out of one of the Arabian Nights is Jesus' name used at the close of our prayers. That would make His name a questionable appendage.

What is it that I associate with the name of Jesus? His name means *Savior!* He loves me to the giving of Himself upon the cross. It means *power!* All things are possible to Him. It means *victory!* He has conquered sin, and fear, and death. It means *obedience!* He was obedient to His heavenly Father, and His prayer was, "Not My will, but Thine be done."

When I pray in Jesus' name I pray as the child of the King who knows my needs, and who gives me the key to the boundless and inexhaustible treasury of God. Whatever I ask the Father in that name, consistent with His will and spirit, He will give me.

Living Lord, through Thy name I link myself with the riches of heaven. Thy name has broken the power of my enemy. All things are possible through Jesus' name. Amen.

June 10

THE LORD'S PRAYER — INTRODUCTION

Our Father, who art in heaven

He is truly our Father, and we are truly His children

READ: Matthew 6:5-13.
TEXT: Abba! Father! Romans 8:15.

✣

No greater honor could have come to George Washington than for the sons and the daughters of American liberty to call him "The father of his country." We are the sons and the daughters of God through faith in Jesus. No greater honor can come to us than to belong to God's family circle. We can truly say, "Father!"

God is the rock of our religion, and we need not fear to stand upon it. If a natural father knows how to give bread and meat to a hungry child, certainly the divine Father will not let His children go hungry.

The marsh hen builds her nest on the watery sod and ties it to the marsh grass so that it rises and falls with the tide. It always floats on the water. It never overflows or floats away. It is always there, safely tied when the marsh hen returns—protected by God.

So our nest, our house, our life will be if it is tied to the Father God by faith in His Son Jesus.

Abba! Father! may we ever be tied to Thy fatherliness, Thy loveliness, and Thy providence, in Jesus' name. Amen.

THE LORD'S PRAYER — INTRODUCTION

Our Father, who art in heaven

We may come boldly and confidently to Him in prayer

June 11

READ: Matthew 7:7-12.

TEXT: Let us therefore come boldly to the throne of grace. Hebrews 4:16.

♣

"Except ye become as little children ye shall not enter into the kingdom of heaven." When Jesus said that He must have had in mind the trustful readiness of little children to run to father or mother, sure that everything will be all right.

As we grow older we are more inclined to think we can take care of ourselves. Yet we should remember that in God's sight we are always children. We never really grow up, and we have hurts and needs and problems too difficult for us. We, like little children, should come with all cheerfulness and confidence to our heavenly Father.

If our earthly parents want to give good gifts unto their children, how much more our Father in heaven wants to give good things to them that ask Him. "For as a father pitieth his children, so the Lord pitieth them that fear Him."

O loving, heavenly Father, I am in Thy sight as a little child. I know not what to ask or how to ask. But hear me and help me, Lord, simply because Thou art my Father, and I am Thy child. For Jesus' sake. Amen.

THE FIRST PETITION

Hallowed be Thy name

June 12

We pray that His name may be hallowed also among us

READ: Isaiah 6:1-8.

TEXT: Give unto the Lord the glory due unto His name. Psalm 96:8.

♣

Have you ever asked yourself the question, "What do I owe to my God?" Here is your answer, "The glory due unto His name."

By the name of God we are to understand all that He has been pleased to reveal to us about Himself, His character, His attributes, and "everything whereby He maketh Himself known." Surely, everything related to God and His worship ought to be hallowed, that is, considered and treated with the deepest reverence as holy and sacred.

In fulfilling this obligation we are benefited. Our life is enriched, it is transfigured by His glory reflected in us, and we are counted among that vast multitude among whom the name of God is hallowed.

How great will be our sin if, after offering this petition, we rise from our prayers and treat sacred things in any light, joking, or careless manner!

Dear name above every name, with our life and our lips help us to manifest Thy glory and make Thy love real to all, for Thy name's sake. Amen.

THE FIRST PETITION
Hallowed be Thy name

June 13

Pray that the Word of God may be taught in its truth and purity

READ: John 1:6-14.

TEXT: He that hath My word, let him speak My word faithfully. Jeremiah 23:28.

♣

Since we have the Word of God in our Bible, it is our duty as Christians to speak God's Word faithfully. For that reason our church endeavors to give her children a thorough religious training and lays great stress on preaching the Word of God regularly in her services. She also tries to be faithful in teaching the Word of God in its truth and purity as indicated in the explanation to the First Petition. Only when this is done can we rightly know the Triune God and His great work of creation, redemption, and sanctification and in this knowledge find our salvation and the way to lead a godly life. Only then can we give our God the honor due unto Him and truly hallow His name. We, on our part, must, of course, gladly hear and learn God's Word and live according to it.

Lord God, our heavenly Father, we pray Thee in Jesus' name, keep our church ever faithful in teaching and preaching Thy Word in its truth and purity and help us as Thy children gladly to hear and to do according to it. Amen.

THE FIRST PETITION

June 14

Hallowed be Thy name

Lead holy lives in accordance with it

READ: Romans 1:1-14.

TEXT: Be ye holy in all manner of conversation. I Peter 1:15b.

✤

It is the peculiar excellence and glory of our religion that it has ideals. These are set forth in an infallible guide, the Word of God. We, as Christians, are to live by that guide, for the apostle records this word, "Be ye holy in all manner of living." In this way we honor God and are well-pleasing to Him. With Ruth of old we must say: "Where thou goest, I will go; thy people shall be my people; thy God my God."

Entering harmoniously into God's plans for His people and His world, she gave herself in noble loyalty and consecration to Him. So with us. And such a response lets God into our life, lifts it from the commonplace, brings us into the care of an Almighty Father-God, gives personal peace and joy, and equips us with power to undertake the task of changing lives of other men and nations.

Holy, holy, holy, art Thou, O Lord. Grant that we may live a life according to Thy Word and be well-pleasing in Thy sight. We ask in Jesus' name and for His sake. Amen.

THE FIRST PETITION
Hallowed be Thy name

June 15

Whosoever teaches otherwise profanes the name of God

READ: Galatians 1:1-9.

TEXT: If any man preach any other gospel unto you than that which ye received, let him be accursed. Galatians 1:9.

❧

He that teaches otherwise than the Word of God teaches is like a druggist who changes the doctor's prescription, putting death-dealing poison into the bottle instead of health-giving medicine.

He who changes the prescription spurns the doctor's word and wisdom. Whosoever changes the Word of God makes God a liar in that he contradicts Him. Wrong and harmful use profanes the Word and dishonors the author.

"Another gospel" is not a gospel. For there is salvation in none other than in Christ, the Lord, who was born in Bethlehem and who died for our sins on Calvary, according to Scripture.

As capital punishment is inflicted upon a murderer, so the false prophet who destroys souls with false teachings is cursed by being cast into the lake of fire, which is the second death.

From false prophets, false teachings, false faith, false life, and consequent unhappy, eternal death—from these preserve us, heavenly Father. Amen.

June 16

THE FIRST PETITION
Hallowed be Thy name

Whosoever lives otherwise profanes the name of God

READ: II John 1-13.

TEXT: He that abideth in the doctrine of Christ, he hath both the Father and the Son. II John 9b.

✣

God's name is hallowed by us in three ways: *in pure doctrine, in true faith, and in a holy life.* This third means a life separated from sin and lived unto God. In praying the fundamental petition of the Lord's Prayer we ask our Father to help us by the Holy Spirit to live a life in harmony with the Word and the will of God, a life of personal godliness, loving obedience, and aggressive Christlikeness. "Abide in the teachings" by actually doing the will of God as revealed through Christ. Let others see what Christ is in you, and what He can do for men. In this the purpose is twofold: the glory of God and the salvation of souls. The encouragement? You stand in the mercy of God, realize the love of this Father, and depend on the merits and righteousness of Christ.

"Have Thine own way, Lord! Have Thine own way!
Hold o'er my being absolute sway!
Fill with Thy Spirit till all shall see
Christ only, always, living in me!" Amen.

THE SECOND PETITION
Thy kingdom come
What the kingdom is not

June 17

READ: John 18:33-37.
TEXT: My kingdom is not of this world. John 18:36.

✤

So said Jesus concerning His kingdom. It is not a country, it is not a democracy, it is not a dictatorship, it is not a monarchy. It is not houses or lands, money or position, honors or preferment. It is simply accepting the priority of God's rule in your life. You have stepped out of an earthly government or kingdom into a heavenly kingdom. Have you ever attended a naturalization session in which a group of foreign-born people renounce their allegiance to any other government and pledge allegiance to the United States? When you were confirmed you did just that. You renounced the rule of sin in your life, and you entered (became naturalized into) a new kingdom, the kingdom of God. Now as you go forth you are a citizen of the kingdom of God and you pray, "Thy kingdom come." For you, of course, the kingdom of God must already have come in heart and life. What shall you do now? You must learn the rules of the kingdom so that kingdom may indeed come in you, come into you, and you into it.

Blessed Lord Jesus, I have promised to serve Thee in Thy kingdom. May Thy kingdom indeed come in my life and strengthen me so that in every way I may show that I am a true citizen of that kingdom. Amen.

June 18

THE SECOND PETITION
Thy kingdom come
How the kingdom may come to us

READ: Matthew 3:1-12.

TEXT: Repent ye, for the kingdom of God is at hand. Matthew 3:2.

♣

Here is a quiz for you. A chunk of coal is held before your eyes. To what kingdom does it belong? You answer, "The vegetable kingdom." How would you classify a gold ring? "The mineral kingdom." And now, what about a little baby nestling in its mother's tender arms? *"The kingdom of God."* You are right.

We are all as Christians part of God's kingdom, and we should live in it as God would have us live. That living and growing begins with repentance. Repenting suggests feeling sorry for our mistakes and failures. But it is more than that, for Judas regretted what he had done and then took his own life. We are to do as did Simon Peter who realized that he had failed his Savior and then humbly but trustingly turned to God for forgiveness and ever afterward served the crucified Lord. If we do that daily, the kingdom of God will always be ours.

Gracious Lord, our life is weak, and we often fail Thee. Help us to feel truly sorry for our failures and grant us forgiveness. Give us strength to be true to Thee and serve Thee and especially strive to bring others into Thy kingdom. All this we ask in Jesus' name. Amen.

THE SECOND PETITION

Thy kingdom come

How one may enter the kingdom

June 19

READ: John 3:1-13.

TEXT: Except a man be born of water and of the Spirit, he cannot enter into the kingdom of God. John 3:5.

♣

Luther, we are told, was accustomed to say to himself frequently, "I have been baptized." He thus reminded himself, not only that he was a child of God and belonged to the kingdom of God, but he reminded himself of the way in which he had entered the kingdom. In obedience to Christ's command his parents had presented him to God, and God had accepted him in baptism so that he was born "of the water and the Spirit." Thus had the kingdom of God come to him.

It would be a good habit for each Christian to say to himself often: "I have been baptized. I am a child of God. I belong to God's kingdom. I must live as a child of God, behave as a citizen of the kingdom of God."

It would be good to say that when tempted or discouraged and thus to remember that God is ready to come to our help since we are His.

O God, Thou hast received me into Thy kingdom through the faith and the love of my parents. Help me to remember my baptism and to live worthily as Thy child and a member of Thy kingdom. Amen.

THE SECOND PETITION

June 20

Thy kingdom come

Where to look for the kingdom

READ: Luke 17:20-37.
TEXT: Behold the kingdom is within you. Luke 17:21.

♣

The *kingdom* lives in the mind and the heart. It is a rule which Christ personally exercises over the personalities of the faithful. In this kingdom the Lord rules by His grace and truth and power.

The *kingdom* of God cannot be "spotted" or measured with the eye. It is a kingdom within the heart of the believers. Even all external signs of the presence of the kingdom such as church buildings, religious dress, necklace crosses, and pious looks are not infallible since these same signs may be used by those who are hypocrites.

But the kingdom can be seen at work wherever men are proclaiming the gospel and are letting God's will and power overcome evil, wherever they are letting Christ's love govern their attitudes and relations with others.

Lord Jesus, my blessed King, open my eyes to Thy beauty. Let my soul realize that Thou didst come into the misery of this sin-burdened world a man of sorrows and grief in order to win man for the adoption of sons and an eternal inheritance. Come into my heart and reign there in the beauty of Thy grace as my King and Lord. Amen.

THE SECOND PETITION

Thy kingdom come

Of what the kingdom consists

June 21

READ: Romans 14:16-23.

TEXT: The kingdom of God is not meat and drink, but righteousness, and peace, and joy in the Holy Ghost. Romans 14:17.

✤

Our Lord Jesus Christ was so poor that He said He had no place to lay His head. Yet His was the kingdom. He had a right relationship with God, the Father, who is King of kings and Lord of lords.

The apostle Paul had little of this world's goods. Yet he was content and had the sense of possessing all things, for he wrote to his converts, who were poor indeed, "All things are yours, and ye are Christ's, and Christ is God's."

It is this knowledge which is really the kingdom of heaven within us.

It is righteousness, which assures us a good conscience. It is peace, which is freedom from fear. It is joy because the Holy Spirit says to us, "You are children of God, and if children, then heirs; heirs of God and joint-heirs with Christ."

O God, who holdest the wealth of the world in Thy hand, teach us to know and to love those things which belong to the kingdom of God that we may have that which the world cannot give nor ever take away, righteousness and peace and joy, through our Lord Jesus Christ. Amen.

THE SECOND PETITION

June 22

Thy kingdom come

How the kingdom is spread

READ: Matthew 28:16-20.
TEXT: Ye shall be witnesses unto Me. Acts 1:8.

✤

Like a great stream is the course of the church. Seen as only a spring of fresh water in its beginnings, the kingdom of God on earth has grown to be an ever-widening streams, bringing the water of life to the nations.

Christ sent forth His disciples to be His witnesses. On Pentecost Sunday they preached the Word with power, and the Holy Spirit called three thousand more to be His witnesses. The stream was growing. From Jerusalem into Judea, into Samaria, to the uttermost parts of the earth went these witnesses, telling everywhere of the gospel of Jesus.

Down through history that stream of witnesses has spread through the nations of the world, fulfilling the simple task of proclaiming God's good news. We have heard that witness in our church. We have received the blessings of the gospel. We, too, shall be witnesses and have a part in the great missionary work of Christ that all the world may hear the gospel and join in the prayer, "Thy kingdom come!"

We pray, "Thy kingdom come." So use us, dear Christ, that Thy kingdom may come to many others, too. Amen.

THE SECOND PETITION
Thy kingdom come
When the kingdom of God is consummated

READ: Revelation 11:1-15.
TEXT: The kingdoms of this world are become the kingdoms of our Lord. Revelation 11:15.

✤

The Book of Revelation gives us a picture of what is to happen in the last times. Jesus came to this world to redeem men and to establish His kingdom, but He found many powerful enemies to oppose Him. Satan is the chief of these. He is called the prince of this world, and Jesus must defeat him before He can take the kingdom and reign.

The defeat of Satan was accomplished when Jesus died on the cross of Calvary, but he has not been dispossessed of the kingdoms of this world. He is fighting desperately to maintain his hold. The evil in the world of today is due to his activity.

But there is a day coming when Satan and all his followers shall be finally vanquished and destroyed. Then Christ's rule shall be complete and unopposed. It is that day our text speaks about. Shall we not, by the grace of God, endeavor to be faithful servants of our Savior that we may share the eternal, glorious kingdom with Him?

Lord Jesus, we thank Thee that we may look forward to the complete victory of Thy kingdom. Until that day, help us to be Thy loyal and faithful subjects. Amen.

June 24

THE THIRD PETITION

Thy will be done on earth, as it is in heaven

The good and gracious will of God

READ: II Peter 3:1-9.

TEXT: God would have all men to be saved, and to come to the knowledge of the truth. I Timothy 2:4.

♣

God wants me for "His own." He has done every thing that needed to be done in order that I might actually become His child. He wants all others to have that same privilege.

To want something without making any effort to secure it is just wistful wishing; but to want something so earnestly that one does all in his power to secure it is determination. It is an act of the will. That is just what God has done. Because of the great love with which He loves mankind He gave His Son to redeem men that they might be "His own." So we can say, "God has willed all men to be saved."

In this petition I pray that this good and gracious will of God may be realized in me and in others; that I do truly become His child and may be steadfast in His Word and in faith unto the end. I pray that all those things which are pleasing to Him may be accomplished in the world.

My Father, I thank Thee that Thou hast made me Thy child. Teach me always to be what a child of Thine ought to be. Amen.

THE THIRD PETITION

Thy will be done on earth, as it is in heaven

God destroys every evil counsel and purpose of the devil

June 25

READ: I John 3:1-11.

TEXT: For this purpose the Son of God was manifested, that He might destroy the works of the devil. I John 3:8.

♣

There is a way to defeat the devil. Jesus knew that way. While the devil was talking, He listened to God and refused the evil counsel of the devil.

During the recent war an airplane carrying men and medical supplies, on returning to the home base, found it had been bombed. Hangars were burning, runways were destroyed. It seemed impossible to land. But the pilot circled the field, clamped on his earphones, and said, "We're going down on the field." He did and made a perfect landing. They congratulated him, but he said: "No, it was not I. For I had what you did not have. I had the voice of the commandant saying through my phones, 'Come on in, Bill. You can make it if you do what I say.'"

That's the way God defeats the evil counsel of the devil in our heart. All we have to do is to listen to God and do what He says.

O God, I thank Thee for Jesus Christ who did not yield to temptation. Grant me by Thy Spirit always to listen to Thy Word that I, too, may defeat the evil counsel and purpose of the devil. Through Jesus Christ, my Lord. Amen.

THE THIRD PETITION

June 26

Thy will be done on earth, as it is in heaven

God destroys every evil counsel and purpose of the world

READ: I John 2:1-15.

TEXT: The kingdoms of this world have become the kingdoms of our Lord and of His Christ, and He shall reign forever and ever. Revelation 11:15.

✤

The kingdom of the world of man is dominated by Satan. Its principles are force, greed, selfishness, ambition, and pleasure. Even the best governments of men have the weaknesses of sin, of evil counsel and purpose. When God is left out, they become largely evil like the godless state of communist Russia. Those of the world kingdom say, "My will be done."

In this pagan world order stands the church, telling men of the kingdom of God and proclaiming the will and the love of God and His purpose to save the world. In the end the kingdom of the world shall pass away and the kingdom of God be established.

Though we are still in the world, let us remember that we are not of this world but of God. Then we, too, shall share in the triumph of the kingdom of our Lord and of His Christ.

O God, the King, let me be loyal to Thy kingdom that the world may not prevail against me, but that I may be faithful always, through Jesus Christ Thy Son, my Lord. Amen.

THE THIRD PETITION
Thy will be done on earth, as it is in heaven

June 27

God destroys every evil counsel and purpose of our own flesh

READ: Romans 7:15-25.

TEXT: And they that are Christ's have crucified the flesh with the affections and lusts. Galatians 5:24.

✠

"Thy will, O God, be done," we pray. God's good and gracious will for us is that we be saved. "For God would have all men to be saved and come to the knowledge of the truth." But in direct opposition to the gracious will of God is the will of the devil and the world, yes, that of our own flesh. The opponent named "self," "my will," dwells in our inmost being. Bloody wars have been waged upon the earth. Yet wars do not rage every day, but in the inner world of the believers there is never any suspension of hostilities, never a day when we can relax from being on guard. And every time we, by the grace of God, take up the battle and fight against those inner tendencies and desires and lusts God helps us. A battle in this constant inner struggle is won every time when God's grace and Spirit defeat and destroy every evil impulse and selfish purpose of our own flesh.

O Lord, help in the battle against the evil selfishness within me. Give me light, strength, and grace that I may faithfully persevere until the combat has ended in eternal victory and peace. Amen.

THE THIRD PETITION

June 28

Thy will be done on earth, as it is in heaven

He strengthens us and keeps us steadfast in His Word

READ: Philippians 1:1-11.

TEXT: They continued steadfastly in the apostles' doctrine. Acts 2:42.

♣

Jesus says there are two ways of life. One is a broad and easy way, downgrade, which requires neither strength nor purpose. One needs only to let himself go. The unfortunate thing is that this way leads to destruction.

The other way requires both strength and determination because it is upgrade and is narrow and hard. But it is the better way because it leads to life eternal. Jesus trod this way.

Now since it is not by our own reason and strength that we walk in this better way, we ought to know how to be strong and how to keep on keeping on.

Again we turn to the apostle Paul and find him saying, "I can do all things through Christ who strengthens me." That, then, is a very definite source of strength, Jesus Christ, the strong Son of God.

It is God's will that we should have the victory, and for this we, too, have the Word of God and the help of Jesus Christ every day.

O God, who hast promised that if we endure unto the end we shall receive the crown of life, help me to be faithful day by day in the little things and to walk with Jesus Christ, the faithful, always. Amen.

THE THIRD PETITION

Thy will be done on earth, as it is in heaven

He keeps us steadfast in the faith

June 29

READ: Hebrews 11:1-10.

TEXT: Looking unto Jesus, the author and finisher of our faith. Hebrews 12:2.

✣

In so many of the pictures showing the scenes of Easter morning the faces of the men and the women show signs of the distress they have been through. Likewise they bespeak awe and wonder. They were all looking toward Jesus, but surprise and pain are dominant instead of ecstasy, joy, and delight. Their faith had been through a terrific test. "We trusted that it had been He." We can look to Jesus, look Him right in the eye and see in Him the author of our faith; His life led us to say with Peter, "Thou art the Son of the living God;" His death fulfilled the prophecy of Isaiah 53; His resurrection rolled away the last rock of obstruction; He lives, and we shall live with Him. Thus did He finish our faith. And now He continues to be present with us, reassuring, dispelling doubts, inspiring confidence, enabling us to live our life in harmony with God's will.

Grant, Lord Jesus, that this triumphant faith may grow ever stronger in mercy and help me to follow Thy example of obedience. Amen.

THE THIRD PETITION

Thy will be done on earth, as it is in heaven

Jesus, our perfect example

June 30

READ: Luke 22:39-46.
TEXT: Not My will, but Thine be done. Luke 22:42.

✣

What does God will for me? He wills the best He has to offer me, namely, the salvation of my soul. My salvation is God's chief concern. He wills that I might become and remain His child. Surely, such a will which seeks my best, my highest and deepest need, my eternal happiness, deserves my constant attention, allegiance, and obedience. Christ kept God's will that all this might become and remain eternally true for all men. My surrender to such a love, such a law, such a will makes my life purposeful. Christ's Gethsemane prayer, "Not My will, but Thine be done," can be my prayer because His keeping of it allows my surrender to the same will. His obedience claims mine, and we become partners in keeping God's will together. His obedient love made it possible for me to serve and to love God above all things.

Heavenly Father, for Jesus' sake make my will Thine own. Help me to surrender all that I might serve Thee and Thy kingdom's purpose, after the pattern of Christ. In His name. Amen.

THE FOURTH PETITION
Give us this day our daily bread
Thank God for food and raiment, house and home

July 1

READ: Matthew 6:24-34.

TEXT: Having food and raiment, let us be therewith content. I Timothy 6: 8.

✣

Six of the petitions of the Lord's Prayer deal exclusively with spiritual matters while only one requests "daily bread." From all quarters of the earth goes up the cry for this "daily bread." Man realizes that his very life depends upon it. Everywhere there is a deep-seated consciousness that we are dependent for our daily sustenance on a power beyond ourselves. Many raise their voices and stretch out their hands to an unknown power. It is not so with the Christian. He *knows* to whom he prays, to the Maker of all things visible and invisible. Since we recognize that this "daily bread" is a gift rather than a compensation, it evokes the spirit of gratitude. By this petition we confess and express recognition of our absolute dependency upon God. If we once fully realize that *all* depends upon God we will be more thankful. No one who fully understands this will ever sit down to the table and partake of food without thanking the Giver.

Dear Father, we know Thee as the Author of all our manifold blessings. We pray that we may have the spirit of gratitude, and that we may gratefully receive Thy blessings to Thy glory and our comfort. Amen.

July 2

THE FOURTH PETITION
Give us this day our daily bread
Thank God for fields and flocks, money and goods

READ: I Timothy 6:6-12.
TEXT: Giving thanks always for all things. Ephesians 5:20.

♣

Having put "first things first" in the *Thy* petitions which open the Lord's Prayer, we are now taught by the *us* petitions to think not only of ourselves but also of others.

Our great God is interested in the common wants and needs of our life and our daily necessities. In this petition He wants us to show forth our dependence upon Him from whom cometh every good and perfect gift. We are dependent upon God for all the produce of the soil. Someone has said that each year in the month of August we are within two months of famine, but God, through the ever-recurring cycle of "seed time and harvest," abundantly provides for His people. When there is famine in one part of the earth, there are fullness and plenty elsewhere. So much so that we who have should share in love with others.

Many are the needs of our fellow men today, and we should daily pray, "Give us day by day our daily bread," doubting not that God is able abundantly to satisfy the wants of all His creatures.

"The eyes of all wait upon Thee; and Thou givest them their meat in due season. Thou openest Thine hand and satisfiest the desire of every living thing." We thank Thee, Lord, that Thou hast thus provided for us. Amen.

THE FOURTH PETITION
Give us this day our daily bread

Thank God for pious parents, children, and servants

July 3

READ: I Corinthians 10:26-33.

TEXT: Offer unto God thanksgiving; and pay thy vows unto the most High. Psalm 50:14.

✤

Parents and children and perhaps servants make the home. There is nothing more blessed than a home where the parents are godly and kind, the children obedient and respectful, the servants loyal and faithful. If yours is such a home, thank God for it every day.

Mr. Louis Bromfield says he came to the conclusion that plants were easily destroyed by insect pests, plagues, and blights because their soil lacked the proper elements. It was necessary to use sprays and dusts to defend them against disease. He began to build up the soil by supplying the missing elements. In seven years he had a garden which was free of plant diseases and unaffected by insect pests.

So does the godly home provide a place where we may grow into a life beautiful and strong enough to resist evil. Thank God for such parents, brothers, sisters, and servants.

O God, our heavenly Father, grant us the supreme blessing of a godly home and help us by a godly life to honor our parents evermore. Through Jesus Christ Thy Son, our Lord. Amen.

THE FOURTH PETITION

July 4

Give us this day our daily bread

Thank God for godly and faithful rulers and good government

READ: I Timothy 2:1-8.

TEXT: Giving thanks . . . for kings and for all that are in authority. I Timothy 2:1, 2.

✤

World conditions today teach us how much our life is influenced by the policies of our government and the character of our officials. Even our income and its purchasing power are involved. This does come within the scope of this Fourth Petition.

We do need to pray for godly and faithful rulers and good government. What losses and suffering are caused by ungodly, unfaithful rulers, by bad governments! Let us not merely complain about it; let us pray about it!

We could use more upright Christian citizens in public office, local, state, and national. Could I serve God and His people in that way? The least I can do is to vote intelligently when I am old enough to qualify for it and meanwhile to pray for those who are in office. We face the alternative of government by those guided by God or by those who have ruled out God. America needs our prayer, this prayer, today!

Ruler of nations, King of kings, bless us with godly and faithful rulers, with good government that we may serve Thee and enjoy Thy blessings, through Jesus Christ, our Lord. Amen.

THE FOURTH PETITION

Give us this day our daily bread

Thank God for seasonable weather, peace, and health

July 5

READ: Deuteronomy 8:1-9.

TEXT: He maketh His sun to rise on the evil and on the good, and sendeth rain on the just and on the unjust. Matthew 5:45.

✣

The vitality and the self-reliance of youth are important factors in the development of Christian character. The ability to "hold one's own" with others of our age and background fosters initiative and enterprise. We must realize, however, that these powers and traits are God-given. If we forget this we imagine that we are self-sufficient and not dependent upon God's providence.

The knowledge that God is the Giver is necessary when things go smoothly, but especially when they seem to go seriously wrong for us. We then need a *proved* trust that the Lord will provide.

When St. Felix was pursued by murderers he took refuge in a cave, and instantly a spider wove a web over the opening. The murderers, glancing at the cobweb as they passed by shortly afterward, assumed that no one could have entered there. When they had gone, Felix said, "Where God is not, a wall is but a spider's web; where God is, a spider's web is as a wall."

Lord, open my eyes to see Thy hand in the material abundance which I enjoy. Thy hand is loving and offers blessing. Help me to see it. In Jesus' name. Amen.

July 6

THE FOURTH PETITION

Give us this day our daily bread

Thank God for education and honor

READ: Deuteronomy 8:10-20.

TEXT: I have taught thee in the way of wisdom. Proverbs 4:11.

✣

The ability to learn is a gift of God for which we should ever be grateful. Education is the training of the human mind to use the facts of science, history, and truth to the benefit of ourselves and others. We should be thankful that we live in a land where all may gain such an education because we can know the truth, and truth frees us from the chains of ignorance, superstition, and error.

We recognize in Jesus the wisest of men, that is, the most truly educated. If we would learn of Him we should let the mind of Christ be in us; then we, like Him, will honor our heavenly Father and be honored by Him.

Let us learn all that schools and books and science and experience can teach us. But let us learn that God delights to give true spiritual wisdom to those who seek it.

O God of all truth, lead us into a knowledge of Thy truth that we may live to Thy glory and the service of our fellow men even as our Lord Jesus Christ honored Thee and served mankind. Amen.

THE FOURTH PETITION
Give us this day our daily bread

Thank God for true friends, good neighbors, and the like

July 7

READ: Genesis 13:8-13.

TEXT: There is a friend that sticketh closer than a brother. Proverbs 18:24.

✤

Beyond the home with its love and sympathy is the great world where many men are selfish, thoughtless, and unkind. But here also will be those who are faithful and true, among whom we should seek our friends. Having found them, we should grapple them to our souls with hooks of steel.

True friends may be known in the way they stand by when there is trouble, for friendship is not merely having fun together. It is being faithful in times of need as well.

The friendship of Jesus is the more wonderful because He loved us when we were unworthy. He is the great Friend who sticketh closer than a brother. And He says to us, "I have called you friends."

It is the mind of Christ which makes Christians the finest friends, kind, patient, forgiving, helpful, loving. Thank God for friends, good friends, trusty neighbors, and the like. They are, indeed, the gift of God.

Dear Lord, we thank Thee for our best Friend Jesus and for all true friends and good neighbors. Give us grace to be true friends and good neighbors and to receive all things as gifts from Thee. Amen.

THE FIFTH PETITION

July 8

And forgive us our trespasses, as we forgive those who trespass against us

Pray God not to regard our sins

READ: Psalm 130.

TEXT: There is forgiveness with Thee, that Thou mayest be feared. Psalm 130:4.

✣

Forgiveness is a wonderful word. It means to put away, dismiss, send afar off, and forget any offence. God alone can forgive like that. We can know the full meaning of God's forgiveness only when we understand what a terrible thing sin is. God is holy, righteous, just, and good. He cannot lightly regard any sin, big or little. Disobedience, meanness, hate, impurity, impatience, untruthfulness, selfishness: all these things make us come short of the goodness of God.

Now when we know what sinners we are, our conscience is troubled. We are not right with God, and it makes us unhappy and afraid. How may we get right with God? God Himself provides the way. He says, "I will forgive your sins and remember them no more forever." That is the wonderful thing about the forgiveness of God. He is willing to forgive our sins and to cleanse us from all unrighteousness.

O God, who hast loved us with an everlasting love, and who dost forgive all our sins, grant us to know the wonder of Thy forgiveness that we may forgive those who sin against us. Amen.

THE FIFTH PETITION

And forgive us our trespasses, as we forgive those who trespass against us

July 9

Pray God not to deny our prayers

READ: Psalm 51:1-9.

TEXT: I will confess my transgressions unto the Lord; and Thou forgavest the iniquity of my sin. Psalm 32:5b.

♣

When one is afflicted with a toothache, it is foolish to ignore the decay which causes it. It is useless to fill the cavity without first cleaning out the decayed area, for decay and pain would continue and grow worse.

Sin is a corruption in the soul which hurts like a toothache. The writer of Psalm 32 found that out. He tried to ignore his sin, to hide it from himself and God, but he could not. In his anguish he finally went to God in humble confession and was cured. He received the forgiveness which cleansed his heart and brought a glorious joy.

When we truly repent and seek His forgiveness, God removes the festering guilt from our heart. This is necessary before His further blessings can come to us. We can then go on in the experience of His love and friendship and spiritual power, thus enriching our character and making real progress in Christian living.

Loving Father, cleanse me from evil and lift its burden from my heart. By Thy grace draw me away from all sin and close to Thee. Through Jesus, my Savior. Amen.

THE FIFTH PETITION

July 10

And forgive us our trespasses, as we forgive those who trespass against us

We do not deserve that for which we pray

READ: Psalm 51:1-10.

TEXT: I am not worthy of the least of all the mercies. Genesis 32:10.

✣

These words are from the prayer of Jacob, who was in trouble. He was fleeing from his father-in-law; he was about to meet his brother Esau, from whom he had stolen the birthright. The circumstances compelled him to take stock of himself. He became aware that he had not deserved the blessings which God had given him.

It ought not to require a circumstance like that to make us realize that God grants us everything by His grace, not only daily bread, but this greatest of all blessings, the forgiveness of sins. God is good. He will not cease to be good and to love us even if we sin much every day. God's gifts and God's forgiveness are not because of our merit but because of God's everlasting, unfailing mercy.

We may be sure He will not deny our plea for forgiveness. "God, be merciful to me, a sinner," is a prayer which fits both our unworthiness and God's great mercy.

O God, hide Thy face from my sins and blot out all mine iniquities. Create in me a clean heart, O God, and renew a right spirit within me. Amen.

THE FIFTH PETITION

And forgive us our trespasses, as we forgive those who trespass against us

July 11

He grants us all things through grace

READ: Psalm 25:1-11.

TEXT: According to Thy mercy remember Thou me for Thy goodness' sake, O Lord. Psalm 25:7.

✤

An ancient Christian writer has compared "grace" with a flame that burns downward instead of upward. It is the flame of God's infinite love reaching down into our cold, sinful heart. If God should deal with us according to our sin, we should, indeed, experience a flame from His person. It would be the flame of His holiness which points out and punishes sin. Our only hope, however, is that He will not deal with us according to our sin but according to His "loving-kindness."

Paul writes to Titus: "The grace of God hath appeared unto all men." It, indeed, put in its appearance when Jesus was born. Then the flame of God's grace developed into a "great light," "the light of the world." Jesus is the grace of God in person. In Him the goodness and the loving-kindness of God have come to us. With Him and in Him God would "grant us all." In Jesus, God grants us His undeserved love, His forgiveness, His peace, His presence, His life, His strength.

Heavenly Father, I thank Thee for the grace Thou hast shown me in Jesus. Help me to live in His fellowship so that I may continue to receive from Him daily the manifold gifts of His grace. Amen.

THE FIFTH PETITION

July 12

And forgive us our trespasses, as we forgive those who trespass against us

We sin daily and deserve nothing but punishment

READ: Romans 6:12-23.

TEXT: The wages of sin is death; but the gift of God is eternal life through Jesus Christ our Lord. Romans 6:23.

✣

The need for daily forgiveness arises because of daily sinning. Let us not deceive ourselves. There remains with us what St. Paul calls the "old Adam." The first man, Adam, you will remember, chose to disobey God. He deserved to be punished and was punished. We, too, have a sinful nature so that we deserve to be punished, not only for those daily sins which spring up like weeds, but for our sinful disposition, which is the soil in which they grow.

We need to pray with deep and sincere repentance because there is in us this tendency to sin. But God does not want us to perish. He wants to bestow on us the gift of eternal life. Pray sincerely that God will forgive the sins of this day, and pray that He will forgive you, a sinner, and because of His great love grant you this gift of eternal life through Jesus Christ, our Lord.

O God, deliver me, I pray Thee, from my sinful self and grant me forgiveness that I may bring forth the fruits of holiness and gain eternal life, through Jesus Christ, my Lord. Amen.

THE FIFTH PETITION

And forgive us our trespasses, as we forgive those who trespass against us

We on our part will heartily forgive

July 13

READ: Matthew 18:21-35.

TEXT: I say not unto thee: until seven times: but until seventy times seven. Matthew 18:22.

♣

This Fifth Petition is a dangerous prayer for the impenitent but an encouraging one for the sincere Christian. It is a common experience that we sin in thought, word, and deed against God and our neighbor. Without God's forgiveness there is no peace in the heart. But the will of God is that we should first forgive and then be forgiven. In this petition Jesus puts us on a contingent basis, that is, as we forgive others, so will God forgive us. The parable of the unmerciful servant stresses the great need of forgiveness on our part. We must willingly forgive the small sins committed against us in order that God may forgive us our many sins. When we refuse to forgive others we are closing our heart to our own receiving of God's forgiveness.

So it is imperative that we on our part heartily forgive, and that not only once or a few times "but until seventy times seven," that is, without limit.

Lord, Thou knowest that I have not forgiven everyone who has wronged me. Give me grace to confess these failures. And help me by Thy Spirit to be forgiving that I may be fully forgiven. Amen.

THE FIFTH PETITION

July 14

And forgive us our trespasses, as we forgive those who trespass against us

Do good to those who may sin against you

READ: Matthew 6:5-15.

TEXT: Be not overcome of evil but overcome evil with good. Romans 12:21.

♣

When we are tempted to strike back with fist or tongue or thought at someone who offends us, even though it may seem justifiable and smart, we must remember how God warns us, "Be not overcome of evil."

To resist temptation by the Holy Spirit's help strengthens a young Christian's faith and prepares him to resist even greater attacks from the evil one, the Devil. But a defensive warfare against an enemy merely prolongs the misery. It is necessary here as elsewhere to launch out on the offensive. God says this day to you and to me, "Overcome evil with *good.*" This is an aggressive step and requires immediate action on our part. Being kind and good to one who has wronged us isn't easy, but it is the Christian way. God, who is goodness, brings victory to our side, for goodness disperses evil everywhere. May *we* seek this source of help by our own free choice.

Dear Father, forgive me my trespasses as I forgive those who trespass against me and teach me to be like my Savior in the face of my enemies and say, "Forgive them, for they know not what they do." In Jesus' name. Amen.

THE SIXTH PETITION
And lead us not into temptation
God indeed tempts no one to sin

July 15

READ: James 1:12-22.

TEXT: Let no man say when he is tempted, I am tempted of God. James 1:13a.

♣

Temptation—what a common word, and yet what an important meaning it has! We are all subject to temptation, that is, we are all constantly being led and induced to do things which are opposed to the will of God. Since temptation is always in the direction of sin and wrongdoing, it is foolish to think that God is in any way responsible for it. So in this petition we are asking God to watch over and protect us from temptations that are too severe for us. God is our guide to right living, and we ask Him to guard and keep us so that the devil, the world, and the flesh may not lead us astray. We ask Him to give us strength that we may be able to overcome even though temptations are ever about us. We gain our victory over evil only through the help of God.

Father, in our weakness we look to Thee, for Thou alone wilt make us conquerors through Him who loves us. Give us daily guidance and power that we may be found mightier than temptation. In His name. Amen.

July 16

THE SIXTH PETITION
And lead us not into temptation
God tests us

READ: Genesis 3:1-7.

TEXT: The Lord your God proveth you [tests you] to know whether ye love the Lord your God with all your heart and with all your soul. Deuteronomy 13:3.

♣

Tests are not intended to do harm nor merely to prove; they are intended to *improve*. Much more so are these the intentions of our loving God and Father relative to our spiritual testings.

"A calm sea never makes a strong sailor." Nor does a point of advantage or a stronger army make a skillful general. When a sailor has to sail his ship through a rough sea or into a difficult channel, and a general has to lead his army against a superior force and into a difficult position, skill and courage are not only tested but decidedly improved.

A test brings on experience as practice makes perfect. So faith grows stronger by exercise and patience.

God tests or proves us, not to sin, but to strengthen our faith and to bring us to a conviction that we love Him with all our heart and soul. Read James 1:2,13,14.

O Lord God, let not Satan tempt us overmuch, and whenever he tempts us give us power to resist him that he may flee from us. Give us strength to bear up and grow stronger under the trials of our faith. If it be not Thy will to remove the burden of affliction from us, do Thou strengthen us to bear it. Amen.

THE SIXTH PETITION

And lead us not into temptation

The devil tempts us to sin

July 17

READ: Genesis 3:8-21.

TEXT: Be sober, be vigilant; because your adversary the devil, as a roaring lion, walketh about, seeking whom he may devour. I Peter 5:8.

♣

Lions abounded in rugged sections of the Bible lands. They turned upon people, coming upon them stealthily to attack them. Meeting with a lion was a serious matter. One had to be watchful. In his ways and his intentions the devil is like a lion, and we must be serious about him and on the watch for him. The devil is our "adversary," opponent. He seeks us with his temptations. Yielding to them, we are caught and are in his power. The devil is more dangerous than a lion. A lion can hurt the body only whereas the devil can hurt soul and body. He would destroy souls. Jesus delivers and saves souls from the devil's power. Indifference to the devil, his temptations, and the sins that follow is playing into the hands of the devil. The Lord Jesus, Himself tempted by the devil, warns: "Watch and pray that ye enter not into temptation."

Grant, heavenly Father, that Thy Holy Spirit may keep us ever watchful against the devil. Help us to pray aright when tempted and show us a way of escape. Amen.

THE SIXTH PETITION

And lead us not into temptation

The world tempts us to sin

July 18

READ: Proverbs 1:10-19.

TEXT: My son, if sinners entice thee, consent thou not. Proverbs 1:10.

✤

Have siren voices ever sung to you and said: "Why believe in God? Why go to church? Why read the Bible? Why pray? Why waste time and money on the things of an unseen world? If I must be serious, there will be time aplenty later on to settle down to this business called religion"? Thus Satan through his human subjects sings to tempt you while God leads to test you.

Have you ever planned to go places and do things with the "gang," on which your Lord Jesus would frown? So many of the world's attractions seem both pleasant and desirable. And yet they are used by the evil one to lure you as with a bait. And getting "caught" means breaking a promise. We must remind ourselves again and again of the first question of our pastor on the day of our confirmation, "Do you renounce the devil and all his works and all his ways?" Your answer was, "Yes, I renounce."

Kind Lord, Merciful Father, make me strong, for I am weak. Help me day by day to fight off sin and temptation. Then will I thank and praise Thy name forevermore, for Jesus' sake. Amen.

THE SIXTH PETITION
And lead us not into temptation
Our own flesh (lust) tempts us

July 19

READ: Galatians 5:16-26.

TEXT: But every man is tempted, when he is drawn away of his own lust, and enticed. James 1:14.

✣

God who is holy cannot sin or do wrong. Hence when we are tempted, invited, and urged to commit sin we dare not accuse God of sending the temptation to us or hold Him responsible if we fall. Our text tells us that we are enticed to commit sin by our own lusts that dwell in our heart. We are born in sin, that is, by birth our heart is filled with evil desires of all kinds. We all have inclinations and tendencies to abuse our capacities, to make wrong use of God's gifts, to desire what is not healthy for us and for others. Thus our own sinful flesh, our sinful heart, serves as bait to tempt us and to try to make us do what God forbids. It follows, then, that when we yield to temptation and violate the will of God, we alone are at fault and not God. Let us daily ask God for strength so that the faulty desires of our heart will not lead us away from our Savior nor cause us to lose the blessings of eternal life and salvation which He has given us.

Dear heavenly Father, keep me ever mindful that alone I am weak and unable to resist the temptations of my heart, but that with Thy help no evil desire can overpower me. Give me that strength for Jesus' sake. Amen.

THE SIXTH PETITION

July 20

And lead us not into temptation

How to prevail and gain the victory

READ: Matthew 26:36-41.
TEXT: Take up the whole armor of God. Ephesians 6:13.

♣

In the fight against temptation we are not left without effective aids and weapons. He who has taught us to pray for deliverance from the strategems of the devil will not leave us to our own helplessness. As the Roman soldier donned heavy armor to ward off the poisoned darts and spears of the enemy, so we must steel ourselves against Satan's enticing invitations.

"Take the whole armor of God." Throw yourself with complete confidence upon the power and the grace of God. Let His presence, the strength that He gives protect you. Be able to say with the Psalmist, "Thy Word have I hid in my heart that I might not sin against Thee." Or with Joseph, "How can I do this great wickedness and sin against God?" Sinful pleasure and unrighteous gain bring only shame and remorse, but the victory through Christ of a conscience free from guilt means joy everlasting.

Blessed Savior, Thou wast tempted in all points like as we are, yet without sin. Strengthen me in my weakness and enable me to live according to Thy will. In Thine own dear name. Amen.

THE SIXTH PETITION

And lead us not into temptation

Jesus shows us how to meet temptation

July 21

READ: Ephesians 6:10-18.

TEXT: Take the . . . sword of the Spirit which is the word of God. Ephesians 6:17.

✤

No one of us wants to get into trouble. Temptation means trouble. That is why we pray, "Lead us not into temptation." Yet troubles and temptations come to every one of us. When we feel like telling a lie to escape a scolding, when we think of cheating to pass an examination, when it seems smart to use filthy words—at such times we are being tempted. What can we do then? We can do what Jesus did when He was tempted. He remembered something the Bible says, and He used it. The Bible is so useful as a weapon for defeating evil that St. Paul calls it a sword. We must not be clumsy in using this weapon. We must practice the use of it daily. Then we, too, when temptation comes, can remember our noble Master who was too honorable to lie or cheat, too holy to do wrong.

Heavenly Father, strengthen me by Thy Word to resist each day's temptations and be faithful to my Savior who withstood evil by His life and conquered evil by His death. Amen.

July 22

THE SEVENTH PETITION
But deliver us from evil
Deliver us from all manner of evil affecting the body

READ: Job 5:6-19.

TEXT: He will deliver thee in six troubles; yea, in seven there shall no evil touch thee. Job 5:19.

✣

This petition is closely related to the preceding one. Yielding to temptation results in sin. All suffering in this world and the next is the consequence of sin, immediate or remote. God's children know that He is able by His bounteous grace to lead in ways where evil will not befall. And they know, too, that if it be the Father's will to permit affliction, He provides the strength and the grace to bear it and be strengthened by it. Therefore, when bodily suffering is their lot, they in faith patiently await the removal of that evil in God's own good time and according to His own Holy will. As we use His grace to believe, God draws us closer in divine fellowship through our bodily suffering, for so it was that Job's severe and prolonged troubles became the ministering servants to strengthen his convictions concerning God's infinite and eternal love.

Dear heavenly Father, we thank Thee for Thy loving care. Grant us grace to grow in faith through Thy grace to bear bodily suffering. We pray in Jesus' name. Amen.

THE SEVENTH PETITION
But deliver us from evil

July 23

Deliver us from all manner of evil affecting the soul

READ: Job 33.

TEXT: The Lord God ... breathed into his nostrils the breath of life, and man became a living soul. Genesis 2:7.

✣

It is the living soul of man which needs to be protected and delivered from all manner of evil. Some beautiful souls are to be found in bodies broken and disabled. Some beautiful bodies have souls stained and marred by ugly sins. Some sins apparently have little effect upon the body. But every sin leaves its mark upon the soul and mars it in the sight of God.

You would be shocked if the devil offered you a price for your soul, wouldn't you? Yet each sin committed is part of a process of selling the soul to Satan. Unless I am defended and kept by the power of God I may lose my soul. Let body and material property be affected as circumstances may determine. That I cannot always control. But I can guard my soul by constant prayer and use of the Word of God, which St. Paul calls the sword of the Spirit.

O God, be Thou the strength of my life so that my heart may not fear though Satan and all the hosts of evil rise up against me. Be near unto me, O God, and deliver me. Through Jesus Christ, my Lord. Amen.

THE SEVENTH PETITION
But deliver us from evil

July 24

Deliver us from all manner of evil affecting our property

READ: Job 42:10-17.
TEXT: Give me neither poverty nor riches. Proverbs 30:8.

♣

Christians are deeply conscious of their dependence on the Father, for God has in His infinite wisdom provided for all His creatures. Men should be constant in prayer that evil may be avoided and its effect may not bring calamity and harm. Let men bring their petitions without wavering doubt, confidently believing that the strength they need will come from God.

But for what does the Christian pray in the realm of personal property? He hopes to avoid the pitiable marks of poverty but is not eager merely to amass and retain material riches. He regards all these material assets as blessings that God has given to be used carefully and thankfully, with a desire that others may enjoy those blessings, too. He realizes that want and privation may come but knows that God is able to provide ways that he may be delivered from all the evils to which human flesh is subject.

Gracious Father, Author of every good, we rejoice that Thou knowest our needs before we bring them unto Thee. As Thou hast provided, so wilt Thou preserve unto us whatever things are essential for our effective service of Thee. Through Jesus Christ. Amen.

THE SEVENTH PETITION
But deliver us from evil

Deliver us from all manner of evil affecting our reputation

July 25

READ: Psalm 34:11-22.
TEXT: Man looketh on the outward appearance; but the Lord looketh on the heart. I Samuel 16:7.

♣

What God sees in me is my character, what I really am. What men see is my reputation. It is what they say and think about me. A reputation that will stand the test of the judgment of men must have the enduring foundation of a life lived constantly in the presence of God. The best defense of a good reputation is a good character.

Men who are themselves faulty in behavior and character may judge us unfairly and spread false stories about us. So they judged and bore false witness about Jesus Christ. But God honored Him because Jesus always did His Father's will.

We must pray that God will keep our souls from evil, and it will not matter what men will say about us, or what they will do to us. God is our judge. Let us commit our ways unto Him. Thus shall we obtain a good name which will be honored forever.

O God, the righteous Judge, before whom the lives of men are as an open book, guard the thoughts and the intents of my heart that I may be seen of men as one in whom Thou art well pleased. Through Jesus Christ, Thy sinless Son. Amen.

July 26

THE SEVENTH PETITION

But deliver us from evil

Deliver us from the evil one

READ: I Peter 5:1-11.

TEXT: And the Lord said, Simon, Simon, behold, Satan hath desired to have you. . . . But I have prayed for thee, that thy faith fail not. Luke 22:31, 32.

✣

Christ's warning to Simon Peter is a warning to us. Satan, that old serpent, called the Devil, who deceives the whole world, is our enemy. He seeks to destroy us. This he would do by tempting us to sin.

We need to be on our guard always, for Satan deceives us by suggesting that we may have our own way, be selfish, disobedient, untruthful. These seem like little sins. But little sins lead to great ones.

We are not equal to overcoming Satan. That is why Jesus told Peter that He had prayed for him. That is why we also must constantly pray that God, our heavenly Father, will deliver us from the evil one. This He does through Jesus Christ, who resisted the temptations of Satan and is thus able to deliver us.

O God, be with me, I pray, that when the devil attacks my soul he will find me safe in Thine almighty power. For Jesus' sake. Amen.

THE SEVENTH PETITION

But deliver us from evil

Grant us a blessed end

July 27

READ: Revelation 14:1-13.

TEXT: Be thou faithful unto death, and I will give thee a crown of life. Revelation 2:10.

♣

The major concern of a Christian's earthly existence is to attain the salvation of his immortal soul. Everything, therefore, that we do or ask of God should be directed toward this blessed end. By ourselves alone we can never remain faithful; but "with God all things are possible," and He assures us of that goal if we trustingly, obediently rely on Him.

All that we have asked so far in the Lord's Prayer was for this one glorious purpose, "Our Father who art in heaven, grant us a blessed end." The whole of the Christian race of life is run with the eye fixed on the finish of the course. And there is no greater thrill for us than the anticipation of the Judge's verdict: "Well done, thou good and faithful servant . . . enter thou into the joy of thy Lord."

Dear heavenly Father, help me that nothing in my whole life may ever frustrate or prevent me from being saved and be with Thee in Thy kingdom throughout all eternity. For Jesus' sake. Amen.

July 28

THE SEVENTH PETITION
But deliver us from evil

Graciously take us to Thyself in heaven

READ: Revelation 21:1-7.
TEXT: Lord Jesus, receive my spirit. Acts 7:59.

♣

Stephen, the first Christian martyr, while being stoned to death by the enemies of Christ prayed, "Lord Jesus, receive my spirit." Well he knew that Christ would do so, for Jesus came and died that He might deliver us from the evil consequences of our sins and open for us the way into heaven. Stephen was willing to die for this faith, assured that his spirit would soon be at home with God.

The penitent thief on his cross prayed that Jesus might remember him in mercy when He came into His kingdom, and immediately Jesus said, "Today thou shalt be with Me in paradise." A very wicked man, when he repented and asked for pardon, was forgiven and dying was received into heaven. This is the hope and the confidence of every true Christian. Returning to God means the final deliverance for us of all evil.

Gracious Savior, strengthen my faith to believe that Thou dost pardon all my sins. Lead me safely past all the pitfalls of this world and life and finally receive me into Thine eternal glory. Amen.

THE LORD'S PRAYER — CONCLUSION

For Thine is the kingdom

July 29

READ: Psalm 24.
TEXT: Thine is the kingdom, O Lord. I Chronicles 29:11.

♣

These words were spoken by David as king of Israel. He gave to God the praise for whatever success he had achieved as a ruler and thereby acknowledged the Lord as Ruler over all things. In the concluding words of the Lord's Prayer we confess our faith in God as our King to whom we are ready to submit as loyal subjects. His is the kingdom of grace, power, and glory, and every petition of this prayer embodies principles for the promotion and the consummation of that kingdom here on earth and in heaven forever. As good children of "our Father which art in heaven" we delight to do His will in His kingdom and confidently believe that under all circumstances He will provide for us, protect us from harm and evil, and preserve us in the true faith, and at the last bring us into His kingdom of glory through our Lord Jesus Christ, King of kings and Lord of lords.

O God, rule over my life in Thy kingdom and help me to be an obedient servant, through Jesus Christ, my Lord. Amen.

THE LORD'S PRAYER — CONCLUSION

July 30

For Thine is the power

READ: I Chronicles 29:10-13.
TEXT: With God all things are possible. Matthew 19:26.

✣

What an inspiring confession terminates the Lord's Prayer! Yes, God is *power*. We say in the Creed, "I believe in God the Father Almighty," and repeat this thought in the Lord's Prayer, "Thine is the power," but do we really believe that God is the Almighty power? Is this our confession? Or do we believe that God rules only a part of this world while the rest belongs to "chance" or some other power? Is not this our belief when we speak about good or bad luck, the number thirteen, the Friday superstition? And worry, what is it but our unwillingness to trust God's power for tomorrow? Christ trusted not only God's love but also His power. Must not we do the same? Is not this what we need so much to make our faith complete and strong and our life free from worry and fear?

Lord, keep us from ignorance, superstition, and sin. Strengthen and purify our faith and give us the blessed assurance that underneath are the everlasting arms. Amen.

THE LORD'S PRAYER — CONCLUSION

For Thine is the glory

July 31

READ: John 12:23-33.

TEXT: Thine, O Lord is the greatness, and the power, and the glory, and the victory, and the majesty. I Chronicles 29:11.

♣

To God belongs glory, for He occupies all the universe which He has created. So great is He, yet through His Spirit He lives in the heart of each believer.

There are exhibitions of power on earth, in nature, and in the inventions of men, but God's power is greater than all these visible things. History has had its nights and its days, its times of discouragement and its periods of optimism, but there has been always a hand outside of man that works for righteousness in the world. Eventually He will conquer all things. As King of kings note His divine majesty, "He plants His footsteps on the sea and rides upon the storm."

All that we have that is worth anything has come from Him, and all that we are that is really worth while is the product of His hand. He has made us for Himself; our life is to glorify Him forever.

Our Father, the King of kings, we cannot comprehend Thy glory, but may we ever seek to glorify Thee by lives that constantly speak Thy praise. Amen.

THE LORD'S PRAYER — CONCLUSION

Forever and ever

Aug. 1

READ: John 17:1-5.

TEXT: Now unto the King eternal, immortal, invisible, the only God, be honor, and glory forever and ever. I Timothy 1:17.

✣

Only God's children have and know a Father who is eternal, without beginning or ending. This heavenly Father in whom we believe and to whom we pray is not only an everlasting Father but also an Almighty King. His kingdom like His Fatherly mercy endures forever. There is great comfort and assurance in this for the children of God, not only to pray to Him, but to trust and believe that their heavenly Father can and will answer their prayers.

He who gave His children this prayer of all prayers is the one and only true God, the God who was, is, and ever shall be—the God of Abraham, David, Daniel, Peter, John, Paul, Luther, you, me, and many yet unborn who shall come into His kingdom. Let us honor and glorify with our life this one and only eternal King whom we are privileged to call and have as our heavenly Father.

Our Father in heaven, our eternal and glorious King, we ask Thee to keep us ever faithful to Thee and Thy church, and when life's work is done, take us to Thy home above where we may dwell with Thee forever and ever. Amen.

THE LORD'S PRAYER — CONCLUSION

Amen, such petitions are acceptable and heard by Him

Aug. 2

READ: I John 5:14-21.

TEXT: For all the promises of God in Him are yea, and in Him Amen, unto the glory of God by us. II Corinthians 1:20.

❖

God says what He means. From Him Israel learned to make all promises and agreements binding with an Amen, meaning, "So shall it be."

Amen is God's expression for finality. Whatever precedes that will come to pass. When we pray the Lord's Prayer we are to bear in mind that all we ask in this prayer of His Son is according to His will and agrees with His love-care toward us. When a Christian, therefore, says Amen he tells himself, that by God's own Son I am assured that what I ask pleases the Father, is heard by Him, and He will answer. This Amen links itself with the beginning, with all boldness and confidence to entreat Him as dear children entreat their dear Father.

Heavenly Father, Thy words teach me to say what I mean and to live by what I say. I thank Thee for the promises and the gifts assured to me in Jesus who is Thine own Amen to my prayers. Forgive my neglect, thoughtless and careless use of this word. Teach me to see the sacrifice of Jesus in it, through and for which I am Thy child and heir. Let my trust and confidence shine forth in my daily behavior. In Jesus' name. Amen.

THE LORD'S PRAYER — CONCLUSION

Aug. 3

He Himself has commanded us to pray in this manner

READ: Matthew 6:9-15.
TEXT: Ask, and it shall be given you. Matthew 7:7.

✤

When we have finished praying the Lord's Prayer we have, indeed, asked for many and great things. Does God hear us in all these petitions? Is He willing to be bothered with our constant coming to Him with our requests? Yes, He is even more ready to hear than we are to ask. Furthermore, these petitions have been given us by our Savior Himself. He has bidden us to come to the Father asking Him for all these great blessings which we seek in the Lord's Prayer. We have the promise of the Father that He will hear us. What a privilege we have in prayer! We are, indeed, highly honored by God when He, so to say, gives us the key to the storehouse of His blessings and says, "Unlock the door, go in, and take away those things you have need of." That key is believing prayer. Should we, then, not make good use of this privilege? "Ask, and it shall be given you."

Heavenly Father, we thank Thee that Thou hast made us Thy children in Christ Jesus. We thank Thee for the privilege of coming to Thee daily. Grant us, O Father, courage to seek Thee in all our needs, for Jesus' sake. Amen.

THE LORD'S PRAYER — CONCLUSION

He has promised that He will hear us

Aug. 4

READ: II Corinthians 1:18-24.

TEXT: For how many as ever be the promises of God, in Him is the Yea; wherefore also through Him is the Amen, unto the glory of God through us. R. V. II Corinthians 1:20.

✤

God's promises are affirmative. When He says, "I will hear you," He has already heard. Promising, He fulfills even as He speaks. He is the Giver of all good things. His storehouse is full of blessings. His heart has but one thought, the welfare of His children. As parents desire for their children the very best in life, so He pours out His blessings to His own for the very asking. "The wind is contrary," said Wesley's friend in answer to the question why the ship was going the wrong way. "Then we pray," said Wesley. Kneeling down on the deck, he prayed briefly but fervently, asking God to steer the ship. The prayer finished, he sat down to resume his reading as though nothing were at stake. He took for granted that the God of all winds would command them to lie still. God did. That is our part in prayer. Our Amen is faith's own answer to God's promise. We believe. We trust. We receive.

Our heavenly Father, Thy promises are ever sure. In Thy loving heart there is room for all who wish to come. We pray not for riches or fame but only for a place near Thy blessed presence. Keep us, O Lord, in childlike faith always. Amen.

THE SACRAMENT OF HOLY BAPTISM

Aug. 5

What is Baptism?
Baptism is water used according to God's command and connected with God's Word

READ: John 3:1-17.

TEXT: Except a man be born of water and the Spirit, he cannot enter the kingdom of God. John 3:5.

♣

Christian baptism is the application of water in the name of the Father and the Son and the Holy Ghost. On our part baptism is an act of faith and obedience. On God's part it is a means by which He bestows and seals His grace.

It is a simple thing to do, to apply water thus. God makes His ordinances simple so that all can understand and obey them. But the meaning and the effect of baptism are far beyond our power to understand, for it is through baptism that we become the children of God, that we are born again.

Stop and think what a wonderful thing God does when we obey His commands. Baptism works forgiveness of sin, delivers from death and the devil, and gives everlasting salvation to all who believe what the words and the promises of God declare.

O God, we humbly thank Thee for the faith of our parents and their obedience to Thy command in presenting us in baptism so that we have become Thy children and have entered into Thy promises. Keep us evermore in this loving relationship to Thee, unto eternal life, through Jesus Christ, our Lord. Amen.

THE SACRAMENT OF HOLY BAPTISM

What is this Word of God?
Go ye therefore, and make disciples of all nations, baptizing them

Aug. 6

READ: Matthew 28:16-20.

TEXT: Go ye therefore, and teach all nations, baptizing them in the name of the Father, and of the Son, and of the Holy Ghost. Matthew 28:19.

♣

Nobody consulted us about being born. Life was a gift to us from our parents.

In the same way we begin being Christians. By the gift of God's grace in baptism we become His children. That gift comes through God's Word, wherin lies the power of the sacrament, a power capable of transforming lives. We do not know about it then any more than the soil is aware of the seed, but the life in the heart of the seed says to the soil, "Give me thy strength," and thereby grows into a harvest.

Seed is not sown in the desert. For growth there must be moisture and cultivation.

Now we must live what we know. Christ is the Way, the Truth, and the Life. The great adventure opens before us. Let us engage in it with courage and zest, showing to the world what Christ can do with a life wholly given to Him!

O Christ, Thou hast the secret, answering our questions, solving our problems. Help us to live the changed life of the born-again that alone can lift and save our world. Amen.

THE SACRAMENT OF HOLY BAPTISM

Aug. 7

What gifts or benefits does baptism confer?
It works forgiveness of sins

READ: Acts 2:37-47.

TEXT: Repent, and be baptized every one of you in the name of Jesus Christ for the remission of sins. Acts 2:38.

✤

"Remission of sins," this is our greatest need. By experience we know how dreadfully sin separates from God and from man and takes the joy out of life. There is no escape from the guilt and the curse of sin but by God's pardon, granted to all who are sincerely sorry for sin and humbly accept Jesus Christ as their Savior. By baptism we are transferred into Him, are born anew as children of God. We now have a new life, a new relation to God, and new obligations to our fellow men. "God so loved the world that . . . whosoever believeth on Him . . . should have everlasting life." Out of all nations and races and conditions God is gathering saved sinners who as His children are one great family. By God's grace I belong to this redeemed, forgiven family and by my conduct shall be a credit to it and by my influence help to win others.

Blessed Jesus, Thou hast admitted me into Thy kingdom when I was baptized; help me to be grateful for my forgiveness, to obey Thee, to praise Thee, and to lead others to share with me eternal life in Thee. Amen.

THE SACRAMENT OF HOLY BAPTISM

What gifts or benefits does baptism confer?
Delivers from death and the devil

Aug. 8

READ: Romans 8:1-14.

TEXT: For the law of the Spirt of life in Christ Jesus made me free from the law of sin and death. Romans 8:2. ✤

We are a sinful race and lost but for the grace of God. "The wages of sin is death." We are under condemnation, but God has provided a way to cancel the sentence that rests upon us. "The gift of God is eternal life." In baptism God cleanses us from sin and rescues us from the death that rests upon us. "He that believeth and is baptized shall be saved." God, however, does much more than to deliver us from the sentence of death. He gives us power to live triumphantly, to grow Christlike.

We cannot and need not add anything to assure or complete our salvation. "Not by works of righteousness which we have done, but according to His mercy He saved us by the washing of regeneration and renewing of the Holy Ghost, which He shed on us abundantly through Jesus Christ, our Savior." Not only does God start us on the way of the Christian life, He also sees us through to the end. We are *kept* by the power of God through faith unto salvation."

Blessed Father, I thank Thee that Thou hast begotten faith in my heart. Help me now to grow stronger in faith and in love. Make me "strong in the Lord and in the power of His might." Amen.

THE SACRAMENT OF HOLY BAPTISM

Aug. 9

What gifts or benefits does baptism confer?
And gives everlasting salvation to all who believe

READ: Mark 16:14-20.

TEXT: He that believeth and is baptized shall be saved. Mark 16:16.

✣

Baptism is not an invention of men, it is the institution of God. Baptism is God's way of adopting us as His children and making us heirs of eternal life. How do I know that I am a child of God? I am baptized, and I believe that God is both willing and able to fulfill all His promises in regard to baptism.

One promise is, "For as many of you as have been baptized into Christ have put on Christ," Galatians 3:27.

Of course, faith is necessary, but faith is the gift of God to the receptive heart. As disobedient and rebellious children may be disinherited by earthly parents, so our heavenly Father disinherits those baptized persons who turn away from Him and *live in impenitence and unbelief,* and they lose that glorious crown of life which God gives to the faithful.

O God, we thank Thee that Thou didst make us Thine own in holy baptism; we thank Thee that we now belong to Thy family. Help us always to remember the obligations resting upon those who are Thy children that by the power of Thy grace we, too, may be Thy faithful children now and forever. In Jesus' name. Amen.

THE SACRAMENT OF HOLY BAPTISM

What is the Word and promise of God?
Sealed with the Holy Spirit

Aug. 10

READ: Ephesians 1:1-14.

TEXT: In whom also after that ye believed, ye were sealed with that holy Spirit of promise. Ephesians 1:13.

✤

A seal is a sign of ownership and of authority. A sealed envelope keeps others out. God says that those who trust in Jesus are sealed with the Holy Spirit of promise. By faith in the crucified Savior we become God's own people. When He puts His seal on us, we can depend upon it that we belong to Him. This seal is a living testimony in our heart.

The gift of God's Spirit is His pledge that someday we shall be in His presence in heaven. We are "sealed unto the day of redemption," Ephesians 4:30.

There need be no question or doubt about our salvation. If we have trusted Jesus and His finished work on the cross, God has "given the earnest [guarantee] of the Spirit in our hearts," II Corinthians 1:22. The seal is never separated from the cross. Trust Him, beloved.

Blessed Jesus, I do believe Thou hast died to take away my sins. I thank Thee for the sealing of Thy Spirit in my baptism. Grant me joy in this truth each day. Amen.

THE SACRAMENT OF HOLY BAPTISM

Aug. 11

What is the Word and promise of God?
The word and promise of God includes infants

READ: Mark 10:13-16.

TEXT: Suffer [let] the little children to come unto Me, and forbid them not: for of such is the kingdom of God. Mark 10:14.

✢

Christ's command regarding baptism includes all, without exception. It is something which we need from the very beginning of life. Jesus urged His helpers not to try to stop the little children from coming to Him and receiving a heavenly blessing from Him.

The new life which begins at baptism has infinite possibilities for such who also are privileged to learn to know Jesus as their Lord and Savior and thus daily renew their baptismal covenant in willing service. A little baptized boy in the Primary class in Sunday school said to his mother, "Today the devil doesn't like me because I have been so helpful."

Thank God every day for your baptism and all the privileges which it grants you for time and for eternity. Let us ever remember that we who serve God in true faith and with willing heart are His children and joint-heirs with Jesus Christ. Jesus wants the blessings of the kingdom of God to begin in infancy.

Dear Lord Jesus, I thank Thee for my baptism and Thy gift of salvation. Help me and all believers to serve Thee by keeping Thy commandments and thus by Thy grace to live a helpful life. Amen.

THE SACRAMENT OF HOLY BAPTISM

**How can water do such great things?
The Word of God is connected with the water**

Aug. 12

READ: Ephesians 5:18-27.

TEXT: Christ also loved the church, and gave Himself for it; that He might sanctify and cleanse it with the washing of water by the word. Ephesians 5:25, 26.

✣

There is use in everything but no magic in anything. To say that there is good or bad luck in a thing is superstition. Some have had that thought about baptism, as though water could of itself work magic to protect us from disease and danger. That is not true. The power of baptism is in the cleansing of the soul, and it requires God's Word and promise and our faith and obedience to make it effective.

The Word of God is a living, powerful thing. It makes of baptism a real experience in the life of the Christian. Think of your own baptism. Believe that in your baptism you received and still receive the forgiveness of your sins through the water and the Word of God. Believe that through this sacrament you are now living as a child of God, and that God, your heavenly Father, is giving you strength and grace so to live.

O heavenly Father, since Thou hast called me to be Thy child, continue to me every day thy Holy Spirit that I may live godly here in time and forever in Thy kingdom, to Thy glory, through Jesus Christ, my Lord. Amen.

THE SACRAMENT OF HOLY BAPTISM

Aug. 13

How can water do such great things?
Our faith must rely on the Word of God

READ: II Kings 5:1-14.

TEXT: Go and wash in the Jordan seven times . . . and thou shalt be clean. II Kings 5:10.

✠

Have you read the II Kings passage? Wasn't that altogether too simple a solution to his problem? Was it worth his coming? Shouldn't he demand a more dignified reception? There was that royal letter entailing two nation's friendship, his gold he brought as reward. If water was needed, there were finer rivers in Syria!

Question after question raced through Naaman's mind. On second thought, however, he chose to listen to his charioteer and comply with the order of the prophet. The faith so expressed was rewarded with health for the sick body.

God needs no help. No amount of water will improve baptism, secure greater blessings. It is all God's doing. This only we can do: believe and obey His holy Word.

Father in heaven, untouched by the confusion this day will bring, I come to Thee and ask for that strength of faith I shall need. When confronted by sin and false promises of temptations, then, I plead, remind me of Thy promises given to me in my baptism. Let there be no other guidance for me but Thy holy Word. In Jesus' name. Amen.

THE SACRAMENT OF HOLY BAPTISM

How can water do such great things?
A gracious water of life

Aug. 14

READ: Titus 3:5-8.
TEXT: According to His mercy He saved us. Titus 3:5.

✤

Jesus said to Nicodemus, "Except a man be born of water and of the Spirit, he cannot enter into the kingdom of God," John 3:5. This new birth is brought about "by the washing of regeneration and renewing of the Holy Ghost," as a result of baptism.

The water combined with the Word of God, as used by the Holy Ghost to regenerate, renews and strengthens the faith of the individual so that he may grow in holiness of life. Thus it truly becomes a "gracious water of life."

It is a "gracious water of life" in that it confers upon the individual the gifts and benefits promised in baptism, forgiveness of sin, deliverance from death and the devil, and everlasting life. These are the mercies of God which the Psalmist says are great and everlasting. These great gifts guided Jesus in His ministry and enabled Him to endure the cross. They are the keystone in the redemption of every one who believes as the Word and promises of God declare.

Heavenly Father, help me every day to keep my life pure and clean and to wash away all my sins and help me ever to believe that Jesus is my Savior, and that I am Thy child; in Jesus' name I ask this. Amen.

THE SACRAMENT OF HOLY BAPTISM

Aug. 15

How can water do such great things?

Baptism is a washing of regeneration in the Holy Ghost

READ: John 6:60-65.

TEXT: He saved us by the washing of regeneration and renewing of the Holy Ghost. Titus 3:5.

✣

I have been baptized. What does that mean to me? When I was born into this world I was born "flesh of flesh." My parents, like all others, were sinful, and thus I was born in a state of sin. In fact, the Bible makes it plain that I was "dead in trespasses and sin." It was impossible for me to receive faith and to believe in Jesus Christ as my Savior.

When I was baptized, and water was applied in the name of the Father, and of the Son, and of the Holy Ghost, my original sin was washed away. I was regenerated, born again, made spiritually alive by God's Spirit. The Holy Ghost worked through the Word of God in my baptism, imparting grace, and He made me a child of God.

Just as electricity proves itself by giving light, heat, and power, so every child of God proves his faith by living a Christian life. Am I living such a life?

Almighty God, Thou who hast cleansed me and made me Thine own child in holy baptism, help me to live a Christlike life so that in thought, word, and deed I am worthy of the name—Christian. Amen.

THE SACRAMENT OF HOLY BAPTISM

What does such baptizing with water signify?

The old Adam in us, together with all sins and evil lusts, should be drowned by daily repentance

Aug. 16

READ: Romans 6:1-14.

TEXT: Our old man is crucified with Him, that the body of sin might be destroyed that henceforth we should not serve sin. Romans 6:6.

✢

We have learned that the old Adam in us is the sinful nature that produces all wrong living, and the new man is the new spirit of the Christian who strives to do the will of Christ. Life is a warfare; a struggle between good and evil in us. An ancient writer said that every youth has two steeds hitched to the chariot of his life: one is white representing the good impulses, the other is black representing the evil. St. Paul said, "Be not overcome of evil, but overcome evil with good." Our duty as Christians is to fight against the evil in us and to put it down. "Yield not to temptation, for yielding is sin." Luther wrote, "When Christ said, 'repent ye,' He intended that the whole life of believers should be repentance." Every day we are to be penitent, sorrowful over the evil in our life, and this is to continue till our entrance into the kingdom of heaven.

O Lord Jesus, give me more of Thy good spirit that I may hate evil and love the good and by Thy grace overcome the power of evil in my life. Amen.

THE SACRAMENT OF HOLY BAPTISM

Aug. 17

What does such baptizing with water signify?
The new man should daily come forth

READ: Ephesians 4:24-32.

TEXT: And that ye put on the new man, which after God is created in righteousness and true holiness. Ephesians 4:24.

♣

We were baptized into the kingdom of Jesus Christ. We have been sealed and set apart as His people and, therefore, belong to Him in this world and in the world to come. We really have no right to lay down any rule to live by except what the Lord has given us in example and word. This may seem like a hard program, but Christ is in that program to make it possible.

If this new life in us is to "come forth daily," we must read our Bible regularly, especially the New Testament. The more you read it, the more you will love the Lord, and the more this new life will come forth in you. If there are some things there you don't understand take them to your pastor, and he will help you. Daily prayer is necessary. The Sacrament of the Altar and regular worship should not be neglected. And each day let Christ actively direct your thoughts, attitudes, activities.

Dear Lord, help me to be loyal and true to Thee by being faithful in the use of Thy Word and the Sacrament and daily prayer so that the new life in me may daily come forth. Amen.

THE SACRAMENT OF HOLY BAPTISM

Baptismal covenant renewed at confirmation

Aug. 18

READ: I Timothy 6:11-21.

TEXT: Fight the good fight of faith, lay hold on eternal life, whereunto thou art also called, and hast professed a good profession before many witnesses. I Timothy 6:12.

✤

You have been baptized. You have been taught the meaning of baptism. You know that you are called to be a child of God. Confirmation continues and renews the blessing which your loving parents obtained for you in the sacrament of holy baptism. In confirmation you consciously and voluntarily make your own confession of faith in Jesus Christ. You now tell the world: "This is my faith. By the help of God I will be true, I will fight the good fight of faith."

Confirmation is a very definite step in the process of growing up. You do not want to be a child always. In confirmation you accept and assume and take over some of the privileges and obligations of manhood. From this time on it will be your own increasing responsibility to live a truly Christian life and be personally faithful in the use of the means of grace.

O Christ, Thou strong Son of God, who didst grow in knowledge and stature and in favor with God and man, be my help and my strength as I accept for myself the burdens and the opportunities of life that I also may be found faithful and make a good confession before many witnesses. Amen.

THE CONFESSION OF SINS

Aug. 19

What is confession?
Confession consists of two parts

READ: Luke 15: 11-32.
TEXT: Father, I have sinned. Luke 15:21a.

✣

Luther says, "Confession embraces two parts: one, that we confess our sins; the other, that we receive absolution." The Scripture says, "I said, I will confess my transgressions unto the Lord; and Thou forgavest the iniquity of my sin." The publican said, "God, be merciful unto me, a sinner." He was said to be worthy of forgiveness, for "he that humbleth himself shall be exalted." When we learn this in our catechism and our Bible study, it may seem faraway and theoretical for many of us. We probably have not yet taken upon ourselves much responsibility. Nor perhaps have we felt the anguish of a suffering conscience nor desperately yearned for the comfort of pardon. But each day and year it becomes more wonderful to know that there is pardon for us. "For this is a faithful saying and worthy of all acceptation that Christ Jesus came into the world to save sinners."

Open your heart to God, and His peace will abide with you through the grace of His pardon.

O Christ, Thou Lamb of God, that takest away the sin of the world, have mercy upon me. Blot out my transgression. Amen.

THE CONFESSION OF SINS

What is confession?
That we confess our sins

Aug. 20

READ: Psalm 32.

TEXT: I said, I will confess my transgressions unto the Lord; and Thou forgavest the iniquity of my sins. Psalm 32:5.

✤

You who would let your light shine must keep it clean and bright. The light of God's love cannot shine forth from sin-stained souls.

Because He is our heavenly Father and loves us with a holy love God is always eager to fulfill His promise in cleansing us "from all unrighteousness." Like the Father of the prodigal son, He comes out to meet us as we return to pour out our sins before Him and to beg His mercy. God answers with His forgiveness every sincere confession of sin.

Many millions of Christians, in every worship service, upon hearing their pastor lead them in their confession, saying, "I said, I will confess my transgressions unto the Lord," are ready to respond with their own true testimony, "And Thou forgavest the iniquity of my sin." A forgiven sinner! That is the most beautiful and yet most wonderful miracle of God. Think it over!

O God, Thou hast loved me before I could turn to Thee to call Thee Father. I cry unto Thee, mercifully grant pardon for all my sins that I may fully reflect Thy glory and Thy holy love. Hear me for Jesus' sake. Amen.

THE CONFESSION OF SINS

Aug. 21

What is confession?

That we receive forgiveness from the pastor as from God

READ: I John 1.

TEXT: If we confess our sins, He is faithful and just to forgive us our sins, and to cleanse us from all unrighteousness. I John 1:9.

♣

A man denied that he had leprosy. Experienced physicians were convinced of it. At his death it was said that, if he had not denied he had it in its early stages, modern medical science could have cured him.

Sin is the leprosy of the soul. Whoever persists in and denies he is sinful deceives himself and becomes a victims of his own lying, John declares.

The best thing to do with sin is to confess it to our ever-faithful Father in heaven in joyful expectancy of forgiveness and cleansing of our soul. "For where there is forgiveness of sins there is also life and salvation," concludes Luther. And each Sunday we have that opportunity. In the confessional services of the church we receive God's forgiveness through the pastor who speaks in His name.

Almighty and ever gracious God, prevent us from the lying denial of our sinful selves and all self-righteousness and inspire us to acknowledge and confess our sins with lowly contrite hearts that we may enjoy the favor of Thy approval of our souls for life eternal, both here and forevermore. Through Jesus Christ, Thy Son, our Lord. Amen.

THE CONFESSION OF SINS

What sins should we confess?
Let us confess all manner of sins

Aug. 22

READ: I John 1.

TEXT: God saw that the wickedness of man was great in the earth, and that every imagination of the thoughts of his heart was only evil continually. Genesis 6:5.

✣

What sins should you confess? Why should you judge between sins as though this sin is great, and that sin does not matter? How may one know what is sinful when the imagination of his heart is only evil continually? We need standards other than our own judgment to determine what is sinful.

That is why the Psalmist asked, "Wherewithal shall a young man cleanse his way?" And answered his own question, "By taking heed thereto according to Thy word." Here in the Word of God we find the guide and the measure, the commandments. Here we find the example of the perfect life of Jesus. Jesus makes it very plain that impure thought, anger, hate, unbelief, unforgiveness, selfishness, hypocrisy, envy, pride, untruthfulness are sins. Acknowledge them.

O Holy God, I cannot hide anything from Thee. Help me to hate sin as Thou dost hate it and to love righteousness with the new heart which Thou dost desire to give me, through Jesus Christ, my Lord and Savior. Amen.

THE CONFESSION OF SINS

Aug. 23

What sins should we confess?
Let us confess those that we are not aware of

READ: Psalm 51:1-9.

TEXT: Who can understand his errors? Cleanse Thou me from secret faults. Psalm 19:12.

♣

Secret faults are secret only to the eyes of men. God is the searcher of hearts, and in His sight all sins are plain and open; nothing can be hidden from Him. "There is not a word in my tongue, but lo, Lord, Thou knowest it altogether," Psalm 139:4. Secret faults and sins are real. Not only then is a man guilty of murder when he slays his brother with a club or a gun, but "whoso hateth his brother is a murderer." A lustful leer or a smutty thought amounts to adultery according to the Savior's words. Some people regard secret sins as trivial. That is both wrong and dangerous. If sin is not forgiven, it will bring about your condemnation. God be praised! There is a Savior given to men, Jesus Christ, our Lord, who saves from sin, secret or open. Whoever believes in Him and seeks pardon through Him has the forgiveness of sin.

Lord, Thou knowest my thoughts from afar. Cleanse me from envy, disobedience, unchastity, greed, and all other secret faults and sins that my heart may harbor. Cause my conscience to be sensitive that I may not entertain evil thoughts. In every time of temptation direct my heart that it may resist sin. Lord, make me sincere. In Jesus' name. Amen.

THE CONFESSION OF SINS

In what spirit should we confess our sins?
A broken spirit is pleasing to God

Aug. 24

READ: Psalm 51:10-19.

TEXT: The sacrifices of God are a broken spirit; a broken and a contrite heart, O God, Thou wilt not despise. Psalm 51:17.

♣

David, the king, had sinned great sins. His conscience gave him no rest, he says, when he kept silence, an experience which all have when there are unconfessed sins. The prophet Nathan came to him, reminded him of God's blessings, and pronounced the judgment of God upon his sins. Then David's proud and guilty spirit broke. He acknowledged his sin and confessed it in the words of this Fifty-first Psalm.

This is the broken spirit and the contrite heart. It is the only attitude which is proper in the presence of God.

Don't you see that we should always be repentant and humble in the sight of God? For we sin much every day. There is none perfect, no, not one. But God is holy, and God is perfect. Yet when our spirits are broken, He will come in and dwell with us. Then we may be strong in the Lord and in the power of His might.

O God, who lovest the humble and forgivest the repentant, let me yield my broken heart to Thee that I may dwell evermore with Thee in the glory of Thy holiness. Amen.

THE CONFESSION OF SINS

Aug. 25

No sins so great but God can forgive

READ: I Timothy 1:12-20.

TEXT: Christ Jesus came into the world to save sinners, of whom I am chief. I Timothy 1:15.

♣

To deny that you are a sinner and therefore do not need forgiveness is the greatest foolishness and the greatest sin. This is the only sin which will not be forgiven because it is the sin of unbelief in God and His Word and unbelief in Jesus Christ whom God has sent. It is the denying of the truth. Jesus says that every sin shall be forgiven but this.

Therefore, when you become aware of your sin and repent of it you are on your way to being forgiven and being saved. When you refuse to acknowledge your sin, are unrepentant and unbelieving you are on the way to condemnation. Let no past sin make you fear. You should be ashamed of it, should resolve to do it no more. But be sure that whatever it is, God is able and willing to forgive it and to cleanse you from all unrighteousness. The promise is this: "Though your sins be as scarlet, they shall be white as snow; though they be red like crimson, they shall be as wool."

O God, who dost not desire that any should perish because of sin, and who hast given Thy Son that whosoever believeth on Him should not perish, grant us repentant hearts and believing spirits, we pray Thee, that we may come unto forgiveness and salvation. Through the same, even Jesus Christ Thy Son, our Lord. Amen.

THE OFFICE OF THE KEYS

Aug. 26

What is the Office of the Keys?
The power Christ has given to His church to forgive sins

READ: Matthew 16:13-20.

TEXT: I will give unto thee the keys of the kingdom of heaven; and whatsoever thou shalt bind on earth shall be bound in heaven, and whatsoever thou shalt loose on earth shall be loosed in heaven. Matthew 16:19.

✣

The authority and the power of the church are great. It need not tremble when confronted by hostile men. The church is the militant force of God in the world, delegated to dispense the gospel. It has power to open the storehouse of God as the steward who has keys to the master's granary. It has power to bind and to loose as one has the ability to open and to close a door. The true church has the keys of doctrine and the power of discipline.

The minister of the church exercises this authority "of binding and loosing" each time he offers absolution to the penitents of his church. The world, the flesh, and the devil make their assault, but even the "gates of hell shall not prevail." The word of the church shall be final.

I do thank Thee, O God, for Thy church and its teaching ministry and its authority on earth. Grant that it may help me and all men to know Thee, the Triune God, Father, Son, and Holy Spirit. Amen.

THE OFFICE OF THE KEYS

Aug. 27

Who exercises this power?
The ministers of Christ

READ: Hebrews 13:17-25.
TEXT: Obey them that have the rule over you; and submit to them. Hebrews 13:17.

♣

Keys lock and unlock. An unlocked, unguarded property is easy prey. The homeowner can exercise control over his property by using keys. So the church watches over her God-given home.

If we would grow in grace and favor before God and among men we must submit to the church and her discipline, we must obey the rules which govern her. Our school report card is evidence of our willingness or unwillingness to fit into the school program. The teachers exercise authority by virtue of their office. So also, we must give account of our conduct to the minister whom God has placed over us. It is in our own interest that he concerns himself about our welfare. Through him Christ would lovingly shepherd our life. And such shepherding requires not only feeding and comforting but also warning and disciplining. As faithful members of the flock we gladly respond and follow, seeing in the work of the pastor the hand of Him who cares.

Dear Lord Jesus, Thou didst humble Thyself and wast obedient even unto the cross. Make me ever more like Thee. Make me willing to listen and to learn. So shall I follow in Thy footsteps. Amen.

THE OFFICE OF THE KEYS

What is the result of the Office of the Keys?
A good conscience

Aug. 28

READ: II Corinthians 5:17-21.

TEXT: Now then we are ambassadors for Christ, as though God did beseech you by us: we pray you in Christ's stead, be ye reconciled to God. II Corinthians 5:20.

✚

Recently I sat with one of the nicest Christians I have ever met during a long ministry. She was 83 years old. As she talked, her mind went back over the years to the time of her confirmation. Her face lighted up, and there was something of the heavenly in her countenance as she told me of her confirmation.

Jesus will always keep His word and honor our confession of Him as "the Christ, the Son of the living God." Because of this the pastor is enabled to pronounce the blessing, "The Father in heaven, for Jesus' sake, renew and increase in thee the gift of the Holy Ghost, to thy strengthening in faith, to thy growth in grace, to thy patience in suffering, and to the blessed hope of everlasting life." There is no greater satisfaction in life than having the clear, undisturbed conscience of those who know they are at peace with God.

Lord, help me to keep my confirmation promise. May the covenant I made with Thee help me to carry something of the fragrance of the Christian life in all the walks of this work-a-day world. Amen.

THE OFFICE OF THE KEYS

Aug. 29

What do you believe in accordance with these words?
If your brother sinned against you, go to him alone

READ: Matthew 18:15-20.

TEXT: Moreover if thy brother shall trespass against thee, go and tell him his fault between thee and him alone; if he shall hear thee, thou hast gained thy brother. Matthew 18:15.

✣

"He did the wrong; let him make it right." That is the way of the world. But it is not Christ's way. Christ's way is this: "He did the wrong; I must make it right." The responsibility for making things right rests with the follower of Christ even when he is wronged.

It takes courage, great courage, to go to one who has offended you and in gentle speech to try to recover a damaged friendship. It requires faith to believe that by so doing you may overcome evil with good and regain your brother. It can be done only when you love your brother more than your pride and love peace more than strife. You must have control of your feelings, your thought, and your speech.

Yes, that is Christ's way, and Christ can help us to make peace, to gain our brother, and thus to open to both of you the kingdom of heaven.

O God, help me to understand how wonderful it is to make peace, to gain back a lost brother, and to open the kingdom of heaven by reason of love and forgiveness; grant me the spirit of Christ to do this at all times; for His name's sake. Amen.

THE OFFICE OF THE KEYS

What do you believe in accordance with these words?
If he will not hear, go with several witnesses

Aug. 30

READ: Luke 17:1-5.

TEXT: Whose soever sins ye remit, they are remitted unto them, and whose soever sins ye retain, they are retained. John 20:23.

✣

When a young Jewish scribe was authorized to teach he was presented with a key as the symbol of his office. Thus when Jesus gave His disciples the "keys of the kingdom," they understood that they were empowered with the *key of knowledge* to teach the truth about God and the Christian way of life to mankind everywhere. "Go ye, therefore, and teach."

A second key committed to the Church of Jesus Christ is the *key of discipline*. This key is to bind or loose souls in earth and in heaven. Children of God are authorized peacemakers. This is no small responsibility. It is often too great a thing to be undertaken alone. If the offender will not yield to the efforts of one alone, the love and the fellowship of others may help to bring about peace. Therefore, says Jesus, take others with you.

You hold two keys in your hand. Use them faithfully and be blessed.

O Christ, Thou Prince of peace, who hast commanded that we love one another, pour Thy love into our heart that all discord may cease, and we be Thy children indeed. Amen.

THE OFFICE OF THE KEYS

Aug. 31

What do you believe in accordance with these words?
If he refuses, tell it to the church

READ: Galatians 6:1-8.

TEXT: And if he shall neglect to hear them, tell it unto the church; but if he neglect to hear the church, let him be unto thee as an heathen and a publican. Matthew 18:17.

✣

Are you still at odds with your brother? He came to you and humbly sought to be at peace with you. You would not listen to him alone. He came then with some of your friends who pleaded with you to make peace with him. You refused to hear them, too. What should he do now? Jesus says, "Let him tell it to the church."

But the discipline of the church is not intended to condemn. It is meant to make you think, repent, confess your sins, and be restored to Christian fellowship and the saving means of grace; and to be at peace with your brethren.

Listen to the church when it speaks, for it is the church of the living God, divinely appointed to bring peace and salvation to men and to warn those who will not forgive that neither will they be forgiven.

O Thou who judgest the hearts of men and lovest them who seek peace with their brethren, grant me humility of spirit that I may hear the admonitions of my brethren and be at peace with them. Through Jesus Christ, the giver of peace. Amen.

CONFIRMATION

Confirmation is not graduation

Sept. 1

READ: Philippians 3:7-14.

TEXT: Not as though I had already attained, either were already perfect: but I follow after, if that I may apprehend that for which also I am apprehended of Jesus Christ. Philippians 3:12.

✣

Paul's great privilege!

Each new day with this servant of God was an effort to make it a better day. Goal? Prize? "That I may apprehend." That Michaelangelo grit: working a whole week without taking off his clothes! That Paul endurance. No coasting, no loafing. But each day pushing harder toward the goal and the crown of victory. To grasp the beauty of life is to grasp the opportunity of daily spiritual advancement or progress.

Afflicted with serious lung trouble, Cecil Rhodes left Oxford to go to South Africa. Home and friends, love and happiness were the price as he said, "Goodbye" on a gray and stormy morning. He won. "It is what you do with what you have." Every one? Yes, every one who has been "apprehended of Jesus Christ." If we have been laid hold of, claimed by Him, then to the end of our life we are learners, strivers, workers with Him, for Him, by His guidance and His power.

O God, we thank Thee for our young people and the newly confirmed. Inspire them. Keep them in the love of God and let Thy blessing rest upon them by day and by night. Through Jesus Christ, our Lord. Amen.

THE SACRAMENT OF THE ALTAR

Sept. 2

What is the Sacrament of the Altar?
It is the true body and blood of our Lord Jesus Christ

READ: I Corinthians 10:16-26.

TEXT: The cup of blessing which we bless, is it not the communion of the blood of Christ? The bread which we break, is it not the communion of the body of Christ? I Corinthians 10:16.

✤

What a privilege to receive and confess my Lord at His table! O that I may not find it in my heart to remain away from this feast of love, so sweet and so precious, and thus deprive myself of the comfort and the hope which are imparted there! To remain away from the Lord's Table is equivalent to saying that I prefer to continue in sin; that I do not desire divine pardon. I must not permit anything to keep me away. Even a sense of unfitness and unworthiness must not hinder my coming; on the contrary, this should be an incentive to urge me to come. I have wandered in forbidden paths. I have sinned and done evil. I have grown cold in my zeal and my love. But Thou dost invite me to Thine own sacrament. I return to Thee, blessed Jesus, confessing my sins and seeking to have my faith rekindled by Thee.

O Spirit divine, preserve me in union with Jesus Christ in the true faith and ever prepare me in mind and in heart worthily to receive this sacrament of Christ's body and blood every time it is administered by the church. Amen.

THE SACRAMENT OF THE ALTAR

The words of institution (first part)
Our Lord Jesus Christ, in the night in which He was betrayed, took bread

Sept. 3

READ: I Corinthians 11:23-34.

TEXT: Take, eat; this is My body which is given for you. I Corinthians 11:24.

✣

Jesus and His disciples came to an upper room to celebrate the flight of their ancestors from Egypt, that land of bondage. When they ate the unleavened bread they were reminded of the hasty meal of which the children of Israel partook before their flight. When they ate the Passover lamb they remembered the lamb that was slain, whose blood was sprinkled on the doorposts so that the angel of death might pass by.

But when Jesus took bread and brake it and gave it to His disciples saying, "This is My body, take and eat," He gave a new meaning to the Passover. He made it the memorial, not of an escape from the land of Egypt, but of a deliverance from the bondage of sin.

When you come to the altar of the Holy Communion, remember then, that Christ offered Himself for us that we might be delivered from sin and death and the power of the devil into the glorious liberty of the sons of God.

O loving Savior, who hast given Thyself to deliver us from the bondage of sin, give us grace so to eat of this bread that by faith we may obtain forgiveness of sins and enter into life eternal. For Thy name's sake. Amen.

THE SACRAMENT OF THE ALTAR

Sept. 4

The words of institution (second part)

After the same manner also He took the cup

READ: Matthew 26:26-35.

TEXT: Drink ye all of it; for this is My blood of the new testament which is shed for many for the remission of sins. Matthew 26:27, 28.

♣

Jesus said, as He gave the cup to His disciples, "All of you drink of it." Thus He made the Lords' Supper a com-munion, that is, a union of all in one common fellowship. Today those who receive the Sacrament of the Altar are said to belong to the same communion, for they show that they are brethren of the same faith.

Jesus called this cup the "New Testament." Now a testament is a declaration of intention. We may know what good intention God has toward us because this New Testment was written in the blood of Christ. God's love for us is shown in that He spared not His own Son but freely gave Him for us all.

We should, therefore, come thoughtfully, seriously, faithfully to the altar of the Holy Communion, remembering that here is the place where Christian brotherhood is established.

We rejoice, O heavenly Father, in the fellowship and common faith of others. Help us to remember at what cost this has been obtained that we may never lightly regard or despise the Sacrament of the Altar and the communion of saints. Amen.

THE SACRAMENT OF THE ALTAR

What is the benefit of such eating and drinking?

Where there is remission of sins, there is also life and salvation

Sept. 5

READ: John 6:48-58.

TEXT: I am the living bread . . . if any man eat of this bread he shall live forever. John 6:51.

❖

God has given us our physical life. To sustain this life He has provided the necessary food. Bread is called the "staff of life." When it is taken into our bodies it becomes a part of our physical being. It supplies us with health, strength, and energy.

God is also the Giver of our spiritual life. He alone can supply the necessary food for our spiritual growth, strength, health, and energy. God, the Father, sent His Son into the world that we might have life and salvation. Hence Jesus speaks of Himself as "the living bread which came down from heaven." In the Lord's Supper we receive His body and His blood. They provide the spiritual nourishment we need. And the Sacrament reassures us that we have been forgiven and have received His gift of life.

Let us come often to the Lord's Table; then we shall have confidence that "abundant life" is ours for time and for eternity.

> "O dearest Lord, receive from me
> The heartfelt thanks I offer Thee,
> Who through Thy body and Thy blood
> Hast wrought my soul's eternal good." Amen.

THE SACRAMENT OF THE ALTAR

Sept. 6

How can the bodily eating and drinking produce such great benefits?

The words produce them, "Given and shed for you for the remission of sins"

READ: John 6:63-71.

TEXT: This is My body which is given for you: this do in remembrance of Me. This cup is the new testament in My blood, which is shed for you. Luke 22:19b, 20b.

✣

As we approach the Communion Table we enter into the Holy of Holies of our Christian religion. Here the Lord Jesus enters into the closest communion possible with us, for He makes us partakers of His holy body and of His precious blood. Satisfying peace fills our heart when we hear the words, "Given and shed for you for the remission of your sins." "And, where there is forgiveness of sins there is also life and salvation." Now life flows into our soul like a stream of living water. Through the life-giving Word which comes to us in this sacrament we receive power, power to resist temptation; power to fight and to win; power to carry our burdens patiently; power to labor and pray; power to believe and love. Endowed with this power, we face the future courageously.

Lord Jesus, grant that Thy Holy Sacrament may strengthen me in my earthly pilgrimage till I reach my home above and am seated at Thy table in heaven. Amen.

THE SACRAMENT OF THE ALTAR

How can bodily eating and drinking produce these great benefits?

He who believes these words has the remission of sins

Sept. 7

READ: Matthew 8:5-13.

TEXT: As thou hast believed, so be it done unto thee. Matthew 8:13.

✣

Like the water of baptism, which is of no effect without the Word of God and faith which trusts the Word of God in the water, the bread and the wine do not become a sacrament without the Word. The blessed experience of the forgiveness of your sins comes through your faith in what the words and the promises of God declare.

Now faith is not just saying, "I believe." Faith is doing what Christ asks us to do. Faith without obedience is dead. You cannot expect to receive the blessing of the remission of sins unless you do what Christ commands: "Take and eat; take and drink." When you obey you let the Word of Christ work through your faith to the forgiveness of your sins.

Faithfulness in coming to the Holy Communion brings you more blessings than you can understand. Be obedient. Be faithful in attendance at the Lord's Table. It is a means of grace.

Lord, help me to believe that when I receive the Sacrament of the Altar, Thou dost come to me with pardon, cleansing, and renewing, according to Thy promise. Amen.

THE SACRAMENT OF THE ALTAR

Sept. 8

Who, then, receives the Sacrament worthily?

He who is well prepared and believes: "Given and shed for you for the remission of sins"

READ: Matthew 26:17-25.

TEXT: But let a man examine himself, and so let him eat of that bread, and drink of that cup. For he that eateth and drinketh unworthily, eateth and drinketh damnation [judgment] to himself, not discerning the Lord's body. I Corinthians 11:28, 29.

♣

"Wash you, make you clean," cried the prophet Isaiah (Isa. 1:16). And that is good advice. "Examine yourself," said the apostle Paul. See that your heart is right. And that is good advice, too.

What do you find when you examine your heart? Sin, of course. Unworthiness, yes. We have all sinned. But if you find also in your heart a humble faith which believes that God can forgive and wants to forgive, and that in the Sacrament Christ gives evidence of God's good intention toward you, then, in spite of your sin, you are worthy and well prepared to come to the Lord's Supper.

O God of pity, God of grace, teach us to know that to be worthy to come before Thee we need to be conscious of our unworthiness but confident of Thy good will toward us and Thy desire to cleanse us, through Jesus Christ, our Lord. Amen.

THE SACRAMENT OF THE ALTAR
The traitor pointed out

Sept. 9

READ: John 13:18-30.

TEXT: Verily, verily, I say unto you, that one of you shall betray Me. John 13:21.

♣

Jesus had to dismiss Judas Iscariot from His sacred presence because, in spite of his privileges, he rejected Jesus' purpose and opposed His true mission. Instead of being a good servant, he tried to make the Master serve his purpose.

Dear friends, the Savior has chosen you to be good stewards of the mysteries of God. You have responded with your confirmation promise, and for the power to perform that promise be determined to maintain an uninterrupted and faithful contact with your Lord through His Word and the Holy Communion. Seek those things which are above where Christ sitteth at the right hand of God; conform your will to His. Fly high in your course above this sordid, sinful world. A good aviator always inspects his plane before he attempts a take-off. So let us examine ourselves continually that we may never once lose altitude but sail serenely and magnificently on until at last beyond the flaming beauty of the sunset we behold the towering splendor of the City of God.

O heavenly Father, help us unto the end of our days to make our ways consistent with the ineffable love of Him who traveled the road to the cross that we might live eternally unto Thee. In Jesus' name. Amen.

THE SACRAMENT OF THE ALTAR

The foot washing

Sept. 10

READ: John 13:1-17.

TEXT: If I wash thee not, thou hast no part with Me. John 13:8.

✣

In the Lord's Supper we have a bequest which benefits us only when we qualify for its reception by our contrition and sincere reliance on God for cleansing and strengthening. To receive the forgiveness of our sins we must have the faith that will enable us to receive what God has provided. In the person of Jesus Christ God provided an object-lesson for Peter through the washing of his feet. Peter misunderstood when he was unwilling to accept the washing of his feet at the hands of the Lord. The Lord had to tell Peter that, if he did not accept that washing, he was also rejecting the cleansing fellowship of Christ. If we accept not the forgiveness of our sins by faith we have no part in the Supper of our Lord but enter into judgment. Let us do as Peter eventually did: accept by faith what God has to offer.

O Thou Christ, wash us and cleanse us from all our sins in Thy precious and holy blood so that by faith we come worthy to eat Thy Holy Supper. Amen.

THE SACRAMENT OF THE ALTAR

A Passover feast

Sept. 11

READ: I Corinthians 5:7-13.

TEXT: Therefore let us keep the feast, not with old leaven, neither with the leaven of malice and wickedness; but with the unleavened bread of sincerity and truth. I Corinthians 5:8.

♣

The apostle tells the Corinthians to "purge out the old leaven." Those who prepared the Passover meal in Old Testament times always did that, but the apostle means the *leaven of sin*.

Man does not have to purify himself. Has not a Passover Lamb been sacrificed for every man? That Passover is Jesus Christ, and by the sacrifice once made for all on the cross He has brought mankind from the bondage of sin to the glorious liberty of the sons of God.

Jesus Christ is our living Passover. In Word and Sacrament His presence is brought to us. For that reason there ought to be in heart where He will come no malice, no evil thoughts, no jealousy, no wickedness. Our heart ought rather to be full of love to God and love for our fellow men.

The plea of the apostle is of great significance when we prepare for the Lord's Supper. This ought to be a feast of genuine, thankful, wholehearted gladness.

Come, Lord Jesus Christ, and make my heart Thy habitation and dwell there forever more. Amen.

THE SACRAMENT OF THE ALTAR

Sept. 12

A thanksgiving feast

READ: Deuteronomy 16:1-8.
TEXT: And He took bread and gave thanks. Luke 22:19.

❧

Someone has pointed out that the words *think* and *thank* come from the same root. A Christian understands that *right thinking* and *sincere thanking* are related, vital parts of his life.

For 1,500 years the Jewish families gathered at a feast of thanksgiving known in sacred history as the Passover. It reminded them that days of slavery were passed. They were a free people, led and guided by the hand of their heavenly Father.

Now in the upper room the Savior was observing the Passover for the last time. How would His disciples fare after He had gone? As a farewell gift He instituted the Last Supper. In this Holy Sacrament we are assured that we are not left alone; that our sins are washed away through Christ's blood. We are saved! Is it possible to think of all these things without responding in thankfulness to our Great Benefactor? Let us *think* and *thank!*

Dear Jesus, we thank Thee that Thou dost give Thyself to us in the Holy Supper. May we approach Thy table with a spirit of true thanksgiving. Amen.

THE SACRAMENT OF THE ALTAR

A fellowship feast

Sept. 13

READ: I Corinthians 12:18-27.

TEXT. We being many are one bread, and one body: for we are all partakers of that one bread. I Corinthians 10:17.

❖

We often speak of the mystical body of Christ. By it we refer not to Jesus' physical body but to ourselves as Christians, united in Him. The mystical body of Christ is the church. It is the communion of believers. "For as the body is one, and hath many members, and all the members of that one body, being many, are one body, so also is Christ. For by one Spirit are we all baptized into one body," I Corinthians 12:12, 13. Through the work of God's Spirit in faith and our common spiritual labors Christians are bound together under their great Lord and Head; especially so through the Lord's Supper. In the Lord's Supper we not only commune with Christ by receiving His glorified body and blood but also through Him our organic ties are strengthened with one another.

When we think, therefore, of the body relationship that exists between all believers, then love should not be difficult but easy and joyous.

Heavenly Father, we thank Thee that we may commune with Christ and through Him with our fellow believers. Grant, therefore, that we may walk humbly with these and with all men at all times. For the sake of Jesus Christ. Amen.

THE SACRAMENT OF THE ALTAR

Sept. 14

A mystical feast

READ: Mark 14:12-25.

TEXT: The cup of blessing which we bless, is it not the communion of the blood of Christ? The bread which we break, is it not the communion of the body of Christ? I Corinthians 10:16.

✤

Why should such a simple thing as eating a morsel of bread and drinking a sip of wine be of importance? It is not a meal sufficient to satisfy hunger and thirst. Yet true believers gather about the Lord's Table as hungry folk come to a feast. And the church has learned by experience that, when a Christian neglects the Sacrament of the Altar, he is in danger of drifting away from the faith; and when the church neglects the Sacrament it becomes weak and famished and unable to do the Lord's work. This is a great mystery, and the world does not understand it.

Jesus said, "I am the bread of life." Here He offers Himself to us in a very special way so that by faith He is really present when we eat of this bread and drink of this cup. No, I cannot understand. I can only believe the words and the promises, and obeying, be blessed.

O Christ, Thou standest at the door of my heart, ready to come in and to sup with me. Let me open to Thee. Come and dwell with me ever. For the salvation of my soul and for Thine eternal glory. Amen.

THE SACRAMENT OF THE ALTAR

A memorial feast

Sept. 15

READ: Luke 22:7-19.
TEXT: This do in remembrance of Me. Luke 22:19b.

♣

Can you ever forget when you first knelt at the Lord's Table? That was a never-to-be-forgotten experience. It was then that you realized more than ever the price Christ paid for man's salvation. We are dearly bought, "Not with silver and gold but with His holy and precious blood."

As a feast of remembrance this Sacrament brings vividly before us the image of the crucified Savior. We see Him on the cross, paying "the wages of sin" for us. He has paid it all. At the Lord's Table He offers us the pardon He won.

> In memory of the Savior's love
>   We keep the sacred feast
> Where every humble, contrite heart
>   Is made a welcome guest.

Gracious Savior, we thank Thee for Thy great love for us sinners. Help us to receive the Holy Supper in true faith that we may effectively memorialize Thy sacrifice. Then strengthen and preserve us unto eternal life. Amen.

THE SEVEN WORDS FROM THE CROSS

Sept. 16

The first word from the cross

READ: Acts 3:12-21.

TEXT: Father, forgive them, for they know not what they do. Luke 23:34.

♣

Those who saw and heard our Master there on the cross that day were moved by nothing so much, it seems, as by this prayer of His for forgiveness to be granted to the men who crucified Him. Forgiveness with God and forgiveness granted for us is not merely a matter of letting bygones be bygones; forgiveness is of the very essence of God's creative love. It changes and re-creates. Christian forgiveness seen in us can be the means, as it was in this case, of making evil or indifferent men look Godward and exclaim with the centurion, "Surely, this is the Son of God."

We have the word from Jesus that we are to love one another even as He loved us. Men and women without the love of Christ in their heart cannot be forgiving persons. This is what we do "more than others." It is our holy duty and privilege to which we are "confirmed."

Father, "Forgive us our trespasses as we forgive those who trespass against us." Fill us, we beseech Thee, with Thy Spirit that we may be drawn closer to Thee and to each other. Amen.

THE SEVEN WORDS FROM THE CROSS

The second word from the cross

Sept. 17

READ: Luke 23:34-45.
TEXT: Today shalt thou be with Me in paradise.
  Luke 23:43.

✤

Today is the important day for salvation. Yesterday is gone. Tomorrow is yet to come. Thus the decision made today will determine the course of the three days. On that fatal day the one thief reviled the Savior of man. The other thief made a decision for his own glory. He humbly, penitently, confidently asked to be remembered, and paradise was promised.

Today is the time to part company with evildoers. Today is the time to resolve to be with our Lord. To be with Him is worth more than the perishable things of the world. The eternal home with Jesus as our host is the assurance from the cross. Today's choice of companions may mean rest or ruin as on that first Good Friday.

Do not revile God's servants. It was dangerous then, and is so to this day. Ask your Savior to remember you, a sinner. He has prepared a place and calls it paradise. To be with Him today and every today as we journey on should be the purpose of every Christian life.

Lord Jesus, Thou art merciful to all who call upon Thee. Remember me as I select my companions for today. Be with me and guide me that today may be a day lived to Thee. Amen.

THE SEVEN WORDS FROM THE CROSS

Sept. 18

The third word from the cross

READ: John 19:23-27.
TEXT: Behold, thy son! ... Behold, thy mother!
John 19:26, 27.

✤

Jesus, who is "fairer than all the children of men," hangs on the cross in unspeakable agony, death on His brow. Why must the Perfect One thus suffer? "He was wounded for our transgressions"—including our transgressions of God's commandment, "Honor thy father and thy mother." Who among us is guiltless in this? Thinking alone of all the sins of disrespect and disobedience of sons and daughters, young and old, what a tremendous load for our Savior to bear!

What a sublime example of loving considerateness He here sets for children to follow. His mother stands beside His cross, the "Simeon sword" (Luke 2:35) piercing her soul. No one understands this better than Jesus, and though steeped in agony, He makes provision for her care, adopting His beloved John as brother and substitute son of Mary.

Tokens of love mean much to parents—and to God!

I thank Thee, Lord Jesus, for Thy great sacrifice. Bless me that I may be faithful in my love to Thee and in all things follow Thy example. Amen.

THE SEVEN WORDS FROM THE CROSS

The fourth word from the cross

Sept. 19

READ: Mark 15:29-38.

TEXT: My God, My God, why hast Thou forsaken Me? Mark 15:34.

✤

As our Savior hung on the cross of Calvary, suffering all the brutalities which men could heap upon Him, there came from the depths of His sorrow-laden soul this anguished cry, "My God, My God, why hast Thou forsaken Me?" Darkness above Him, darkness around Him; but far deeper was the darkness which engulfed His soul as He felt Himself cast into the outer darkness of God-forsakenness. We can never understand it all, but we can know and believe that there He endures what we have deserved; that He suffers the agonies of hell which we should have suffered. He is forsaken that we might never be.

Son! Daughter! Someday your hopes may be crushed; your dreams lie dead; you may feel lonely and forsaken. In those dark moments turn to that cross, cling to that Christ, and you will find in Him a companionship and a power to lead you through trial to triumph.

O Christ, give to me the assurance that through faith in Thee I shall never be forsaken whether in the trials of this life, the struggle of death, or in the days of judgment. Amen.

THE SEVEN WORDS FROM THE CROSS

Sept. 20

The fifth word from the cross

READ: John 19:28-30.
TEXT: I thirst. John 19:28b.

✤

Notice the perfect humility of our blessed Lord as shown by this fifth word from the cross. He, who is the Fount of living waters, who could say, "If any man thirst, let him come unto Me and drink," and who did promise rest for the weary and heavy-laden, has so completely emptied Himself and laid aside His divine power that in the likeness of all mortal men He cries out for a drop of water to slake His thirst. So completely did Christ "take upon Him the form of a servant" and for us men did make Himself in the "likeness of man." Deeper still than any bodily thirst was His thirst, His earnest longing for souls. A burning desire for the salvation of the world was what moved our Savior to pour out His blood upon the cross that so at last He could bring His redeemed people to that place "where they shall hunger no more; neither thirst any more."

O Jesus, unfailing spring of love, who in the giving of Thyself didst say upon the cross, "I thirst," kindle in us a desire for the good and worth while and remove the yearning for all that is evil. Amen.

THE SEVEN WORDS FROM THE CROSS

The sixth word from the cross

Sept. 21

READ: John 19:30-37.
TEXT: It is finished. John 19:30.

✣

It is good to be able to say, "It is finished," when a task is done. Jesus could say, "It is finished," because He had completed the work He had been given by His Father to do. This means He had finished the task of fulfilling God's law to the last detail. It means that He had suffered to the utmost for the sins of the world. It means that the Good Shepherd was now giving His life as the final ransom for His sheep. This declaration of our Lord's is, therefore, our great comfort. We can be absolutely sure that Christ's atonement for our sins is complete. These words are gospel, good news. We accept them in faith to our salvation. We reject them in unbelief to our damnation. If we accept these words at face value we shall someday be able to say with Paul: "I have fought the good fight. I have finished my course. Henceforth, there is laid up for me a crown."

We thank and praise Thee, our Redeemer, for a finished redemption. Help us to accept it in faith. Finish also our sanctification by Thy Spirit until we are fully restored to Thy image. Amen.

THE SEVEN WORDS FROM THE CROSS

Sept. 22

The seventh word from the cross

READ: Luke 24:46-49.

TEXT: Father, into Thy hands I commend My spirit. Luke 23:46.

✣

Behold our Savior now about to lay down His life to pay the last full measure of His devotion to His Father's will! He had lived in full membership with His heavenly Father. A prayer was ever in His heart and on His lips. Even from the bloody cross His first words were a prayer. His last words are a prayer, too. Again He turns to His Father in calm assurance that all is well because all things are in His Father's hands. Death has no terrors for Him. His victory is complete.

Behold yourself. Is your fellowship with your heavenly Father such that it will bear up under the tests of life and of death? Can you with calm assurance say, "Though He slay me, yet will I trust in Him"? Practice prayer so that, living or dying, you may move on to the victory that is the sure possession of those who rely on God through Christ.

O God, the Father of all who trust in Thee, grant me a full measure of faith so that, living or dying, I may turn to Thee with the calm assurance that the victory is mine through the Victor over life and death, even Jesus Christ, my Savior. Amen.

THE BEATITUDES

READ: Luke 6:20-26.

TEXT: Blessed are the poor in spirit, for theirs is the kingdom of heaven. Matthew 5:3.

Sept. 23

♣

Philosophers and human leaders do not reckon humility among their moral virtues, but Christ put it first. The foundation of all other graces is laid in humility. Blessed are those who are conscious of their spiritual poverty, who are of a contrite and humble spirit, who are always in want of God's grace, and who desire to become rich in faith. The Psalmist declares, "The Lord is nigh unto them that are of a broken heart; and saveth such as be of a contrite spirit." Christ was ever opposed to the spiritually proud, to those "just men" who felt no need of repentance, and He told them, "Repent ye." Those who would build high must first lay a sure foundation. Those who rightly humble themselves shall by Him be exalted and shall by Him be made to be heirs of the kingdom of heaven. Paul says, "For ye know the grace of our Lord Jesus Christ, that though He was rich, yet for your sakes He became poor, that ye through His poverty might be rich."

Eternal God and Father, grant unto us such a sense of true humility that our life may be patterned after the likeness of Thine only-begotten Son, and that in lowliness we may be made partakers of that grace which is so freely bestowed upon us through our blessed Lord and Savior, Jesus Christ. Amen.

THE BEATITUDES

Sept. 24

READ: Isaiah 61:1-3.

TEXT: Blessed are they that mourn, for they shall be comforted. Matthew 5:4.

✤

There is a juniper tree for every son of man. Most men hang their harps on the willows. David cried out, "Would God I had died for thee!" Job exclaimed, "Let the day perish wherein I was born!" Jeremiah lamented, "O that my head were waters, and mine eyes a fountain of tears, that I might weep day and night for the slain of the daughter of my people!" Jesus declared, "Blessed are they that mourn, for they shall be comforted." This beatitude grows out of the first; happy are those who are deeply sorry for their sins and about all evil and misfortune. Here is the paradox. How can one be sad and glad at the same time? Paul presents the same problem when he says, "We are troubled on every side, yet not distressed; we are perplexed, but not in despair."

The second half of Jesus' statement holds the answer. *Comforted* means an answer from God. This explains our joy in the midst of sorrow. Our Savior is standing with us; therefore, regardless of outward circumstances or inward state, we are sustained.

Dear Savior, Thou didst say unto Thy disciples, "Ye shall be sorrowful, but your sorrow shall be turned into joy." Strengthen me in the hour of grief that I may go on conquering and to conquer. Amen.

THE BEATITUDES

READ: Psalm 37:1-11.

TEXT: Blessed are the meek, for they shall inherit the earth. Matthew 5:5.

Sept. 25

♣

Youth admires the brave, the bold, the daring. Meekness appears to be the very opposite of these. One would expect to find the meek man pushed around, taken advantage of, deprived of his portion of the earth. Many are careful to avoid developing the quality of meekness, thinking it to be almost the same as weakness.

The greatest Teacher who ever lived on this earth said, "Blessed are the meek, for they shall inherit the earth." When Jesus came to the Holy City, greeted by the cries of the multitude, He came in the guise of a meek King. Yet no stronger, more determined person ever lived. His kingdom is the largest and the most powerful in the world. How grateful we should be to have a place in it!

Jesus' meekness meant "going all out" for God and for others but never for self. Because Jesus is meek He is interested in the least of those in His kingdom. He says: "Come unto Me, all ye that labor and are heavy laden and I will give you rest. Take My yoke upon you, and learn of Me; for I am meek and lowly in heart, and ye shall find rest unto your souls." Meekness is a virtue of real worth. Let us cultivate it.

My Father in heaven, help me to be meek and unselfish. May I not seek the best for myself but put others first; through Jesus Christ, my Lord. Amen.

THE BEATITUDES

Sept. 26

READ: Isaiah 55:1-5.

TEXT: Blessed are they which do hunger and thirst after righteousness, for they shall be filled. Matthew 5:6.

✤

Hunger and thirst are natural and necessary functions. They tell you that your body needs food and drink. So it is with the soul. Since it was made by God in His own image its natural hunger and thirst should be for the food God intended for it.

Jesus was talking with some Jews one day about bread. "My Father," He said, "giveth you the true bread from heaven." They said unto Him, "Lord, evermore give us this bread."

Jesus said, "I am the bread of life; he that cometh unto Me shall never hunger; and he that believeth on Me shall never thirst."

How wonderful to know that we need never to be unhappy or discontented or to have hunger of the soul! How foolish to seek after things that do not satisfy! They that hunger and thirst after righteousness shall be filled. Try it and see.

O God, who hast made us for Thyself and given us souls that can receive and enjoy the better things, help us to seek first the kingdom of God that, as Christ has promised, all other things may be added unto us. Through Jesus Christ, the Bread of life. Amen.

THE BEATITUDES

READ: James 2:1-13.

TEXT: Blessed are the merciful: for they shall obtain mercy. Matthew 5:7.

Sept. 27

✣

To be merciful is to be kindhearted even to those who may not deserve our kindness. It is not natural for human beings to be merciful. By nature we find it easy to be cruel, unforgiving, and ready to take revenge. We find it hard to forgive and forget.

Yet God tells us here that we, as His children, must be merciful. Only Christians can be truly merciful, for their heart has been changed by God, and hatred has been replaced by love. To the Christian, God's will is also more important than his own will.

A Christian is merciful to others because God was first merciful to him. God saved him when he deserved punishment and not salvation, and so the Christian is anxious to show that same merciful spirit toward his fellow men. Furthermore, Jesus' parables teach that only the merciful can receive and profit by God's mercy.

"Be ye therefore merciful as your Father also is merciful."

We thank Thee, dear Father, that Thou hast not dealt with us as we have deserved. Make us to love others as Thou dost love them, to be as merciful to them as Thou art to us. Amen.

THE BEATITUDES

Sept. 28

READ: Psalm 15.

TEXT: Blessed are the pure in heart: for they shall see God. Matthew 5:8.

✤

In all ages men have longed for God, for clean hands and pure hearts, for holiness without which no man shall see the Lord. They have prayed, "Create in me a clean heart, O God, and renew a right spirit within me," because they felt that the only thing that stands between them and God and happiness is sin, sin in the heart, the very source of life. "Keep thy heart with all diligence, for out of it are the issues of life." How, then, can we be chaste and pure in our words and our deeds when the "heart is deceitful above all things and desperately wicked," and, "out of the heart proceed evil thoughts, murders, adulteries, fornication"? Right here is where we need God most. He alone can give us a *new heart* and put a *right spirit* within us; He can make us wholehearted, truly sincere toward Him. Jesus does not want part of us, a divided loyalty. He wants a "pure product," a heart cleansed of its impurities and rival interests. God's Spirit will do that in our life—if we let Him—and the result will be seeing and knowing God as He is in all His glory.

Dear Father in heaven, give me that faith in, love for, and hope through Christ that will enable me to overcome the temptations of the devil, the world, and the flesh and to live only to Thee. Amen.

THE BEATITUDES

READ: Matthew 5:43-48.

TEXT: Blessed are the peacemakers: for they shall be called the children of God. Matthew 5:9.

Sept. 29

✦

Jesus, our precious Savior, is the true source of all peace. He came to establish peace in a sinful world by establishing it first in the individual's heart. The cause of strife and unrest in the world is the result of man's alienation from God through disobedience and refusal to accept Jesus Christ. From God comes love. Men oppose this love and hence have no peace. Christ is our peace, and in Him we are to sow love where there is hatred, urge peace where there is strife. We are also to go about proclaiming His peace by living like Jesus.

This is a service that will be richly rewarded. The reward is beyond great measure! "They shall be called the children of God." Who will call us children or sons of God? Let John answer, "Beloved, behold what manner of love the Father hath bestowed upon us that we should be called the sons of God." But never forget—peace takes more than wanting; it requires "making," first by God and then by ourselves.

Dear Father in heaven, create in us the mind of Jesus, our Lord and Savior, that we, like Him, may be ambassadors of peace. In His precious name we pray. Amen.

THE BEATITUDES

Sept. 30

READ: II Corinthians 4:7-18.

TEXT: Blessed are they which are persecuted for righteousness' sake: for theirs is the kingdom of heaven. Matthew 5:10.

♣

The world is going away from God. We want to go the other way, toward the kingdom of heaven. We may know that we are going in the right direction when the world pushes us around and persecutes us. It makes us understand the cruelty, sin, and meanness of the world.

Life is like a game in which you develop your strength against the opposing team. All the coaching in the world does not make you an efficient player until you come up against the other team. So is the strength of the Christian revealed by the persecution of the world.

It was said of Jesus that He, the Captain of our salvation, was made perfect through suffering. This means that we are able to see the perfection of Jesus even when all the evil of the world tempted and tried and persecuted Him. He still kept going in the right way and could say, "I have overcome the world."

The promise to you and to me is this, "Be thou faithful unto death, and I will give thee a crown of life." Then ours will be the kingdom of heaven.

O God of all grace, who hast called us unto eternal glory by Christ Jesus, grant that after we have suffered a while we may be made perfect, established, strengthened, and settled in our faith. Amen.

THE BEATITUDES

READ: I Peter 4:12-19.

TEXT: Blessed are ye, when men shall revile you [reproach you], and persecute you, and shall say all manner of evil against you falsely, for My sake. Rejoice and be exceeding glad, for great is your reward in heaven. Matthew 5:11, 12.

Oct. 1

♣

While it is true that a good name and reputation is worth more than riches, Jesus teaches us not to base our joy and deepest satisfaction on what other people think and say about us. In fact, He goes a step farther and warns us, "Woe unto you when all men shall speak well of you." If we live according to the ways of the world, and if the people of the world approve of us, there is danger that God disapproves. I will, therefore, seek to know my Savior's will and His plan for my life through the study of His Word and through meditation and prayer. Then by His help I will strive to follow His pattern and have His approval regardless of what men say or think about me. "We ought to obey God rather than men."

Blessed Lord Jesus, help me to be faithful to Thee and to Thy way of life in the midst of the world. Give me grace to be a witness for the truth in a kindly spirit even when good friends oppose it. Fill me with courage and love. Amen.

SINGING

Oct. 2

Service in singing

READ: Ephesians 5:14-20.

TEXT: Let the word of Christ dwell in you richly in all wisdom; teaching and admonishing one another in psalms and hymns and spiritual songs, singing with grace in your hearts to the Lord. Colossians 3:16.

✤

Our church is a singing church. From our first days in Sunday school we have learned to sing "psalms, hymns, and spiritual songs." As we grow older, many of these songs become very dear to us.

We must not keep these songs to ourselves, nor let other, so-called "popular" songs, take their place. Let us sing them as we go about our work helping mother and father at home. Let us sing together with our brothers and our sisters and with our playmates and our friends. We can also sing for people who can't go to church very often, for those who are sick and shut-in. By doing these things we "sing with grace in our hearts unto the Lord."

Let us remember that our voices belong to God, and that we should praise Him in word and in song.

"Take my voice and let me sing
   Always only for my King;
Take my lips and let them be
   Filled with messages from Thee."

Jesus Christ, even though I may not have a beautiful voice, let me use it to praise and serve Thee from a heart that is pure. Amen.

SINGING

Confession in singing

READ: Romans 15:4-13.

TEXT: For this cause I will confess to Thee among the Gentiles, and sing unto Thy name. Romans 15:9.

Oct. 3

✣

The word "confess" here means to bear witness, to testify, to tell. Long before men wrote stories they sang them, and they were remembered. The Psalms were written for worshipers to sing. The church has used song to witness to its faith. Luther wrote both words and music of hymns, for he understood the value of song in witnessing to the truth. It has been said that the Reformation sang its way into the hearts of the people. Today the gospel story is effectively told everywhere by song.

For we have so much to sing about: the goodness, greatness, grace, and mercy of God, His love and compassion, and His wonderful salvation. It is good to have great hymns and to make right use of them in the church, both in understanding the words and in joining in the singing of them. Through all the world the Christian story is being told while we sing,

"I will tell the wondrous story, of the Christ who died for me."

O God, we thank Thee that Thou dost give Thy children songs, songs of faith, hope, and victory. Let us sing before all the people and make melody in our heart unto the Lord that the whole world may praise Thee. For Christ's sake. Amen.

SINGING

Oct. 4

The church and singing

READ: Hebrews 2:11-18.

TEXT: In the midst of the congregation will I sing praise unto Thee. Hebrews 2:12b.

✤

Song and worship have always gone hand in hand. Our Christian religion particularly has found music, the language of the heart, a powerful means to express prayer and praise. Christ sang together with His disciples on the night of His betrayal. Paul sang even in the dungeon, and he exhorted his fellow Christians to "make melody in their hearts unto the Lord" in "psalms and hymns and spiritual songs." The church of the Dark Ages forgot this injunction for a thousand years, eliminating congregational singing, and Christian life largely died out. Luther and his followers found Christian song one of the effective means to restore spiritual appreciation and the Christian life. The hymns they gave us are acclaimed universally as the finest of all time. Thy are our heritage, to sing to the glory of God and our own spiritual strengthening. Let us ever be mindful of Isaiah's solemn warning, lest we draw nigh only with our lips when our hearts are far away.

Dear Lord, we thank Thee for the privilege of bringing Thee our prayers and our praise on the wings of song. May we ever worship Thee rightly and sincerely. Amen.

SINGING

Praise in singing

Oct. 5

READ: Psalm 106:1-12.

TEXT: Then believed they His words; they sang His praise. Psalm 106:12.

❖

From the early pages of the Old Testament where we find Moses and the Israelites offering a mighty chorus of praise to God for deliverance from bondage to the book of Revelation where we read of the anthems that perpetually fill the vast arches of the New Jerusalem, we hear again and again of sacred song. We can conclude only that God Himself must surely have devised singing that it might pour out from man's lips as the purest expression of the many emotions that fill his breast. The apostle Paul, who sang praise through many dark nights in Roman prisons, urged the early Christians to "pour forth psalms and hymns and spiritual songs," and so "make melody in their hearts to the Lord!" His wisdom is just as appropriate for us Christians of today, and all of us should avail ourselves always of this noblest means to express our praises and our prayers.

Dearest Lord Jesus, who Thyself didst sing hymns with Thy disciples, fill my heart with such knowledge of Thy precious love that my lips may everlastingly pour forth Thy praise. Amen.

SINGING

Unity in singing

Oct. 6

READ: I Chronicles 16:4-23.

TEXT: Sing unto the Lord, all the earth; show forth from day to day His salvation. I Chronicles 16:23.

✣

Your voice may not have solo qualities, but God wants you to use it to the best of your ability. Perhaps you cannot sing in the choir but will be restricted to sing with the congregation or merely "hum to yourself." Still you can praise God with your voice.

"How many of us ever stop to think
 Of music as a wondrous magic link
 With God; taking sometimes the place of prayer
 When words have failed us 'neath the weight of care.
 Music, that knows no country, race, or creed
 But gives to each according to his need." *Anon.*

It is inspiring to realize that each Sunday Christian families throughout the whole world are gathered in their churches worshiping God in music, singing the same hymns and the beautiful liturgy which is our heritage. Be sure to be a part of that grand chorus!

Oh, Triune God, we unite with all the members of Thy church in singing praises to Thee for the joy that is ours in the knowledge of our salvation, through Jesus Christ, our Savior. Amen.

SINGING

Rejoicing in singing

Oct. 7

READ: Proverbs 29:6-16.
TEXT: The righteous doth sing and rejoice. Proverbs 29:6b.

❦

Were you ever *really* happy? What did you do? You just had to sing; you couldn't help yourself; you had to give some expression to that joy within your heart. When we hear people going about their work singing we know that they must be happy because "singing and rejoicing" go together just as they are together in our Bible verse for today.

There are certain kinds of joy which even the children of the world can know, and there are other kinds of joy which only "the righteous," that is, God's children, can find. Should we not be happy when we remember that God loves us, that He gave His Son to die for us; that we were made God's children in baptism, that we are heirs of everlasting life? Such a joy will want to express itself in song, not in the mere singing of popular song hits, but in the singing of the beautiful hymns of our church.

I am happy, Lord, to be called Thy child. Help me to sing Thy praises in hymns and sacred songs and to rejoice in Thy salvation. Through Christ, Thy Son. Amen.

Oct. 8

SINGING

Faith in singing

READ: Isaiah 52:1-10.

TEXT: Thy watchmen shall lift up the voice; with the voice together shall they sing; for they shall see eye to eye, when the Lord shall bring again Zion. Isaiah 52:8.

✤

To encourage our heart we sing, "My faith looks up to Thee." For assurance of our faith we sing, "How firm a foundation, ye saints of the Lord." When danger threatens, we sing, "A mighty fortress is our God." When we think of the church as one in all the world we sing, "Elect from every nation, Yet one o'er all the earth." When we would think of the divinely appointed purpose of the church we sing, "O Zion, haste, thy mission high fulfilling."

As you in your own church sing these and other great hymns of faith try to imagine that you hear the whole Christian Church on earth singing with you, raising a great anthem of praise. Listen to the church throughout the world singing, singing, singing.

"Great is the Lord, our God, and let His praise be great." Your faith will be strengthened, your zeal rekindled, and your heart thrilled at the grand chorus of faith which is being sung.

O God, let us with heart and voice join in the great assertion of faith and praise which Thy church on earth is singing even as the angelic hosts are praising Thee on high. Through Jesus Christ, our Lord. Amen.

CHRISTIAN LITERATURE: AN AID TO GROWTH

Growth in the love of God

Oct. 9

READ: Ephesians 3.

TEXT: That ye, being rooted and grounded in love, may . . . know the love of Christ, which passeth knowledge, that ye might be filled with all the fulness of God. Ephesians 3:17-19.

♣

Christian literature had its beginning in the letters of the apostles. They were written, as St. Paul says, that men might know the love of Christ which passeth knowledge. Then the Gospels were written, as St. John says, that men might know and love God.

Today there are many forms of Christian literature, Sunday school and church papers, Bible stories, missionary stories, books, and tracts, all of which are useful and should be found in the Christian home. The world uses literature, too, which teaches us nothing and turns our heart away from the truth and the knowledge of God. It is good for us to read good literature that we may discover how great and good is God, and how we may grow in our love of Him.

O Father in heaven, as by Thy Holy Spirit Thou didst inspire men to write for our guidance and instruction, continue, we pray Thee, to put into the heart and the mind of gifted men to write for us those things which will lead us to love Thee more and serve Thee better. Through Jesus Christ, our Lord, who is Himself the living word. Amen.

CHRISTIAN LITERATURE: AN AID TO GROWTH

Growth in love of the Bible

Oct. 10

READ: Revelation 1:1-6.

TEXT: Blessed is he that readeth, and they that hear the words of this prophecy, and keep the things which are written therein: for the time is at hand. Revelation 1:3.

✤

Intimate association is necessary for growth in love. Repeated hearing of a piece of music will bring out the beauty of its melody and its lovely harmonies. In like manner only those can truly love the Bible (God's Word) who associate themselves with it daily. Read your Bible faithfully, and as the Psalmist says, "It will become sweeter also than honey and the honeycomb."

Go to God's house Sunday after Sunday; listen attentively to the preaching of God's Word, and you will grow more and more appreciative of the sweet tones of the Savior's voice; you will rejoice in the beauty of His promises. Do these things, for your time on earth is short.

But all this reading and this hearing will not bring the desired blessing unless you "keep those things that are written therein."

Dear Father, help me to love Thy Word so that I shall gladly hear and learn it. May Thy Holy Spirit engender love in my heart for Thee and Thy Word. For Jesus' sake. Amen.

CHRISTIAN LITERATURE:
AN AID TO GROWTH

Oct. 11

Growth in love of our home

READ: II Timothy 1:1-10.

TEXT: When I call to remembrance the unfeigned faith that is in thee which dwelt first in thy grandmother Lois, and thy mother Eunice, and I am persuaded that in thee also. II Timothy 1:5.

♣

What a blessed privilege for a child to be reared in a Christian home, to grow up in a distinctively Christian spiritual atmosphere! The apostle Paul calls our attention to this when he speaks of the home in which his spiritual son, Timothy, was reared. He speaks of the faith of Lois, the grandmother, of Eunice, the mother of Timothy, and the influence they exerted upon the life of the young child. A beautiful galaxy of God's children is here presented in grandmother, mother, and child. No wonder Timothy became a great worker together with God in and for His kingdom!

We, the confirmed youth of our beloved Lutheran Church, have, no doubt, come from similar homes. Let us thank God for them. And in a day when the stability of the home is being threatened in so many ways, let us stimulate our love for it by what we read, what we think, and how we live.

Heavenly Father, we thank Thee for the blessings which we enjoy in our home. We pray Thee, preserve them and our love for them. In Jesus' name. Amen.

Oct. 12

CHRISTIAN LITERATURE: AN AID TO GROWTH

Growth in love of the church

READ: Luke 4:16-21.

TEXT: And He came to Nazareth, where He had been brought up; and, as His custom was, He went into the synagogue on the Sabbath day. Luke 4:16.

♣

The Old Testament is one of the greatest books in the world. It tells the story of a people who called themselves the chosen people. Every child knew the stories of Abraham and Moses, of David and the prophets, and of the glorious history of their nation.

The church has these great stories and also the stories of Jesus, of Peter and Paul, of martyrs and preachers and missionaries; of great achievements by the followers of Christ; of works of mercy, hospitals, schools, and homes established by the church because the love of Christ dwells in the heart of Christian believers. The church has gone out into all the world, and we ought to know the stories of its mighty works. And when we read the Christian literature prepared for us to bring us the knowledge of the church and its great works, our heart will be thrilled with a sense of belonging to the greatest institution on earth, the church of the living God.

O Lord God, as I learn of the church and its works of love and truth, help me to grow in love for the church and to serve humbly in any service to which I may be called. For the glory of our Christ. Amen.

CHRISTIAN LITERATURE: AN AID TO GROWTH

Growth in love of our country

Oct. 13

READ: Psalm 33:12-22.

TEXT: Blessed is the nation whose God is the Lord; and the people whom He hath chosen for His own inheritance. Psalm 33:12.

♣

David wrote these words with the Jewish nation in mind. God had chosen it for His own inheritance.

How well these words apply also to our nation! Every child knows something about the marvelous growth and prosperity of our country. Thrifty, home and liberty-loving people from all nations of the earth have come here and have made their contributions. It is because our founding fathers placed God first, and because worship of Him has always been permitted and encouraged that God has so richly blessed us. How we have been favored above other nations! Of course, there are many improvements to be hoped for in our nation, our churches, and in our own heart. And only true repentance on our part can make more room for increased blessings.

The best citizen is the Christian citizen. True patriotism requires that we see our country through God's eyes, and fulfil our obligations as He requires.

Our dear God, who hast loved us and chosen us in Jesus Christ, keep us in right relation to Thee that Thy blessing may flow through us to our nation. Amen.

CHRISTIAN LITERATURE: AN AID TO GROWTH

Oct. 14

Growth in love of our fellow men

READ: Hebrews 11:32-40.

TEXT: This is the message that ye heard from the beginning, that we should love one another. I John 3:11.

✤

St. John the Evangelist, when he was very old, was asked frequently to give a last message and benediction. He would say only, "Little children, love one another."

Indeed, all Christian literature should have this same purpose: to aid us to grow in love of our fellow men. There are no more thrilling stories than the stories of men who for the love of Christ have gone out to give their life for those for whom Christ died, the poor and the ignorant and the sick and the suffering peoples of the earth. We have heroes of the faith, and, like the writer of the Epistle to the Hebrews, time would fail us to tell of them. Missionaries and workers in the slums and among the underprivileged of the earth, great men who loved greatly. When we read of their love we, too, will be moved to love and to serve. Grow in grace and knowledge and love by learning how men, having the love of Christ in their heart, have served.

O loving Christ, who because of Thy love didst serve and minister unto men, fill us with Thy spirit that we may obey Thy new commandment and love one another sincerely. For Thy name's sake. Amen.

CHRISTIAN LITERATURE: AN AID TO GROWTH

Growth in love of heaven

Oct. 15

READ: Colossians 3:1-9.

TEXT: Set your affection on things above, not on things on the earth. Colossians 3:2.

♣

Heaven and earth! In our text we are told that heaven is more important than earth and the things of heaven more important than the things on earth. We are also told to "set our affection" on the things above, the things of heaven. That is, we are to set our heart and our mind on heavenly things.

One of the important ways to do what this text asks of us is to *read* the right kind of literature. Many things that are printed deal altogether with the things of the earth. Some printed material is downright vile and filthy. Christian literature—good Christian books, Sunday school and church papers, prayer books, hymnbooks, and the like—deal with the things of heaven. If we read Christian literature regularly and faithfully we shall find that more and more our thoughts and our heart are set on things above, not on things on the earth. We shall become homesick for heaven. That is a very fine kind of homesickness, for heaven is our true home.

Our Father in heaven, help us more and more to set our heart upon the things of heaven. Increase our love for Thy Word and for all that draws us to heaven. Amen.

OUR GLORIOUS COMMON SERVICE

Oct. 16

Confession and absolution

READ: Psalm 95.

TEXT: O come, let us worship and bow down: let us kneel before the Lord our Maker. Psalm 95:6.

✤

What a glorious privilege is ours that we may worship the Lord and kneel before our Maker! What a pity that so many must be urged and pushed before they will come to worship! Surely, a Christian will say, "I was glad when they said unto me, Let us go into the house of the Lord."

Just to go and worship is not enough. Much depends upon the spirit in which we enter the house of God. Remember, we have come to meet and commune with the just and holy God. "Draw not nigh hither," said the Lord to Moses, "put off thy shoes from off thy feet, for the place whereon thou standest is holy ground." Certainly, we are told in the Epistle to the Hebrews, "Let us therefore come boldly unto the throne of grace." This, however, we can do only in the consciousness that our sins are forgiven through Christ, our Savior. The confession and the absolution in our Common Service are the true preparation for our worship.

Heavenly Father, instil in me a sense of unworthiness and strengthen my faith in Thy forgiveness, through Jesus Christ, my Savior. Amen.

OUR GLORIOUS COMMON SERVICE

Introit and Gloria Patri

Oct. 17

READ: Psalm 100.

TEXT: Enter into His gates with thanksgiving, and into His courts with praise. Psalm 100:4.

✤

Have you observed that the word *Introit* is very similar to the word *enter?* They are not only similar, they are the same. After the confession of sins and the declaration of forgiveness the pastor in the name of the congregation *enters* the sanctuary, the holy place, to stand before the altar. As he enters, the pastor and the people use the words of a Psalm. Then follows the Gloria Patri, praising God, not as He was known in the Old Testament, but as we know Him: Father, and Son, and Holy Spirit.

How appropriate it is that we should enter only after we are thus prepared! And how fitting that we should praise God the Father who created us; God the Son who redeemed us; and God the Holy Spirit who sanctifies us! Let the meaning of this order of the service and the acts of our worship remind you always of the reason for our coming together in common worship. It is that we may enter into His gates with thanksgiving and into His courts with praise, knowing that our prayers will be acceptable, and that God will bless us.

Let the words of my mouth and the meditations of my heart be acceptable in Thy sight, O Lord, my strength and my redeemer. Amen.

OUR GLORIOUS COMMON SERVICE

The Kyrie

Oct. 18

READ: Matthew 15:21-28.
TEXT: Have mercy on me, O Lord. Matthew 15:22.

✣

The *Kyrie* follows the *Gloria Patri*. Its complete name is *Kyrie eleison,* the words in the original Greek version of the New Testament that signify, "Lord, have mercy." They voice the plea of the Syrophoenician woman. Countless souls in all generations of mankind have turned to God in life's needs, sorrows, and afflictions with the cry, "Lord, have mercy."

That plea has never been in vain when made in humble self-surrender to God and coupled with spirit-wrought faith in His Word.

God's mercy is offered in Christ wherever the gospel is preached in truth, and the Holy Sacraments are properly administered.

My soul, in public worship and private devotion seek God's mercy, and you will find it.

O Thou for sinners slain, let it not be in vain that Thou hast died! Thee for my Savior let me take; my only refuge let me make Thy wounded side. Amen.

OUR GLORIOUS COMMON SERVICE

Gloria in Excelsis and Collect

Oct. 19

READ: Psalm 51:15-19.

TEXT: O Lord, open Thou my lips, and my mouth shall show forth Thy praise. Psalm 51:15.

✣

Praise is a part of prayer and of Christian experience. In our Common Service we have reached the moment of praise, and we break forth in the Gloria in Excelsis, the song of the angels at the birth of Christ: "Glory be to God on high."

The pastor now blesses the people, "The Lord be with you." The people respond with a prayer for the pastor, "And with thy spirit." Thus pastor and people with united hearts are ready for the prayer we call the Collect, the common prayer of the congregation, expressing the thought of the Gospel and the Epistle and the circumstances of the season and the day.

Not only in the congregation but in lonely and difficult situations believers have been moved to worship. I shall never forget giving the Holy Communion to an aged lady blind and deaf for twenty-three years. When she received the Communion she knew I was one of God's undershepherds, and she opened her lips to bless me and to praise God for His goodness.

"Glory be to God on high." Let us worship God in prayer, praise, and thanksgiving.

Blessed Lord, have mercy upon us and accept our praise, for Thou only art holy; Thou only art the Lord. Amen.

OUR GLORIOUS COMMON SERVICE

Oct. 20

Epistle and Gospel

READ: I Corinthians 2:1-13.

TEXT: God, who commanded the light to shine out of darkness, hath shined in our hearts, to give the light of the knowledge of the glory of God in the face of Jesus Christ. II Corinthians 4:6.

♣

The truths and the facts we learn are not useful to us until we apply them to our life situations. In our worship service each Sunday we hear the Gospel story. We learn of Christ, who is the Way, the Truth, and the Life.

We also listen to the Epistle, which tells how the apostles and evangelists brought to men and explained the gospel story that it might be applied to their life.

And so we may get the entire story of the life of Christ and practical applications of the gospel to our life, we have the lessons of the church year that we may learn of His birth, His growth, His ministry, His sufferings, death, and resurrection. It is well for us to be faithful and regular the whole year through in our attendance upon the Word, for thus we hear the whole gospel and see its application to men.

We thank Thee, O God, for the revelation of Thy will and grace in the life of Jesus Christ and for the bringing of the gospel to us through the writings of evangelists and apostles. Let the light shine upon us that there be no darkness in our souls. Through Jesus Christ, Thy Son, our Lord. Amen.

OUR GLORIOUS COMMON SERVICE

Sermon and Offertory

Oct. 21

READ: Romans 10:9-17.

TEXT: So then faith cometh by hearing, and hearing by the word of God. Romans 10:17.

♣

To have faith means to trust in our Redeemer, to rely on Him unconditionally. The Christian's hallmark is faith. Faith is an active power. It can grow and can dwindle. Hence the admonition, "Examine yourselves, whether ye be in the faith," II Corinthians 13:5.

How is faith brought about? Paul says, by hearing. Christ commanded to preach the gospel of salvation to all mankind. Each Lord's Day offers the opportunity to hear the good tidings and learn of the good and gracious will of God. Our duty is to listen attentively. The sermon is not for entertainment; it shall ground us in faith, increase our faith. Such hearing comes through the message about Christ. It depends on our attitude toward the word of God whether, "Christ dwells in our heart by faith," Ephesians 3:17.

The congregation therefore responds to the sermon by singing the offertory, "Create in me a clean heart, O God, and renew a right spirit within me." (Psalm 51:10-12).

Dear Lord, open our hearts to hear Thee and trust in Thee. Thou hast the words of eternal life, and when Thy servants proclaim Thy gospel, help us through Thy Spirit to keep it and increase our faith! Amen.

OUR GLORIOUS COMMON SERVICE

Holy Communion

Oct. 22

READ: Luke 22:7-20.
TEXT: This do in remembrance of Me. Luke 22:19c.

✤

Holy Communion is for all who desire spiritual strengthening and assurance of fellowship with the Lord. Christ invites us to commune frequently when He says, "This do." He also tells us how to commune, "in remembrance of Me." We are to remember His love, agony, suffering, and death and the awfulness of our guilt with the assurance, however, that our penalty has been fully paid by Him. To erase the least shadow of doubt He gives us His body and His blood to eat and to drink. Through this gift of love He strengthens our faith and our love in Him, and by entering into the most intimate union with Him we renew the bond of Christian love with all the saints in heaven and on earth. Here the Lord also offers us the opportunity to confess, honor, and praise Him before men, as St. Paul says, "As often as ye eat of this bread, and drink of this cup, ye do show the Lord's death till He comes."

Lord Jesus, grant that I remain true to Thee. When temptations assail me, may I remember Thee. Let me be a frequent and worthy guest at Thy table. Amen.

THE GREAT I AMS

READ: John 8:46-59.

TEXT: Jesus said to them, before Abraham was, I AM. John 8:58.

Oct. 23

In the mount of the burning bush Moses asked God by what name He was to be known. God replied: "I AM that I AM. Say that I AM hath sent you."

So when Jesus said to the questioning Jews, "Before Abraham was, I AM," they understood the tremendous meaning of those words. Jesus was saying, "I AM. I lay claim to the name which you say belongs to God alone."

All through the Gospels we find great I AMS as though Jesus was trying to bring down to our level of understanding the wonderful meaning of this term, I AM. I AM the only real existence, upon which all other existence depends.

In John 6:35 He says: "I AM the Bread of life. He that cometh to Me shall never hunger; and he that believeth on Me shall never thirst."

There are other great I AMS. They give us a little understanding of the glory and the beauty and the wonder of the existence of our Lord Jesus, by whom all things were made, and without whom nothing was made.

O Christ, who art all things to those who trust in Thee, let me commit my life to Thee, for Thou art able to supply all my needs, now and evermore. Amen.

THE GREAT I AMS

Oct. 24

READ: John 1:1-9.
TEXT: I am the light of the world. John 8:12.

✤

A magnificent word! Spoken either by a self-deluded enthusiast or a person high above all human experience, God. You have to make a choice. Blessed he who chooses Him as his Lord and God. Not so much His words, matchless though they will ever be, but the divine "I," His person, sacrifice, and resurrection make Him the world's light. Light kills germs and brings health and life although many prefer the closed shutters of stuffy dens of sin. Light melts ice and wakes spring flowers and slumbering seeds to new life, but the same sunlight also hardens the clay and produces Death Valley. Only he who follows Me, Jesus said, "shall not walk in darkness but have the light of life." Only he who prayerfully uses this light will be warmed, guided, blessed by it. Otherwise it will destroy him.

Lord Jesus, Thou light of the world, melt the icy crust of my sins, awake in me a new life, and keep me away from the utter darkness of hell. Amen.

THE GREAT I AMS

READ: John 10:1-10.
TEXT: I am the door. John 10:9.

Oct. 25

✣

Jesus as the door provides for us an entrance into the kingdom. Through Him alone we enter upon a nobler, more meaningful life. Through Jesus we come to God, and God comes to us.

Jesus gives protection. As a door keeps out thieves and robbers, so Jesus as the door protects us from the evil powers that destroy the soul. He is our Savior who saves us from sin, death, and hell. His love offers us forgiveness that frees us from despair and remorse.

Jesus as the door symbolizes activity. "He shall go in and out and find pasture," said He. We go in for rest and inspiration; we go out to serve. It is a free life because we have fellowship with both God and man.

May Jesus open to us that abundant life with God that means joy now and peace and happiness throughout eternity.

O Lord Jesus, Thou who art the door to God and eternal life, open to us that we may enter upon that abundant life that shall have no end. Amen.

THE GREAT I AMS

Oct. 26

READ: John 10:11-18.
TEXT: I am the good shepherd. John 10:14.

♣

What an amazing assertion, this statement of Jesus, "I am the Good Shepherd!" What an abundance of loving concern it carries for the sheep of His fold! The Good Shepherd who has bought His flock with the price of His precious blood is ever leading, feeding, and keeping watch over it with tender care. When a sheep has gone astray, He seeks to find and bring it back to the fold. David of old who believed in Him and prophesied of Him exclaims joyously in the Twenty-third Psalm, "The Lord is my Shepherd, I shall not want!"

Could you, my dear friend, ever forget your Good Shepherd? By His grace you have been redeemed, and in holy baptism you have been returned to the Shepherd and Bishop of your soul. In your confirmation you have gladly promised to remain His forever. With Him you will always find security, peace, and joy. How happy you can be!

O Lord Jesus, my good and faithful Shepherd, I thank Thee that Thou hast redeemed me! By Thy grace keep me from going astray and let me be Thine forever! Amen.

THE GREAT I AMS

READ: John 11:1-25.
TEXT: I am the resurrection and the life. John 11:25.

Oct. 27

✤

What do these words of Jesus mean? They mean that no man lives except by the will of the Lord. He is the life. "Without Him was not anything made that was made." They mean that, when the dead arise on the last day, it will be because He raises them. He is the resurrection. They mean that, if I am His friend, and He is my Savior, I need fear nothing. Sickness and death will be my lot in time, but it does not matter since Jesus is my Friend. When the right time comes, He will say the word, and my body will rise from the dead, and my soul once more dwell in my body. This time it will be forever. No more death, no more pain, no more sin! Peace and joy and love in the presence of my King who died that I might live will be my portion. So I can say with St. Paul, "I am persuaded that neither death nor life . . . shall be able to separate us from the love of God, which is in Christ Jesus, our Lord."

Lord Jesus, I am Thine. While I live in this world I will live to Thee, and when I die I will give myself, body and soul, into Thy hands, for Thou art the Lord, my God. Amen.

THE GREAT I AMS

Oct. 28

READ: John 14:6-14.

TEXT: I am the way, the truth, and the life. John 14:6.

✤

The end of life is the gateway to eternity. In eternity there are two places which we can enter, heaven or hell. There is a road through life leading to each. We can't get to heaven by taking the road to hell, nor shall we go to hell if we take the road to heaven. We need help to find the road to heaven. We can find the road to hell without help.

Thomas asked about the road to heaven. Jesus answered him, "I am the way, the truth, and the life." He didn't only tell him where to go and how to reach heaven, but that He Himself was the way to heaven. That was an amazing assertion, but a true one, for Jesus is that way. When we believe in Jesus and live daily with Jesus we are on the road to heaven. And all along the way we find truth centering in Him. Life is no longer a question mark; it has found its purpose in Him who has made us truly alive.

Dear Lord, we thank Thee for showing us the way to heaven. Help me so to live this day that I will not lose the way nor depart from truth nor lose my hold on life. Amen.

THE GREAT I AMS

READ: John 15:1-8.
TEXT: I am the vine, ye are the branches. John 15:5a.

✣

Cut a branch from a vine, and it will wither and die. Separate the disciple from Jesus, and he will die spiritually. He may still prosper in the world, but his spiritual life will be gone. Saving faith is not merely intellectual knowledge about certain religious things; it is not even appreciation of the salvation in Christ; it is nothing less than intimate communion with Christ.

As husband and wife are one, so Christ and the believer are one. In fact, Christ lives in the heart of the believer. Take that literally. The invisible though ever-present Jesus is the source of our spiritual life just as life streams from the vine into the branches. This makes it imperative that the disciple avoid everything harmful to his relation with Christ, and that he do everything which sustains that life which derives from Him.

Fount of every blessing, source of all spiritual life, Jesus, our Savior, keep us unto Thyself that we may truly live and serve Thee in gratitude in time and in eternity. Amen.

OVERCOMING

Oct. 30

READ: Revelation 2:1-7.
TEXT: To him that overcometh I will give to eat of the tree of life. Revelation 2:7.

✣

Have you ever noticed those signs, "Why not? Everybody's doing it!" Although few people buy those things, many of them think that way. Maybe some of your chums have that idea of life—"follow the crowd"—"the majority is right"—"express yourself." Maybe you have had it yourself at times, but our verse points us to something higher and better than animal life. It points us to *real life*. You are young, you want to enjoy life. Nobody wants you to enjoy it more than Jesus. Find it in Him.

But do you notice the words, "To him that overcometh"? That means a battle! You ask, "With whom?" Have you noticed how often you want to do evil, and how seldom you care to pray? That is the devil fighting against your accepting Christ as your life. Don't fight him alone, you can't win. Pray to Jesus in such moments to be your strength. Rely on Him, and you shall eat of the tree of life.

Dear Lord Jesus, I desire that life which can satisfy all my wants. I pray Thee, be my strength that I may overcome. Amen.

OVERCOMING

READ: Revelation 2:8-11.

TEXT: He that overcometh shall not be hurt of the second death. Revelation 2:11.

Oct. 31

✤

These words of our Lord Jesus indicate that there is something for a Christian to overcome if he is to be saved from eternal death. He will be opposed by the devil, the unchristian world, and his own sinful impulses. He will meet with persecution and suffering. He must face temptation, unbelief, and wrong religious ideas.

Many a young Christian has started out bravely as a good soldier of Jesus Christ, but when he has found out how strong his enemies are he has surrendered to the foe. It is not enough to start the Christian life, no matter how good the start.

Notice that word *overcometh*. It speaks to us of patience and endurance and steadfastness. It takes more than a vague longing or a weak desire to go to heaven. The death of total, permanent separation from God awaits those who do not find Christ and persevere in Him.

Who, then, is it that overcometh? Every Christian will overcome if he does not fall away from the faith. There is no defeatism in true Christianity.

Dear Lord Jesus, we thank Thee that Thou hast said, "Be of good cheer, I have overcome the world." We thank Thee that we may say, "And this is the victory that hath overcome the world, even our faith." Amen.

OVERCOMING

Nov. 1

READ: Revelation 2:12-17.

TEXT: To him that overcometh will I give to eat of the hidden manna, and I will give him a white stone, and in the stone a new name. Revelation 2:17.

✣

Here is a threefold promise: *the hidden manna, the white stone,* and a *new name.* The first and the last appear to be the most important. The middle one alludes perhaps to some secret mystery of evil in the city of Pergamos and is set in contrast to the promise here of a secret mystery of life to the faithful church.

The faithful church is secretly preserved. The manna which fell from heaven in the wilderness suggests the symbol of her heavenly food, and those who feed on it shall experience complete satisfaction. Normally physical hunger is satisfied for only a few hours; then the need for food reoccurs. Not so with this food because He gives Himself as a perpetual answer to need: "I am that bread of God."

The East attaches great importance to names. Names become condensed expressions of character and calling. Here a new name is promised because of a walk with Christ, and thus the possessor becomes a citizen of another realm which only he knows.

Help us, O Lord, to fight the good fight of faith in the confident hope that Thou wilt at last receive us unto Thyself, who livest and reignest with the Father and the Holy Ghost, ever one God, world without end. Amen.

OVERCOMING

READ: Revelation 2:18-29.

TEXT: He that overcometh and keepeth My works unto the end, to him will I give power. . . . and I will give him the morning star. Revelation 2:26-28.

Nov. 2

✣

Energy and action are qualities of life. Properly directed, they will lead to rich rewards.

Spiritual life must also reveal these qualities. Spiritual life is not static. The word *overcometh* in the text summons the Christian to action.

For the right action Christ is our example and our guide. His life is a driving force against sin and all that estranges us from our heavenly Father. Follow Him—forgiving, loving, but ever unrelenting against sin.

This is not beyond us when we accept Him in faith. With Him we can overcome, for His power conquers all. "I have overcome the world," He tells us.

Rich are our rewards as we overcome temptations and sin. In overcoming we retain the works and the blessings of Christ. Power and the morning star, the brilliant goal so far beyond us now, shall be ours. Within this range all things are possible. Now and on to eternity we can hourly and daily be filled with an abundance of blessing.

Father in heaven, fill us with the Holy Spirit to overcome all sin and temptation that Christ, our Savior, may abide in us and we in Him. Amen.

OVERCOMING

Nov. 3

READ: Revelation 3:1-6.

TEXT: He that overcometh, the same shall be clothed in white raiment; and I will not blot out his name out of the book of life, but I will confess his name before My Father. Revelation 3:5.

♣

Life is a struggle. Temptations constantly try you. Your whole thought and energy must be given to the winning of the game or the battle. Yet ever present is the knowledge of what comes after—the cleansing and refreshing shower, the clean clothing, the pleasant fellowship, the good word from the coach, and the assurance that your name will be remembered as one who played a clean, hard game, who put everything he had into it. Because you know that you play harder, fight more bravely, try more earnestly.

St. John was trying to encourage his fellow believers in these messages to the churches. They were having a difficult time of it. There were few to encourage them. But remember this, St. John writes, "The Lord Jesus says, To him that overcometh the same shall be clothed in white raiment; and I will not blot his name out of the book of life, but will confess his name before My Father." What greater reward can we ask than this? Let us so fight the good fight of faith that we may overcome.

Give me, O Lord, a strong and a brave heart for the battle of life. Help me by Thy good Spirit to stand fast evermore. Through Jesus Christ, my Helper. Amen.

OVERCOMING

READ: Revelation 3:7-13.

TEXT: Him that overcometh will I make a pillar in the temple of My God. Revelation 3:12.

Nov. 4

✣

Our text suggests struggle and victory. Victory apart from struggle is impossible. As a sober-minded youth you are determined to overcome, cost what it may. The enemy you must overcome is sin beginning with your own personal life. Remember that the seemingly small and apparently insignificant sins are your deadliest enemy. The postconfirmation years are the most crucial time of life, for at this point the enemy exerts his utmost power to defeat you. Are you depressed by past defeats? Friend, do not lose courage. You shall overcome, not by any effort on your own but by faith in the word committed to you, "And they overcame him by the blood of the Lamb, and by the word of their testimony," Revelation 12:11.

And look at the prospect for the victor—glorious distinction in God's presence. However weak and unimpressive his life may be here, the "overcomer" shall be a pillar in the eternal temple of God.

My God and my Father, I want to overcome sin, but I have not the strength. Grant Thou me grace to trust in Thy Word for strength. Amen.

OVERCOMING

Nov. 5

READ: Revelation 3:14-22.

TEXT: To him that overcometh will I grant to sit with Me in My throne. Revelation 3:21.

✣

We Christians need to remember who is the captain of our salvation. He is the strong Son of God, the Lord of glory, the King eternal. Though He has been in all points tempted just as we are tempted He overcame the world. He has been exalted by God the Father. What, then, does He promise us?

He promises us the marvelous privilege of sitting with Him on His throne, in the very presence of God the Father and the entire company of heaven. This is the reward of being faithful unto death and overcoming. And He is able to fulfil His promise.

I can't imagine *all* that means. No one can. But it does mean this, that I shall share His victory, enjoy His triumph, and be forever in the happy company of my Lord and of those who have overcome the evil of the world by the power of His might.

He will help me to overcome because He wants me to share with Him the eternal blessings of His kingdom.

O Lord Jesus Christ, who dost offer to those who overcome such joys as pass man's understanding, be near to help me in all trials and temptations that I may be found faithful even unto the end, for Thy name's sake. Amen.

A SUCCESSFUL LIFE

My habits

READ: Galatians 5:16-26.
TEXT: But the fruit of the Spirit is . . . temperance. Galatians 5:22, 23.

♣

An act repeated again and again becomes a habit. If the deed is good, the habit will be good. If it is bad, the habit will be bad.

We are thinking today of the good habit of self-control, which we learn by being temperate in our actions, our thought, and our speech. If we think hastily, speak rashly, or act violently we are intemperate and may hurt both ourselves and others.

It is good to be temperate in our use of food and drink. Excessive indulgence is harmful. Habits are meant to be our servants, but they can become our masters, such as the habit of drink. Here we should be very careful, for the Word of God says that no drunkard shall inherit the kingdom of heaven.

Paul says that the Holy Spirit produces good habits like fruit, in lives which are surrendered to Him. He names nine wonderful virtues or habits, and one of them is temperance. Yield to the Spirit through the Word of God, and He will work this wonder in your heart, to make you the possessor of good habits.

O Holy Spirit, develop in me those habits which are well pleasing in Thy sight that I may know to do always the right thing in the right way at the right time after the example of our Lord Jesus Christ. Amen.

A SUCCESSFUL LIFE

Nov. 7

My amusements

READ: Psalm 1.

TEXT: Blessed is the man that walketh not in the counsel of the ungodly. Psalm 1:1.

♣

Blessed means "happy." My heavenly Father wants me, His child, to be happy. He has placed in my heart a desire for pleasure. He has made it possible for me to satisfy this desire by taking part in amusements.

Some amusements are sinful, and God punishes those who take part in them. Ungodly people do not keep God's Word nor do His will. Some of them find satisfaction in leading other people into sinful amusements which bring them sadness instead of happiness.

There are many amusements in which I can take part without harming my body, mind, or soul; without giving offense to my neighbor; or without dishonoring God. There are good books, magazines, programs, and music that I can enjoy by myself. There are games, puzzles, contests, and clean motion pictures as well as many kinds of outdoor recreation that I can enjoy with Christian friends. I will remember the words of a wise man who said: "Happiness is unrepented pleasure."

Lord Jesus, lead me to choose only those amusements which are pleasing to Thee and good for me. Help me to shun the counsel of the ungodly who would rob me of happiness. Amen.

A SUCCESSFUL LIFE

My vocation

Nov. 8

READ: Genesis 3:8-21.
TEXT: In the sweat of thy face shalt thou eat bread. Genesis 3:19.

✣

God placed man in Eden to "dress it and to keep it." After Adam had been driven out of the garden, work was still a privilege, but it involved a strain, a struggle against hardship that he had not known before. God now has something for all people to do, and when we work faithfully we are in this respect like God, for Jesus said, "My Father worketh hitherto, and I work." The satisfaction that comes with the consciousness and the acknowledgment of work well done is called success.

As man lived on in the world he found many things to be done. He found also that God had endowed people with different talents so that all might enjoy their labor, however different their activities. When we do the work for which we are best fitted by our abilities and interests we may be said to follow our vocation, and when we pursue that vocation with the intent of serving God and our fellow men we shall be blessed, and successful, and happy.

Dear heavenly Father, help me to thank Thee for life and for the opportunity of doing what Thou hast planned for me. Graciously direct and strengthen me for Jesus' sake. Amen.

A SUCCESSFUL LIFE

My friends

Nov. 9

READ: Proverbs 1:10-19.
TEXT: My son, if sinners entice thee, consent thou not. Proverbs 1:10.

♣

One of the weaknesses of professing Christians is the effort to please both God and man. Such compromisers live too close to the world and "walk unworthy of the vocation wherewith they were called." It is right to please others, but when they do wrong and try to entice you to things you know are wrong, learn to give a firm *no*. Else you will soon "walk in the counsels of the ungodly, stand in the way of sinners, and sit in the seat of the scornful." Many a soul has been lost, many a life wrecked by consenting to evil; and not the bitterest tears could wash away the record.

Choose Christians for your friends, remembering that a true friend is one who holds you up to your best. Let Christ be your constant companion and best friend. When your youthful blood is hot with passion, when sinners tempt you, think of Him. He will calm your heart as He stilled the Galilean sea. Say, "yes" to God; say, "no" to sin.

Lord, let me hear and follow Thy voice above the confusing, tempting suggestions of those who would lead me into evil. Strengthen my weak heart that nothing may separate me from Thee now and in eternity. Amen.

A SUCCESSFUL LIFE

My courtship and my engagement

Nov. 10

READ: Matthew 1:18-25.
TEXT: Mary was espoused to Joseph. Matthew 1:18.

♣

Our life is successful to the degree in which God enters into and controls it. This is especially true in the important "growing-up" period when we have dates, fall in love, and eventually become engaged and are married.

In the expectant spirit of Mary and Joseph let us treasure each new experience in the realm of friendship and affection as a God-given opportunity for growth and development. Enter into it joyfully yet *reverently*. May we be aware of the sacredness of each individual personality which we may influence and alive to the promised happiness where body, mind, and spirit are dedicated to God's will.

Before our dating and engagement may we *seek* and then *obey* divine guidance. Daily let us pray for the mind of Christ and His scale of values as we share life with those we love. May the Holy Spirit direct us as our Father moulds our life and helps us to build our future home *now*.

Our heavenly Father, make us to fear and to love Thee that we may be pure in thought and word and need, and in the strength and the love that is Christ's fulfill the plan and the purpose of our life for which our Savior lived and died and rose again. In His name we pray. Amen.

A SUCCESSFUL LIFE

Nov. 11

My marriage

READ: John 2:1-11.

TEXT: And the third day there was a marriage in Cana of Galilee . . . and Jesus also was bidden, and His disciples, to the marriage. John 2:1, 2.

♣

The bridal couple in Cana was fortunate to have Jesus bless their wedded life. It makes a world of difference whether or not Jesus is invited to our weddings and into our homes. He is able to provide for all our needs and to transform our homes into havens of laughter and cheer. There is no spot on earth so beautiful as a home with loving parents and happy, obedient children, united in the bond of Christ's love.

Jesus, no doubt, was a friend of the bridal couple. It is of utmost importance that we learn to know Jesus early in life and begin to seek His guidance when we are young. I recall a home of a young couple. It was a little bit of heaven on earth. Long before their marriage they had sought God's guidance. Already as a boy the young man had prayed God to guide him in finding his life's partner. God heard his prayer and blessed his home. So, too, He will bless the marriage estate of all who seek His aid.

O Christ, our heavenly Bridegroom, grant that the youth of our land may turn to Thee for guidance and grace to build homes that will be an honor to Thee and a blessing to mankind. Amen.

A SUCCESSFUL LIFE

My home

Nov. 12

READ: I Timothy 5:1-16.

TEXT: Let them learn first to show piety at home. I Timothy 5:4.

✦

The home is the foundation of the church and the state and of civilization itself. God gave to Adam and Eve the Garden of Eden, commonly called Paradise, as their first home. As long as it was a pious home where God could "walk and talk to them in the cool of the day" (Genesis 3:8), it was a blessed home. As soon as this home lost its piety, its obedience to God and His Word, it was wrecked, and sin entered, followed by expulsion.

By placing the Fourth Commandment at the head of the list of the second table of stone with its seven commandments on "our duty to our neighbor" God wants us to know that piety in the home requires that we honor, serve, obey, and love *all* our superiors in the home, the state, the church, and the school.

Paul, who wrote these words above to his student Timothy, knew that Timothy had such a pious home. His mother and his grandmother were both pious women. May we have such pious homes where all members show the proper respect for God and holy things, hearing Him, and talking with Him.

Lord, we thank Thee for our home. Preserve in our home a deep respect for Thee and Thy Word and all things holy. We ask it in Jesus' name. Amen.

MISSIONS

Social welfare

Nov. 13

READ: Matthew 25:31-46.

TEXT: Inasmuch as ye have done it unto one of the least of these My brethren, ye have done it unto Me. Matthew 25:40.

✣

"By grace are ye saved through faith." This is a great and glorious truth which we must ever hold fast and high, but it is quite as true that "faith, if it hath not works, is dead." In other words, *saving* faith is *living* faith which expresses itself in *action* such as witnessing for Christ and obeying His word, "Thou shalt love thy neighbor as thyself."

By personal service and by supporting the welfare agencies of the church we should "do good unto all men, and especially unto them who are of the household of faith." The Lutheran Church in the United States maintains about 450 welfare agencies such as children's homes, home finding societies, welfare societies, homes for the aged, institutions for epileptics, sanitoria, hospitals, hospices, deaconess' institutes, and various missions.

Whatever we do for others personally or by supporting such Christian welfare agencies Christ will accept as service unto Himself.

O Lord, give me a kind, sympathetic, and understanding heart so that I may see human need about me and gladly work and share to give relief and comfort. For Jesus' sake. Amen.

MISSIONS

Home missions

Nov. 14

READ: Acts 1:1-8.

TEXT: Ye shall be witnesses unto Me, both in Jerusalem, and in all Judaea, and in Samaria, and unto the uttermost part of the earth. Acts 1:8.

✤

Jesus instructed the disciples as the nucleus of His church to begin their mission work at Jerusalem and then to keep on enlarging the territory until they had reached the uttermost part of the earth. This means that the early Christians began to preach the gospel at home. They then went to the neighboring towns and cities, then to the towns, cities, and nations farther and farther away.

Christian home missions, following the example of the early Christians, is an endeavor to win souls for Christ and gather them into congregations, first in the home neighborhood, then in the next town or city, and then in the towns and cities farther and farther away until the entire country has been covered. The home mission program of the church challenges our interest and demands our prayers and our support.

Heavenly Father, who desirest that every person in America be won for Christ, by the power of the Holy Spirit enable us to spread Thy gospel in every part of our land. Amen.

MISSIONS

Nov. 15

Missions among the Jews

READ: Romans 1:1-16.
TEXT: To the Jew first. Romans 1:16.

✠

What about the Jew? Israel turned away from God in disobedience and finally rejected even the Son of God with the words, "His blood be upon us and our children." How fearfully God's threat (Leviticus 26) and their own words are fulfilled even recent Jewish history tells us plainly.

Is there any hope for the Jew? "Yet for all that . . . I will not cast them away . . . to destroy them utterly and to break My covenant with them, for I am the Lord their God," Leviticus 26:44. We still have the assurance that "the gospel is the power of God unto salvation . . . to the Jew first and also to the Greek."

Think of Jesus' tears when He saw Jerusalem spread out before Him as He was about to make His triumphant entry in the Holy City! Israel is included in the world which "God so loved," and for which Christ died. God makes it plain that He would save also the Jew. Filled with the Spirit of Christ, we are constrained to bring His gospel both to the Jew and to the Gentile. In His name and by His power we must learn to love and to seek the welfare of *all* men.

Lord Jesus, fill our heart with Thy love and the Holy Spirit. Make us willing to bring Thy gospel to Israel also that it, too, may know Thee as Savior and Lord. Amen.

MISSIONS

Missions in India

Nov 16

READ: Mark 16:14-20.
TEXT: And they went forth, and preached everywhere. Mark 16:20.

✠

Our Lord commanded that the whole world should be considered one great mission field. In the text selected we are told that the disciples went everywhere preaching the Word. In India they have a tradition that the Disciple Thomas preached the gospel on their shores. There is even a group of Christians in that country who call themselves the "Thomas Christians." We shall not try to verify this tradition, but India continues to be one of the great mission fields in the world.

We Lutherans have the largest missions in that country. But even if we have a million Christians, what are they among the three hundred and sixty million people who are still without Christ and the gospel?

Mission work in that country is very largely a work for young people. Ordinarily we do not send people to the mission field above the age of thirty. Think it over and in prayer try to find out whether you can qualify as a foreign missionary. The doors are open in India and in many other lands for those who bear the good tidings of the gospel.

O Lord, help us to direct our thoughts to the great good we can do in the world by joining the great Christian throng that is willing to go anywhere and bring the gospel to all people. Amen.

MISSIONS

Missions in China

Nov. 17

READ: John 4:31-42.

TEXT: Lift up your eyes, and look on the fields; for they are white already to harvest. John 4:35.

✤

Their recent war with Japan has shown how remarkable a people the Chinese are. During the war years they built the Burma Road, not with steam shovels, but with picks and shovels and even bare hands. They moved schools and colleges hundreds of miles to escape bombings. They made progress in manufacturing and developed distant and backward parts of the country.

Let us thank God that during these terrible years many Chinese have become Christians. One reason is that many missionaries remained in the country and helped the people in many ways. Another reason is that the Chinese Christian Church has been very active in the alleviation of distress, the treatment of the wounded, the care of the homeless and the orphans, and the promotion of health and reconstruction. The Chinese pastors and the church members have not only maintained the Christian work but have made significant advances.

Heavenly Father, bless the brave, patient, industrious, suffering, and determined millions of China. Bless the Chinese Christian Church and its missionaries, pastors, and leaders. Inspire us to help all Thy children everywhere. Amen.

MISSIONS

Missions in New Guinea

Nov. 18

READ: Isaiah 60.

TEXT: Can the Ethiopian change his skin, or the leopard his spots? Then may ye also do good, that are accustomed to do evil. Jeremiah 13:23.

♣

The only answer to these questions is a decisive *no, he cannot.* In like manner an ungodly person cannot be converted into a pious child of God by his own strength or reason. But while this is impossible with men, with God all things are possible (Matthew 19:26).

A Papuan in New Guinea complained to the visiting mission secretary, saying: "Why do the people in your country call us Papuans *the black?* Our skin is only brown." "However," he added, "we Papuans will not complain because, though our skin is not black, our soul is; the devil made it so with sin and its shame but," he added, "Jesus makes our soul white by His crimson blood, for we know and believe that 'the blood of Jesus Christ His Son cleanseth us from all sin,'" I John 1:7.

Oh, Lord, we thank Thee that Thou cleansest us from all our sin by Thy holy and precious blood and also the Papuans of New Guinea and all the heathen who become Thy children. Bless us, we pray Thee, and all mission work of our church among all people. Amen.

MISSIONS

Missions in Africa

Nov. 19

READ: Acts 8:26-39.
TEXT: **Then Philip opened his mouth ... and preached unto him Jesus. Acts 8:35.**

✤

All human beings descended from the first human being, Adam, whom God created an immortal soul. So all human beings, whether they are dark-skinned or white, have a soul, a soul that never dies. Furthermore, our Savior Jesus Christ has prepared salvation for all colored and dark-skinned people, too. He shed His holy precious blood and died on the cross for their sins also.

This love of Jesus for the souls of the colored races naturally kindles in us followers of Christ a similar love. Our Lord gave us the commission to make disciples of all nations (races). So it becomes our Christian duty to do our part so that the colored races learn to know the good news, too, that Christ has prepared salvation for them also. How can we do our part? By praying for the salvation of the colored races, by supporting with our gifts and our time the mission work which our church does among them in Africa and elsewhere, and, possibly, by going to them ourselves as missionaries.

Increase, O God, my zeal and desire in fulfilling my Christian duty in helping my church to bring the good news of salvation to the natives of Africa and other heathen lands. In Jesus' name. Amen.

MARTIN LUTHER AND OUR GENERATION

Luther and thinking

Nov. 20

READ: Proverbs 23:1-19.
TEXT: As he thinketh in his heart, so is he. Proverbs 23:7.

♣

He is a great thinker who can follow a line of thought straight through to its conclusion without being turned aside by that which does not apply. He is a great thinker who can take profound truths and state them simply. He is a great thinker who recognizes a greater wisdom, even the thoughts of God which are higher than the thoughts of men.

Luther was a great thinker. He was able to put aside all that did not apply to the question, "What is it that makes a Christian?"

He could state great truths so simply as to bring them within the understanding of all. Today, after these centuries, we use his catechism in the instruction of young and old in the church.

With all his powers of mind he recognized the truth of the Word of God and would not permit himself to think otherwise than as the truth was found in that Word.

Yes, Luther was a great thinker. We shall do well to follow his way of thinking rightly, of speaking simply, and trusting fully in the truth of God.

Give us, O Father, hearts and minds controlled by Thy Holy Spirit that we may love truth, think aright, and turn to Thee for knowledge and wisdom even as Jesus, our Lord. Amen.

MARTIN LUTHER AND OUR GENERATION

Luther and truth

READ: John 8:12-32.
TEXT: Ye shall know the truth, and the truth shall make you free. John 8:32.

♣

Luther was, undoubtedly, the greatest man in his generation. He is known as the Great Reformer of the Sixteenth Century. What made him great was his ability to distinguish truth from error; this coupled with a mighty faith, a fearless spirit, a great devotion, and a complete surrender to the will of God made him the prophet of the truth.

Through painful experience Luther came to know the truth that sets men free, namely, that man is justified by faith alone. In anguish of heart his troubled soul had sought relief in the church and performed the works prescribed, but he found peace only when he discovered that "the just shall live by faith," and when faith became for him the sole avenue of escape.

The truth which our faith must grasp is that Jesus Christ is the Way, the Truth, and the Life. "Thou art the Christ, the Son of the living God." For me Thou didst die and rise again and hast become my advocate at God's throne of grace. To know Christ is to know the truth that sets men free.

Dear Jesus, we thank Thee for the revelation of Thy saving truth, and that Thou art our Savior indeed. Give us the faith of Luther and keep us steadfast in Thy truth. Amen.

MARTIN LUTHER AND OUR GENERATION

Luther and courage

Nov. 22

READ: Acts 28:11-31.
TEXT: He [Paul] thanked God and took courage. Acts 28:15.

❖

What a hero was the apostle Paul! Though he knew that death awaited him in Rome "he thanked God and took courage."

How would you like to be a hero? The world honors heroes today. Heroism demands courage. It requires that we stand up for our convictions. This is what Jesus expects of us. No one can be a Christian who has not the faith to stand fast.

What a hero was the great Reformer, Dr. Martin Luther! Recall his statement at the Diet of Worms, "Except I be convinced by the Word of God that what I have spoken and written is false I cannot recant." Luther could never have shown this heroism except for his faith in God. Our heavenly Father can make heroes out of cowards.

The greatest hero of all times was Jesus, our Savior, who endured the cross for us. If we keep our eyes upon Him, strive to imitate Him, and seek His empowerment, we, too, shall have the courage to bear our crosses with fortitude.

Heavenly Father, increase my faith that I may truly trust Thee and have the courage to meet every temptation and trial of life victoriously. Amen.

MARTIN LUTHER AND OUR GENERATION

Nov. 23

Luther and prayer
READ: Psalm 4.

TEXT: I will pray with the spirit, and I will pray with understanding also. I Corinthians 14:15.

✣

True prayer is conversation with God. The desire to pray is the best evidence of a reborn soul. When there was a question as to whether or not it was safe for the prophet of the Lord to visit Saul of Tarsus, the Lord told Ananias of Damascus, "Behold, he prayeth."

Luther, like Paul, was a man of prayer. Like Paul, he, too, failed for a long time to pray aright. He prayed to the Virgin and to the saints. These prayers were ineffective; but when he found Jesus as his Savior and his Mediator with the Father he began to pray in the Spirit and with understanding. Now his prayers availed much. Luther's constant communication with God in prayer explains him as the power he was and still is. While people and prayers do not perform miracles, God does perform miracles for praying people. This Luther discovered at Melanchthon's bedside. Luther told his students that to have prayed well over a lesson is half of the study of the lesson. Let students and others try this with faith and trust.

Jesus, our Lord, teach us to pray aright. Show us how to ask acceptably and how to accept according to Thine own prayer, "Thy will be done." Amen.

MARTIN LUTHER AND OUR GENERATION

Luther and serenity

READ: Isaiah 26.

TEXT: Thou wilt keep him in perfect peace, whose mind is stayed on Thee. Isaiah 26:3.

Nov. 24

✤

It is not so easy in these days to feel secure, especially when the future is so uncertain and full of danger as it is now. We cannot plan ahead so calmly as people did forty years ago. Twice in that time the world has been upset, and now it is again being threatened with upheaval. The very truths of religion and the rules of morality are being questioned, and we are tempted to go with the crowd; but there is One who remains unchanged, God and His holy purposes. We can always rely on Him if we keep our mind fixed on His promises. He is always the final Victor; He will speak the last word, and His plans are all for our good. In the words of the prophet that Luther was fond of quoting, "In quietness and in confidence shall be your strength," Isaiah 30:15.

Grant, O Lord, that amidst the manifold changes of this world my heart may be fixed in Thee. Through Christ, our Lord. Amen.

MARTIN LUTHER AND OUR GENERATION

Nov. 25

Luther and friendship

READ: I Samuel 18:1-4.

TEXT: The soul of Jonathan was knit with the soul of David, and Jonathan loved him as his own soul. I Samuel 18:1.

✣

What Jonathan was to David, Melanchthon was to Luther. They taught together, and together they labored to find and give others the truths of God. The Augsburg Confession is Melanchthon's work but bears the stamp of Luther's faith. They often prayed together to Christ; it proved to be the tie to hold them together.

To play, to hike, to read, to dream with one's friend is fine, but not until friends worship together, spurn what is base, and seek what is high and holy are they friends after the heart of God.

At one time Melanchthon was desperately sick. All signs indicated that death was near. Luther felt that he could not spare his friend nor the church her worker. So he knelt down at Melanchthon's couch and told the Lord that His disciple must live. God heard him; Luther's prayer saved his friend.

Do I pray for my friends? Then my soul is truly knit with theirs.

I thank Thee, Father, for my friends and the gladness, brightness, and guidance they mean for me. Grant that I may never harm them but ever show them the way of life. Amen.

MARTIN LUTHER AND OUR GENERATION

Luther and family life

Nov. 26

READ: Proverbs 31:10-31.

TEXT: Who can find a virtuous woman? For her price is far above rubies. Proverbs 31:10.

✣

When Dr. Martin Luther left the Catholic monastery he advised monks and nuns to become married. He hesitated for a long time to take such a step himself. In 1525, when he was in his 42nd year, he suddenly made up his mind to do what he had recommended to others. He was married to Katharina von Bora, a former nun. Theirs was a happy marriage. Luther often spoke of his wife as a "virtuous woman." Luther had three sons and three daughters. One daughter died when she was but eight months old. Whenever he speaks of his wife and his children he is filled with gratitude toward God.

God bless our country with good wives and God-fearing mothers. Their "price is far above rubies." Who can count the blessings that have gone out into the world from Christian homes in which the wife, the heart of the family, is virtuous in her living?

Dear Father in heaven, bless our country with Christian wives and mothers who make home life pleasant and together with their husbands bring up their children in the fear of the Lord. Amen.

STEWARDSHIP
God the owner

Nov. 27

READ: I Corinthians 4:1-8.

TEXT: For who maketh thee to differ from another? And what hast thou which thou didst not receive? Now if thou didst receive it, why dost thou glory, as if thou hadst not received it? I Corinthians 4:7.

✤

From the beginning of time, yes, even before time began, God has been giving things to men. He made the world for men to dwell in. He placed into that world everything that we need and said, "Use it; it is all for you."

He gave life to every one of us and keeps and protects us every minute. If He were to withdraw His divine help from us but for a moment, we could not exist.

When sin separated us from God, He gave us the Savior who gives us forgiveness. He gives me everything that I need and keeps me a child of His. What I am and have is a gift of God, and, therefore, I am His completely and entirely.

Heavenly Father, whose gifts and blessings are new to me each morning, help me to see and understand that all things come from Thee, and that I must always be deeply and sincerely thankful to Thee. Amen.

STEWARDSHIP

Man the manager

READ: Matthew 25:14-21.
TEXT: Moreover it is required in stewards, that a man be found faithful. I Corinthians 4:2.

✣

In the context these words are applied to the gospel ministry. It is, however, in perfect accord with many Bible passages to apply them to old and young alike.

To everyone God has given certain talents of mind, body, and earthly possessions. These talents are, indeed, variously distributed, but everyone has received some. Over these God has set us to be stewards, and to a certain extent we have the power to use them as we choose, but someday He is going to ask an accounting. We dare not, therefore, use them selfishly but must employ them to His greater glory in our own life and for the good of our fellow men.

How great are the opportunities for loving service about us daily if only we have eyes to see! Oh, the happy satisfaction it gives to have been a faithful steward!

Lord Jesus, make me conscious of my dependence upon Thee with all that I am and all that I have. Help me to use daily what Thou hast given for Thy greater glory in my own life and for the good of others. Amen.

STEWARDSHIP

The workshop of the world

Nov. 29

READ: Matthew 21:28-32.

TEXT: Son, go work today in my vineyard. Matthew 21:28.

✤

A departing soldier said: "Pastor, I do not fear overseas duty. I am more prepared to die than many others if that is God's will. I look forward to my journey across the sea and plan to remain after it is over to continue the fight as a soldier of the Lord Jesus."

Another said: "Pastor, I knelt in the presence of my whole outfit last night and prayed for them and their souls' salvation. They don't call me 'preacher' anymore, they call me 'buddy' and 'friend.'"

A humble shoemaker expressed his viewpoint this way: "My business is the kingdom of God. I mend shoes to pay expenses." Each one of us has a vocation, a job to do, a mission to fulfil in the world. There is work for all. But through that work we can and must serve God. We are His stewards.

> "O, Jesus, I have promised
>   To serve Thee to the end.
> Be Thou forever near me,
>   My Master and my Friend." Amen.

STEWARDSHIP

Divine tools in human hands

Nov. 30

READ: James 1:5-12.

TEXT: If any of you lack wisdom, let him ask of God, that giveth to all men liberally, and upbraideth not, and it shall be given him. James 1:5.

✣

All who desire to do things will need tools with which to do them. They would be helpless without these. This holds true also of us Christians who should be active in Christian stewardship.

The tools you need are at hand. God has prepared them for you. It should encourage and help you to know that you need not shop around a long time for these. Pray God, and He will give liberally to you.

Sincere love for God, for the fellow man, and for the work of winning souls for Jesus, the Word of God, which alone is the power of God unto salvation, the church with all her facilities, her services, Sunday school and societies, her home and foreign mission projects and her charities—these and many others are the divine tools which are entrusted to human hands for use in Christian stewardship. Will you make good use of them?

Heavenly Father, for Jesus' sake give me, Thy steward, the wisdom, willingness, and strength to use Thy tools successfully in winning souls for Thee. Amen.

STEWARDSHIP

Dec. 1

A heavenly teacher

READ: Psalm 32.

TEXT: I will instruct thee and teach thee in the way which thou shalt go: I will guide thee with Mine eye. Psalm 32:8.

✣

God and I are intimately associated. With Christ Jesus I enjoy a beautiful companionship. He is my heavenly Friend. We become partners together even though I am the steward accountable to Him for every thought and act. He is my instructor who teaches me the ways which I should go. He has given me the one textbook, the Holy Bible, and bids me to search its sacred pages diligently. The more carefully I study life's daily lessons in the light of His Word, and the more intimate my association with Christ becomes, the more apparent will be the hand of God that leads me on. I am not "as the horse or as the mule which have no understanding." Like the loving mother who guides with her eyes her first grader on the way to school morning after morning, so God promises me, "I will guide thee with Mine eye."

God, our Father in Christ Jesus, our Lord, guide us and lead us. Through the Holy Spirit working in heart and mind give us the strength and the courage to follow Thee. Amen.

STEWARDSHIP

The way of love

Dec. 2

READ: II Corinthians 5:9-17.

TEXT: For the love of Christ constraineth us. II Corinthians 5:14.

✤

The above seven words give us the key to the Christian's way of life. God's people of the New Covenant are constrained *to do* according to the love of Christ. We, as Christians, are constrained to do things for Christ and His cause because we love Him.

To be more specific let us consider the matter of worship. All of us have covenanted with God in our confirmation to be faithful in our church attendance. We find, however, that it is not the promise which we made that keeps us faithful in our church attendance but the love of Christ. Loving Christ, we love His cause, and we find deep spiritual joy in honoring His name in sincere worship. We have also experienced, that in worshiping Christ as Lord and God in prayer, praise, and thanksgiving, He has blessed us with power to overcome the sinful impulses of the flesh, the temptations of our world, and the subtle influences of Satan and his servants.

The Christian's stewardship of life is based on this *way of love*.

Lord Jesus Christ, we thank and praise Thee for the love with which Thou hast first loved us, and we pray for grace to love Thee with all our heart, mind, soul, and strength. For Thy name's sake. Amen.

STEWARDSHIP

Divine increase

Dec. 3

READ: Isaiah 40:28-31.

TEXT: And to them that have no might He increaseth strength. Isaiah 40:29.

♣

My gifts to God and my efforts for Christ are so small and so weak.

Five thousand men have followed Jesus faraway from their homes to hear Him speak and watch Him work. It is now far past the dinner hour. They have no bread. Andrew suggests, "There is a lad here with five barley loaves and two small fishes, but what are they among so many?" Wait! "Make the men sit down," said Jesus. Then He took the five small loaves and the two fishes and, looking up to heaven, gave thanks and blessed them. He began to hand them to the disciples, and they kept distributing them among the people until every hungry stomach was satisfied. In the hands of Jesus one small gift from one little boy fed more than five thousand people!

Do not be discouraged with the smallness of your service, rendered in love to Christ. He will add to your strength, increase your opportunities, and multiply the results of your labor in His name.

My precious Savior, Thou hast given Thyself into death for me; give me a happy heart as I lay my efforts, works, and money into Thy holy and almighty hands. Amen.

FEEDING CHRIST'S LAMBS AND SHEEP

The task of feeding

Dec. 4

READ: John 21:15-17.
TEXT: Feed My lambs. . . . Feed My sheep. John 21:15-17.

✤

Three times, but each time with a somewhat different meaning, Jesus asked Simon Peter, "Lovest thou Me?" And three times Jesus followed Peter's "yes!" with the admonition, "Feed My lambs," or, "Feed My sheep."

He also gave Peter the charge that, on the basis of a genuine and abiding love for Him, Peter should "feed" the Lord's "lambs" and His "sheep." The "feeding" was to be done, of course, with the bread of life, the Word of God.

An understanding of the original words used by Jesus suggests the possibility that He was asking Peter to feed His "lambs" (the children), His "half-grown sheep" (the young people), and His "full-grown sheep" (the adults). The Lord here provides for a complete program of Christian education that includes everyone.

Lord Jesus Christ, Thou art the wonderful Shepherd of Thy sheep. I thank Thee for the great task of Christian education which Thou hast assigned to Thy church and to all who love Thee. Help me to appreciate the fact that I have had the great privilege of being fed on the bread of life. Amen.

FEEDING CHRIST'S LAMBS AND SHEEP

Feeding in the home

Dec. 5

READ: Ephesians 6:1-4.

TEXT: Ye fathers . . . bring them up in the nurture and admonition of the Lord. Ephesians 6:4.

♣

We can never thank God enough for Christian parents and for having been brought up in a Christian home. The best inheritance we can receive is to have Jesus as our Lord and Savior from earliest childhood. All earthly treasures are less important than a living faith in Christ. The religious instruction and the guiding example of devout fathers and mothers will continue to grow in meaning as the years go by. The greatest tribute which anyone can give to his parents is this, "They brought me to Christ."

Let us gladly receive the spiritual food which they desire us to have. Just as our bodies need to be fed daily, so likewise do we need spiritual food day by day. Let us thankfully join our parents in daily family worship, in the reading of the Bible, and in prayer.

Heavenly Father, fill my heart with appreciation and love for my parents, and may the Christ to whom they brought me be my ever-present Lord and Savior. Amen.

FEEDING CHRIST'S LAMBS AND SHEEP

Feeding in the church

Dec. 6

READ: Acts 2:41-47.

TEXT: Teaching them to observe all things whatsoever I have commanded you: and, lo, I am with you alway even unto the end of the world. Matthew 28:20.

✣

We are very careful about the whole process of eating. Vitamins and calories must be considered, restaurants must pass government inspection, pure food laws protect us, and books on etiquette tell us how properly to handle our food.

One would almost believe that our only essential need is food for the body. If that were true, we should not be different from animals, should we? Material food is the only kind that animals require. A person is more than an animal, isn't he? A person is more than a body; he is a spirit. You are a spirit. Jesus said by way of quotation, "Man shall not live by bread alone." He can't because his soul also needs food if it is to live and be strong.

Truth, courage, hope, forgiveness, love, beauty, and joy are not available at a restaurant, soda fountain, or grocery store. For these you must come to church. There you will be fed God's spiritual vitamins.

My spirit is hungry, O Christ, for the food that will make me strong with love, courage, joy, and peace. Feed me in Thy church with Thy truth and Thy strength. Amen.

FEEDING CHRIST'S LAMBS AND SHEEP

I have been "fed"

Dec. 7

READ: II Timothy 3:15-17.

TEXT: From a child thou hast known the holy scriptures which are able to make thee wise unto salvation through faith which is in Christ Jesus. II Timothy 3:15.

✤

I, too, have been made wise unto salvation. My knowledge of the Scriptures may be meager. There may be much that I still have to learn; but this I know, that in Jesus I have the assurance of my salvation. This I owe to those who have taught me from the days of my infancy. As a child I learned that "Jesus loves me." Later I learned that "God so loved the world, that He gave His only-begotten Son that whosoever believeth in Him should not perish but have everlasting life." I have learned to know that the Triune God has done and continues to do all this as necessary for my salvation. So God's wisdom has come to me through the years as a spiritual diet adapted to my needs. By His grace I have been nourished and made healthy and strong.

Heavenly Father, as Thou hast made me wise unto salvation through Thy Word in the past, preserve me in the true saving faith through Jesus Christ, my Lord. Amen.

FEEDING CHRIST'S LAMBS AND SHEEP

Fed, but not "fed up"

Dec. 8

READ: II Timothy 3:6-14.

TEXT: But continue thou in the things which thou hast learned and hast been assured of, knowing of whom thou hast learned them. II Timothy 3:14.

♣

Jesus says to all Christian parents, teachers, and pastors, "Feed My lambs." You are one of the young lambs of Christ's flock. You have been nourished and enabled to grow by the Good Shepherd. Through the Word you have been made a child of God, have been given faith in your Savior, Jesus Christ, and your feet set in the way of righteousness and honor. Remember that it was those who truly love you, your parents, pastor, and teachers, who taught you these things. They would not teach you anything that would harm you but that which will do you good. Now God asks you to continue to believe and to do the things you have been taught. He also asks you to guard against the notion that you now know all that you need to know and hence no longer need to read His Word or go to Sunday school and church. Don't be "fed up." Blessed are they that hunger and thirst after righteousness, for they shall be filled."

Dear Lord, I thank Thee for loving teachers who have fed my soul with Thy precious, saving Word. Preserve me from feeling "fed up." Keep me hungry and thirsty for Thy Word and grant me grace to be not only a hearer but also a doer of it. For Jesus' sake. Amen.

FEEDING CHRIST'S LAMBS AND SHEEP
"Feeding" others by teaching

Dec. 9

READ: Daniel 12:1-4.

TEXT: They that turn many to righteousness [shall shine] as the stars forever and ever. Daniel 12:3.

♣

In the midst of the varied problems of life we Christians will again and again thank God and rejoice that we are created in His image. Whenever the Spirit of God brings us into living relationship with the Word of God and the sacraments, this divine image in us is to be clarified and made more and more beautiful.

As Christians we are invited to aid the Spirit in bringing out this divine image also in those with whom we associate. The prophet of God calls this "turning many to righteousness."

Ever and again I must ask myself whether God has given me any special ability to teach, to turn others in the right way, in the way of God, in the way of peace. It is a difficult but a God-pleasing calling for which the sacred writer even promises a gracious reward. May I give ear to the Savior's imperative challenge, "Teach them to observe whatsoever I have commanded you."

Heavenly Father, direct my thoughts and my desires so that I may use my talents to lead others to righteousness. May my Christian life be attractive in this, that it may turn others to fear, love, and trust in Thee, our Lord and Savior. Amen.

FEEDING CHRIST'S LAMBS AND SHEEP

"Feeding" others by a good Christian example

Dec. 10

READ: II Corinthians 3:1-5.

TEXT: Ye are our epistle. . . . known and read of all men. II Corinthians 3:2.

✣

Your certificate of baptism says that you have become a child of God in holy baptism. Your certificate of confirmation says that you promised to be faithful to your God and Savior until death. What does your daily life say? "You are writing a gospel, a chapter each day, by deeds that you do and by words that you say. Men read what you write, whether faithless or true. Tell me, what is the gospel according to you?" You are to be an epistle of Christ, a living message of Jesus to the people around you. People who do not go to church and do not read the Bible can and will read your life. Is it a Christlike life? Does it tell the world, "This is what a young Christian looks like"?

"Let your light so shine before men, that they may see your good works and glorify your Father which is in heaven."

O Master, let me walk with Thee in lowly paths of service, free. Take my life and let it be consecrated unto Thee. Help me, for I cannot do it alone. Amen.

THE WORSHIP OF GOD

Dec. 11

The house of God

READ: Psalm 26.

TEXT: Lord, I have loved the habitation of Thy house. Psalm 26:8.

✣

When Jesus talked with the woman of Samaria, she asked in effect, "Where shall man worship?" Jesus answered, "The day cometh when ye shall neither in this mountain nor in Jerusalem worship the Father." And yet! Of that same Jesus we read, "As was His custom, He entered the synagogue."

A person can worship God in the templed mountains and by the music of many waters, but will he? Only if and after he has learned truly to worship in the place we call the Christian house of God. The Word and the sacraments served there, the response of the heart in song and prayer, the fellowship of kindred hearts, it has been experienced, are the fundamental requirements for the awakening and the cultivating of that sacred experience called worship.

So whether my house of God be a thing of architectural beauty on the city avenue or a simpler structure in the village or by the side of the road, let me think most highly of it.

My Lord and my God, I thank Thee that through the love and the gifts of my elders there has been erected that place that I may call "my church." Help me to appreciate this sacred heritage and in the regular use thereof prove myself worthy of the privilege that is mine by Thy grace. Amen.

THE WORSHIP OF GOD
The altar

Dec. 12

READ: Hebrews 13:9-15.

TEXT: We have an altar, whereof they have no right to eat which serve the tabernacle. Hebrews 13:10.

♣

The altar of the Christian is the cross on which the Lamb of God was slain. It is this cross-altar that was foreshadowed in the altar of burnt offering of the Old Testament Tabernacle and Temple.

Of the cross-altar the altar in our churches is a symbol and a memorial.

It is fitting that at prayer pastor and congregation turn to the altar, for only because of the sacrifice of Jesus may we draw near to God at all.

At the altar in the Holy Communion we also receive the tokens of our Lord's sacrifice, His body and His blood. Receiving these in faith, we are assured of the benefits of His sacrifice, the forgiveness of sins and union with Him.

As often as we pray before the altar or approach it to receive the Holy Supper, let us thankfully remember the cross-altar on which our Savior died that we might live forever.

Lord Jesus, when I pray at the altar of my church, and when I kneel there to receive Thy sacred body and precious blood, help me thankfully to remember Thy sacrifice for me. Amen.

THE WORSHIP OF GOD

The cross or crucifix

Dec. 13

READ: Hebrews 12:1-11.

TEXT: Looking unto Jesus the author and finisher of our faith; who for the joy that was set before Him endured the cross, despising the shame, and is set down at the right hand of the throne of God. Hebrews 12:2.

✤

On entering a Lutheran church the first thing we see is the altar. And on that altar, occupying the central and highest place, is the cross; it is generally a bare cross rather than a crucifix. That cross reminds us that Christ died for our sins, for my sins, according to the Scriptures. Its bareness tells us that He is no longer dead but alive forevermore. We worship not a dead Christ but a living, loving Lord.

We must look to Jesus not only to begin our Christian life but also to continue it all the way through to the end of our earthly career. Think of that cross when you are tempted and when in trouble, but also when you are well and strong and happy. Never do anything you would not wish your Lord to see, nor go anywhere you cannot take Him with you, nor say anything that you would rather He did not hear.

Our dear Savior, we thank Thee for Thy life and death and victorious resurrection. Help us to remember the cross of Thy atonement and to live with Thee each day until we see Thee face to face. In Thy dear name. Amen.

THE WORSHIP OF GOD

The candlesticks

Dec. 14

READ: John 8:12-32.

TEXT: I am the light of the world: he that followeth Me shall not walk in darkness, but shall have the light of life. John 8:12.

♣

Jesus draws a parallel between Himself and one of the familiar items of liturgical furniture of the Temple. In the Court of the Women stood great golden candelabra which were lighted on the evening of the first day of the Feast of the Tabernacles. These candelabra were said to shed their light throughout the whole city of Jerusalem. In our Christian thinking we associate the two natures (the divine and the human) of Christ with the candlesticks on each side of the cross on the altar. These candlesticks serve to remind us of the real presence of our Lord and Savior in the Holy Sacraments and in the life of the true believer. The meaning of Jesus' words in the text is very obvious. He points out that He is the *only* light; those who follow Christ shall not walk in the darkness of this world's sin and destruction but have a constant "lamp unto their feet and light unto their path." It remains but to ask, "Do you walk in His light?"

Dear Lord Jesus, pour the light of Thy love into my sinful heart and keep me ever in the brightness of Thy glorious self that I may steadfastly walk in Thy way until, by Thy heavenly light, I stand in Thy eternal presence. Amen.

THE WORSHIP OF GOD

Pulpit and lectern—God's Word

Dec. 15

READ: Psalm 119:105-112.

TEXT: Thy word is a lamp unto my feet, and a light unto my path. Psalm 119:105.

✣

Our life is a journey through a strange country, and we pass this way but once. God does not want us to lose our way in the dark so He gives us the light of His holy Word. The business of the church is to present that light for our guidance. It is done publicly by the reading of the Word and by teaching.

Here we have the lectern, the place of the reading of the Word without comment so that its unadorned truth may shine forth for us.

Here we have the pulpit, the place of proclaiming, explaining, and applying the Word to life and the situations which we find along life's pathway.

Jesus said: "I am the light of the world. He that followeth Me shall not walk in darkness, but shall have the light of life." We should evermore praise God the Father for His Word and the light it sheds upon our path and for Jesus Christ, for when we walk with Him, no pathway is dark or strange.

> O take my hand, dear Father, and lead Thou me
> Till at my journey's ending I dwell with Thee.
> Alone I dare not journey one single day.
> So do Thou guide my footsteps on life's rough way.

THE WORSHIP OF GOD

The font

Dec. 16

READ: Romans 6:1-11.

TEXT: Know ye not, that so many of us as were baptized into Jesus Christ were baptized into His death? Romans 6:3.

♣

Not far from the altar in my church stands the font. It is a carved stone wherein is set a small vessel for the water of baptism. Here God-fearing parents brought me to the Lord in the sacrament when I was just a babe.

Whenever I see the font, it speaks to me. It says, "You were baptized." It says: "You are baptized into Jesus Christ. You are baptized into His death. You are so closely united with Him that the fruits of His death are yours. The pardon He worked out for you on the cross is yours."

What shall my answer be? My salvation is the gift of the Lord to me. He secured it at the price of His life and gave it to me. Must I not offer my life to Him to use it where and as He wills?

Never, Lord Jesus, can I thank Thee enough for Thy great gift to me. Accept my heart, therefore, and help me to serve Thee according to Thy will. Amen.

THE WORSHIP OF GOD

Dec. 17

The organ

READ: Psalm 150.

TEXT: Praise Him with stringed instruments and organs. Psalm 150:4.

✠

I was confirmed on a Pentecost Sunday. Our class had chosen as a class hymn, "Beautiful Savior," and the organist opened the service with a prelude with variations on that beautiful melody. I had often listened to organ music, but until then it had not greatly impressed me. That day it met a response in my soul, and the echo of that music still lingers in my memory as a message from heaven.

The organ, the queen of instruments, when played by a consecrated musician gives inspiration to worship. No other musical instrument can so inspire the soul to true worship and put it in tune with the infinite.

As the eagle soars aloft toward the sun while the little birds nestle near the ground, so the music of the organ lifts the soul to higher regions above the common things of life. If music is the language of universal brotherhood, the church organ speaks the language of saints and angels.

Heavenly Father, I thank Thee for all gifts which make life happy, for the things that bring peace and joy to my soul. Teach me to appreciate every means which Thou hast provided for worshiping Thee. In Jesus' name. Amen.

THE MINISTRY OF MERCY

Children's homes

Dec. 18

READ: Psalm 27.

TEXT: When my father and my mother forsake me, then the Lord will take me up. Psalm 27:10.

✣

The Lord provides each child with parents who are to give the child security, guidance, companionship, and an opportunity to develop its abilities. The child is to be foremost in the planning of the parents. Only death or maturity shall separate the child from the parent.

The Lord maintains His special watch over the child who loses a parent through death or some other cause. He has planted love for children in the heart of relatives and friends so that good family homes are opened to these homeless. In addition, His church builds children's homes where Christian workers give themselves as substitute parents to the fatherless and motherless children. Through Christian citizens He has influenced the state to assume its share of the responsibility for a dependent child. In this Christian era, by the grace of God, every homeless child shall be provided with a home.

"When my father and my mother forsake me, then the Lord will take me up. . . . The Lord is my Light and my Salvation, whom shall I fear?"

Dear Father, we thank Thee for Thy watchful care over Thy children. May we all share Thy concern for the unfortunate and reflect the kindness of Thy love. In Jesus' name. Amen.

THE MINISTRY OF MERCY

Good works

Dec. 19

READ: Matthew 26:6-13.

TEXT: Why trouble ye the woman? for she hath wrought a good work upon Me. Matthew 26:10.

♣

Mary sat at Jesus' feet, hungrily drinking in words of life. She had learned to love her Lord who had proved to be so great a teacher and comforter. When it was indicated that He was to be taken away, her heart responded in love and compassion, and she lavished upon Him the alabaster box of precious ointment.

"To what purpose is this waste? It might have been sold for much and given to the poor," is the comment of cold and calculating reason though it was the comment of Jesus' own disciple. Poor Mary, like some maiden who had too publicly demonstrated her love, tremblingly blushed in the background.

"Why trouble ye the woman?" Do you not realize that you are condemning love? That you are causing her pain? This is a good work which she hath wrought upon Me!

Let us give of our time, our substance, our service for all who are in need of our mercy; we shall be doing a good work for Jesus.

Lord Jesus, wilt Thou so direct our heart and our mind that not only our well-balanced thoughts and acts reflect Thy glory, but that even our unpremeditated, spontaneous doings find favor in Thy sight. Bestow Thy Spirit to sanctify us thoroughly for Thy great name's sake. Amen.

THE MINISTRY OF MERCY

Healing

Dec. 20

READ: Luke 14:1-6.

TEXT: And He took him, and healed him, and let him go. Luke 14:4.

✤

This Pharisee had arranged a Sabbath evening supper that he and his friends might gain a closer acquaintance with Jesus. Suddenly a man who had the dropsy was brought before them. All were silent and watched Jesus. What would He do? The Master wasted no time. He took the man and healed him.

The church has the mind of Christ. It wants to heal men, their bodies, minds, and souls. To do this it establishes hospitals, sends medical missionaries and trained nurses to witness to the ignorant and suffering and underprivileged people of the world of a Christ who loved men and healed them. It is an effective way to reveal to men the gospel of a God who so loved the world that He gave His only Son to minister and serve them. Christian physicians and nurses take the sick and heal them.

Can you think of a nobler way than thus to serve with consecrated skill of hand and heart and to heal your fellow men because of the love of Christ in your own heart?

Eternal Lord and Father of all mankind, fill me with the spirit and the compassion of Jesus Christ, the Great Physician. Let Thy church have the mind of Christ and engage ever in a holy ministry to the sick and the afflicted in all the world. In Jesus' name. Amen.

THE MINISTRY OF MERCY

The will to help

Dec. 21

READ: Luke 10:25-37.

TEXT: Then said Jesus unto him, Go, and do thou likewise. Luke 10:37.

✤

A lawyer had tempted Jesus, saying, "Master, what shall I do to inherit eternal life?" Jesus had told him the story of the Good Samaritan and concluded the story with the words, "Go, and do thou likewise."

Jesus speaks here of those who are in bodily need, the sick, the blind, the crippled, the orphaned, whoever they may be. He tells His followers that they are to help those who are in need. It is impossible to be a follower of Christ and not feel compassion for those who are dependent upon the love and the support of their fellow men. As the heart of Jesus reached out to the weak, the weary, and the heavy-laden, so also the heart of God's children must reach out and be willing to help at all times. Our hands must become the hands of Jesus, wherewith He blesses and helps others. "Go, and do thou likewise" includes you and me and is meant for every day of our life.

Dear Jesus, help us to be ever more like Thee so that we, too, may ever be willing to reach out a helping hand to all who need our help. Amen.

THE MINISTRY OF MERCY

The diaconate (deaconess)

Dec. 22

READ: Isaiah 49:13-17.

TEXT: The Lord . . . will have mercy upon His afflicted. Isaiah 49:13.

✠

When our merciful Lord walked upon the earth He was keenly sensitive to the needs and the sufferings of those among whom He dwelt. He helped them effectively with His mighty power.

Today Christ lives in the heart of those who love Him. He makes us alert to the suffering of our fellow men and gives us a strong desire to render effectual aid.

The mercy of Christ is the heart of the diaconate. In this service Christian women are banded together for charity and Christian work. It is their aim to bring Christ and the comfort of His blessings into needy lives. In wholehearted consecration and with united efforts they devote all their time and their energy to their tasks.

The diaconate challenges all, both women and men, to help their fellow men. In particular it offers to some an opportunity for a life of full-time Christian service.

Make us sensitive to the needs of Thy suffering children everywhere, dear Lord. Bless, we pray Thee, all efforts to render aid. Prosper the work of all deaconesses. For Thy name's sake. Amen.

THE MINISTRY OF MERCY

Dec. 23

Jesus, our perfect example

READ: Acts 10:34-43.
TEXT: He went about doing good. Acts 10:38.

✣

Our dear Lord started something when He went about doing good. The good He did restored people to a greater enjoyment of life and the possibility of greater service of God. It is the right of all people to enjoy life to the utmost and the responsibility of all to serve God as well as possible. Jesus not only called people to make the most of life but realized His responsibility to help them accomplish their purpose.

Ever since then His followers, striving to think and to act like Jesus, have felt more responsibility for the people who are hindered by ill health or unfortunate circumstances. Jesus set the world to thinking, and there is more work of this nature done now than was ever done before. Much still remains to be done. The sick, the crippled, the orphans, the widows, and many others cry for help. The great wheels of power in the church must turn out even better ways to help them.

O Lord, make us mindful of the needs of those whom cruel forces have hindered. May we not only pity. May we act in Thine own spirit and name who art our perfect example. Amen.

JESUS

Jesus is coming

Dec. 24

READ: Luke 3:1-14.
TEXT: Prepare ye the way of the Lord. Luke 3:4.

✤

Judea's mountainous desert, sloping eastward from Jerusalem to the Dead Sea, is severe and uninviting. Human life seems out of place here. Vultures soar overhead by day; and the jackals pierce the night with their screams. Yet against this background a voice, the voice of John, the forerunner, announcing the coming of the Messiah.

The voice of believers, like that of John the Baptist, should cry out in the desert of every modern city. Some protest that it doesn't make sense to shout, "Prepare the way of the Lord." Neither did it make sense in John's day. For the gospel of repentance, of change of heart, never makes sense to those who lack faith in its remedy, Christ.

Too many of us look trancelike at life, thinking there is nothing we can do. Yet all of us, starting with ourselves, can help to prepare the way by which our Lord may come into the heart of men. Is there any better preparation for Christmas?

Stir up, O Lord, we beseech Thee Thy power and come and with great might succor us that by the help of Thy grace whatsoever is hindered by our sins may be speedily accomplished, through Thy mercy and satisfaction; who livest and reignest with the Father and the Holy Ghost, ever one God, world without end. Amen.

JESUS

Jesus is born

Dec. 25

READ: Luke 2:1-14.

TEXT: Behold, I bring you good tidings of great joy. . . . For unto you is born . . . a Savior. Luke 2:10, 11.

♣

The shepherds were watching their flocks by night. Suddenly they were startled by a great light and the appearance of an angel. They were terribly afraid, but their fear was unwarranted. That which made them afraid was meant to make them glad. The best of all good news awaited them. They received their first Christmas greeting. "I bring you good tidings of great joy. . . . For unto you is born . . . a Savior." They knew that they could not save themselves. Now someone had come to set them free. No news could be greater than that.

We, too, need deliverance from the things that hold us bound and keep us unhappy within. It takes someone from above to reach down to take us by the hand and lift us up. Jesus was born into our world that we might be born into His. "Joy to the world, the Lord is come." Thank God this day, as did the shepherds, for our greatest Christmas gift, the coming of Christ.

Loving Father, Thou who didst so love the world as to give Thy Son, I thank Thee this day for Thy great gift to me. Amen.

JESUS

Jesus is seen by the shepherds

Dec. 26

READ: Luke 2:15-20.

TEXT: Let us now go even unto Bethlehem, and see this thing which is come to pass. Luke 2:15.

✤

If I were to express in one word the greatest fact in the history of the world, that word would be *Christianity.*

Little, perhaps, did the shepherds understand when the angels announced to them the good tidings of great joy, the birth of a Savior which is Christ the Lord and bade them go and find Him lying in a manger. Little did they dream that here was a turning point in the history of the world.

This kingdom with its beginning in the humble manger was destined during the centuries to come to outshine and long to outlast the throne of the Caesars who then ruled the world and to gather in the peoples of many races and languages until nearly all the great nations professed the religion of that "Savior which is Christ the Lord."

Why should we not celebrate His recurring birthday as no other day in the year?

Oh, Thou Almighty God who didst send Thy Son into the world to die for our transgressions and to rise again for our justification, help us to embrace the glorious gospel He gave the world and to remain faithful as long as we live. We ask in His name. Amen.

JESUS

Jesus is named

Dec. 27

READ: Matthew 1:18-25.

TEXT: They shall call His name Emmanuel, which . . . is, "God with us." Matthew 1:23.

♣

Your name, as you are well aware, makes you known as belonging to a certain family and within that family as a certain member; but it means more. Where you are known, the mentioning of your name creates a mental picture of you. That picture tells what you mean to your associates, it reflects what you are.

Though our Lord was given the name of Jesus in the brief Temple ceremony, His presence meant to all who knew Him rightly, "God with us," or as it was expressed in Hebrew, "Emmanuel." He represented and was God come among men that they may know Him and become His children.

Now what do you think your name stands for in the mind of those who know you best? Do they feel in your presence a spirit of goodness and kindness, of friendship and helpfulness? Let your influence cause them to think of you as a worthy child of God, a reflection of Christ, a reminder of "God with us."

Dear Jesus, even Thine enemies called Thee "the Son of God." They could not do otherwise. Let me be known, wherever I am, as belonging to the family of "our Father." Amen.

JESUS

Jesus is presented (at the Temple)

Dec. 28

READ: Luke 2:25-35.

TEXT: Lord, now lettest Thou Thy servant depart in peace.... For mine eyes have seen Thy salvation ... a light to lighten the Gentiles and the glory of Thy people Israel. Luke 2:29-32.

♣

Simeon was an aged man who knew that, when the Lord's Christ would appear, it would be in the Temple. It had been revealed to him also that he should not die before he had seen the Christ. So when the child Jesus was presented in the Temple by His devout parents as was their law and custom, Simeon realized that this promise was fulfilled. He took Jesus in his arms and spoke the words which have become one of the hymns of the church, "Lord, now lettest Thou Thy servant depart in peace."

So Jesus came early to His own place, the Temple of God, even as godly parents today bring their children to present them to the Lord in holy baptism. As a child Christ loved the Temple. As a man He wept over its defiling and cleansed it. He loved the church and gave Himself for it that He might build it for us and our children.

O Holy Father, grant that by Thy Spirit we may find Christ whenever we enter the temple of our worship and rejoice in the knowledge that our Savior is present with us there. Amen.

JESUS

Jesus is worshiped

Dec. 29

READ: Matthew 2:1-11.
TEXT: We ... are come to worship Him. Matthew 2:2.

✤

The wise men came from distant places to worship Jesus. They found a little child in a humble rented house. Yet such was their faith and sincerity that they worshiped Him and presented costly gifts, gold and frankincense and myrrh.

They were the forerunners of those who come today to worship Jesus from the east and the west, from the north and the south; a great multitude which no man can number of all nations and kindreds and peoples and tongues; of men and women, boys and girls and little children who bring gifts and worship Him.

So we come to worship, not a little child, but the risen and exalted Son of God, the Lord of glory, who with the Father and the Holy Ghost is worshiped and glorified, ever one God, world without end. Amen.

O come, all ye faithful, triumphantly sing.
O come ye, come hither, to worship the King.

O God, fill our heart with love and gratitude to our Lord Jesus Christ so that we may praise Him continually with faithful believers in all the world that on the earth, as in the heavens, He may be exalted above all else. Amen.

JESUS

Jesus is taken to Egypt

Dec. 30

READ: Matthew 2:13-23.

TEXT: Arise, and take the young child and His mother, and flee into Egypt. Matthew 2:13.

♣

King Herod sought the life of Jesus. He was afraid that someday Jesus would depose him from his throne. His heart was filled with jealous hate. He typifies the world which seeks absolute rule over mankind. Many hearts, however, have found their personal Savior in Jesus. The world does not love those whom Jesus shepherds through life in a spirit of love and grace. The world seeks to take Jesus away from such hearts, knowing that, where Jesus is found, there worldly ways cannot dictate. The flight into Egypt teaches us that, when such dangers threaten us, we must flee to the sanctuary of prayer and worship which God has given us in this world of danger. In the Christian Church, the fellowship of believers, we are bound together by a sustaining Christian love. In God's presence is our refuge.

Gracious Father in heaven, help us to flee the many dangers that threaten to destroy our faith and our life in Jesus, for in Him alone we have life and salvation. Amen.

JESUS

Jesus is coming again

Dec. 31

READ: Acts 1:1-11.

TEXT: Ye men of Galilee, why stand ye gazing up into heaven? this same Jesus, which is taken up from you into heaven, shall so come in like manner as ye have seen Him go into heaven. Acts 1:11.

♣

The end of this series of devotions. The close of another year. The time when men in general take account of their business affairs to find out exactly where they stand. Of what do these things remind Christians? They bring to our memory the fact, expressed in the text on which our meditation is based, that Christ will come again. He will come on that great day when all earthly activity shall cease, when there will be a final accounting by God concerning our spiritual life. The apostles longed for that day. We express the same longing when we pray in the words of Jesus, "Thy kingdom come." Have we settled our affairs? Are we ready for His second coming? Where do we stand? Only true faith in the Christ will find us on the right side of the ledger. Without Him we have reason to dread that day. But trusting in Him, we may confidently and expectantly look forward to His glorious return.

Lord Jesus, give us a full measure of Thy Holy Spirit that in true faith we may look forward to Thy second coming when we shall stand at the right hand of Thy throne. Amen.

INDEX OF CONTRIBUTORS

	Page		Page
Abrahamson, A. L.	67	Bergener, A. G.	297
Ackermann, John B.	143	Billheimer, Stanley	88
Albert, R. A.	214	Bischoff, M. L.	302
Allbeck, Willard D.	215	Blegen, Allen R.	235
Altpeter, Sebastian J.	329	Boatman, Wm. J.	144
Amend, Edward	221	Bock, G. M.	49
Andeen, G. K.	60	Boerger, E. J.	142
Anderson, O. V.	152	Boomhower, W. G.	145
Anspach, Howard A.	222	Bosch, Fred H.	151
Appel, E. G.	108	Bostrom, Otto H.	287
Atkinson, Thomas	251	Boulton, R. L.	71
		Brachna, G.	31
Bachmann, E. F.	232	Brake, Donald F.	209
Bachmann, E. Theo.	371	Bramkamp, John M.	36
Baer, Dallas C.	233	Braun, F.	307
Baetke, August	369	Braun, K. Wm.	104
Baisler, Geo. J.	112	Bream, Charles S.	43
Bakken, E. M.	242	Brede, H. J.	308
Baringer, P. S.	196	Brobst, Charles F.	372
Baumgartner, Paul L.	353	Brueckner, Bruno	244
Bean, Arthur N.	257	Buch, Theo.	56
Beck, Charles G.	269	Buntz, Theodore G.	268
Becker, C. H.	368	Burman, A. L.	38
Becker, John H.	40	Busse, C. N.	348
Behrens, William F.	278		
Beiswanger, Geo.	280	Carl, Robert E.	131
Belter, R. R.	140	Carlsen, Sam	116
Bengtson, C. O.	68	Carlson, Walter E.	123
Berg, Alex.	25	Chamberlin, E. Allan	225

Name	Page	Name	Page
Clark, Harvey	102	Flesner, D. A.	352
Clark, Robert R.	169	Foege, H.	336
Conrad, F. L.	174	Foelsch, Charles B.	42
Creager, Harold L.	203	Foulk, Paul L.	154
Crouse, R. J.	218	Framstad, A.	321
Curran, George J.	137	Frederick, David H.	239
		Frey, Edward S.	272
Davis, W. C.	241	Fritsch, Robert R.	170
Decker, C. Aug.	345	Fritschel, W.	354
Defenderfer, C. R.	246	Froeberg, Peter	364
Deibert, Arthur S.	255	Fry, H. C.	95
DeLauter, Paul W.	311		
Dell, J. A.	313	Glasoe, P. M.	193
Dierolf, Claude O.	281	Glick, H. H.	94
Dietz, J. C.	284	Goedeking, E. J.	275
Dorn, J. George	318	Goeken, John A.	195
Dort, Charles H.	319	Gohdes, C. B.	342
		Grabau, Harold T.	100
Ebert, Adolf P.	51	Gresh, Ralph R.	139
Egbert, W. C.	261	Grosshans, L. J.	89
Ekerberg, H. R.	271		
Elson, H. W.	373	Haberaecker, J. J.	115
Engberg, Emmer	75	Hafermann, C. F.	128
Engdahl, C. Geo.	82	Hafermann, Herbert	135
Epple, Chas. E.	22	Halvorson, H.	32
Erbes, Henry C.	339	Hammer, Em. W.	76
Ermisch, Karl	315	Hamrick, S. A.	163
Ernst, Wilton D.	84	Hansler, George C.	330
		Hanson, Felix V.	285
Fedders, J. F.	165	Harman, J. Paul	134
Ferne, W. J.	120	Harrison, James	141
Firnschild, F. J.	326	Hartwig, Theo. G.	17
Fjelstad, Olin C.	179	Hauge, Melvin E.	81
Flachmeier, Wm. A.	363	Hauser, E. Roy	48
Flack, E. E.	44	Heckman, C. L.	133

Name	Page
Hieronymus, W. P.	351
Hightower, C. H.	113
Hiltner, John	357
Hoeppner, Martin J.	29
Hoff, T. A.	46
Hoh, E. J.	148
Hollensen, M. E.	213
Holtan, Walter	207
Hoyer, A. J.	124
Hull, Rubert A.	236
Jech, Herbert	327
Jones, Dan K.	291
Kaitschuk, Walter E.	361
Kammeyer, Carl D.	35
Keller, Martin C. H.	296
Kelly, James	27
Kern, Rufus E.	99
Kibler, R. F.	350
Killmer, Andrew H.	54
Klinksick, T. G.	37
Knudsen, Arthur M.	360
Koehler, Geo. C.	69
Koski, Onni A.	377
Krauss, Paul H.	62
Krebs, G. P.	347
Krueger, George W.	105
Krumbholz, C. E.	24
Kumpf, Paul J.	184
Lang, John O.	293
Lange, C. J.	61
Langholz, Arthur G.	65
Lauffer, George N.	132

Name	Page
Leas, J. Allen	70
Leatherman, C. G.	34
Liefeld, W. C.	150
Liemohn, E.	288
Lindemann, H.	310
Lindenmuth, A. W.	210
Linder, C. E.	355
Long, Ralph H.	18
Longacre, David F.	279
Loreen, Albert	187
Lotz, Benjamin	267
Magelssen, N. S.	283
Malmin, G. J.	290
Manges, Lewis C.	162
Mardorf, C. J.	191
Mattes, John C.	341
Mees, O. C.	52
Melby, C. A.	153
Meuser, E. H.	331
Meyer, H. M.	58
Meyer, J. T.	93
Michelfelder, S. C.	66
Michelke, H. A.	325
Mueller, Karl A.	178
Mueller, Luther C.	111
Narveson, B. H.	208
Naugle, V. D.	273
Neal, Clarence A.	64
Neumann, A. M.	176
Nicholson, Elmer	370
Nies, William H.	240
Noren, Paul H. A.	173
Odden, A. C.	277

Name	Page
Odell, M. A.	33
Oden, Joshua	110
Olander, C. Martin	349
Olson, Christian G.	317
Ott, John W.	78
Otto, J. Frederick	359
Palmquist, Wilbur N.	138
Paulus, Clarence E.	118
Peterson, James C.	328
Pflum, Henry J.	21
Pinkall, A. H.	258
Ploetz, R. W.	227
Poppen, Em.	304
Poppen, Eugene	248
Proehl, Theo.	171
Pugh, W. E.	223
Pura, Walter S.	224
Putman, Dwight F.	127
Rath, David	228
Read, Charles E.	338
Reents, J. B.	79
Rembold, Carl	122
Reuter, F. C.	226
Rhode, H. O.	238
Riechmann, G. R.	92
Rieke, Marcus C.	346
Rockey, Carroll J.	217
Roehner, Henry C.	13
Romstad, Alf	314
Roth, C. C.	41
Roth, William W.	126
Rowe, Charles I.	305
Rudisill, J. E.	161

Name	Page
Running, A. S.	299
Ruoss, G. Martin	146
Rydbeck, T. L.	159
Sandeen, Enoch	229
Schaeffer, W. C.	231
Schalkhauser, H.	366
Scharf, E. P.	324
Schellhase, Fred. J.	114
Schiffler, H. C.	177
Schildroth, H. E.	216
Schlueter, Roland	212
Schmidt, H. G.	340
Schmieder, John	77
Schramm, Edw. W.	301
Schroeder, Martin	374
Schuh, Fred O.	73
Schumacher, Wm.	262
Sheatsley, C. V.	333
Simonsen, A. M.	155
Simonson, Joseph	23
Snyder, Ellis, E.	292
Sodt, Wm. G.	344
Sorenson, M. A.	59
Spiegel, Wm.	312
Stamets, A. Maxwell	253
Stauffer, E. E.	157
Streng, Adolph C.	356
Streng, John F.	252
Streng, Wm. D.	156
Strock, J. Roy	334
Strommen, P. A.	316
Stubenvoll, C. F.	378
Stull, Maynard A.	245
Suechting August G.	136

	Page		Page
Sund, W. E.	205	Weihe, LeRoy F.	365
Swanson, Herbert	180	Weltner, P. G.	343
Swinehart, H. W.	86	Weng, Armin G.	19
Swoyer, Grover E.	182	Whiting, Henry J.	367
		Wiggert, Walter	101
Taeuber, Richard	335	Wilke, Otto J.	47
Tallakson, Lloyal E.	107	Winterfeld, K.	274
Tallakson, Selmer L.	130	Wittenstrom, C. F.	103
Tappert, W. C. H.	55	Wittig, F. A.	72
Tetlie, Joseph	362	Wolf, Carl G.	30
Thompson, G. S.	199	Worth, J. Howard	266
Tinberg, Albert C.	194		
Tome, John S.	147	Ylvisaker, J. W.	186
Topness, S. M.	158	Ylvisaker, N. M.	15
Tweet, Gabriel	276	Yochum, Harold	198
		Young, D. Bruce	188
Venable, Charles L.	91		
		Zeidler, C. H.	119
Wackernagel, F. W.	211	Ziegler, W. D.	96
Walck, A. W.	332	Ziehe, H. C.	358
Walter, Lloyd W.	97	Zimmann, Wm. C.	181
Walz, M. F.	265		
Weeks, Earl R.	234		